WITHOUT FEAR

Susan McKay, described by the late Mary Holland as 'one of Ireland's finest journalists', is the author of two critically acclaimed and bestselling books: *Sophia's Story* (1998), the biography of child abuse survivor Sophia McColgan, and *Northern Protestants — An Unsettled People* (2000). Awards for her work include the ESB National Media Awards, Print Journalist of the Year 2000 and Feature Writer of the Year 2002 and Amnesty International Irish section Print Journalist of the Year 2001. She writes for *The Irish Times* and the *Irish News* and is a regular contributor to news and arts programmes on RTÉ and the BBC. She has also written for *The Guardian* and *The Washington Post*, was formerly the Northern Editor of the *Sunday Tribune* and has made several television documentaries. Her articles appear in several anthologies including *The Field Day Anthology of Irish Writing*.

Before becoming a journalist she was the director of a centre for young unemployed people in Sligo and before that a founder member of the Belfast Rape Crisis Centre, where she worked for several years. She is from Derry.

WITHOUT FEAR

25 YEARS OF THE DUBLIN RAPE CRISIS CENTRE

Susan McKay

NEW
ISLAND

WITHOUT FEAR: 25 YEARS OF THE DUBLIN RAPE CRISIS CENTRE
First published 2005
by New Island
2 Brookside
Dundrum Road
Dublin 14
www.newisland.ie

ISBN 1 904301 87 8

British Library Cataloguing in Publication Data. A CIP catalogue record for
this book is available from the British Library.

'Reclaim the Night' © Harmony Music Limited, written by Peggy Seeger, used
by permission.

Index compiled by Gráinne Farren
Typeset by New Island
Cover design by New Island
Printed in the UK by CPD, Ebbw Vale, Wales

10 9 8 7 6 5 4 3 2 1

'Reclaim the night and win the day
We want the right that should be our own
A freedom women have seldom known
The right to live, the right to walk alone, without fear.'

Peggy Seeger

Contents

Acknowledgments

I am grateful to all the many people who helped me to research and write *Without Fear*. Some are quoted, others are not. I hope I have made good use of the information and insights all of them gave me. Thanks in particular to those who spoke about their own difficult experiences.

Hundreds of people have contributed to the work of the Dublin Rape Crisis Centre over the 25 years of its history. I trust the many people I did not interview will understand that it implies no slight.

I am honoured that Mary Robinson has written a preface to the book, and thank her for her gracious words.

Thanks to that fine and generous photographer, Derek Speirs, to Ivana Bacik, Olive Braiden, Anne O'Donnell, Bernie Purcell, Brid Rosney, Mary Quinlan, Audrey Middleton, Gemma Hussey, Rosemary Daly, Sophia McColgan, Dorothy Morrissey, Fiona Neary at the excellent Network of Rape Crisis Centres, Maud McKee, Audrey Conlon, Ruth McKay, Anne Marie Hourihane, Ciara Robins, Carolyn Fisher at RTÉ, Esther Murnane and Irene Stevenson at *The Irish Times* library, and to *The Irish Times* picture desk.

Thanks to everyone at the DRCC, especially Maria Byrne and Angela McCarthy, and to my agent, Jonathan Williams, my editor, Deirdre Nolan and everyone else at New Island. Thanks to Peggy Seeger for permission to quote from her wonderful song, 'Reclaim the Night'.

Breda Allen did much to get this project off the ground. Joe Robins was meant to write this book; sadly, he died while researching it. He is much missed at the DRCC.

Finally and above all, my love and gratitude to Mike Allen and to Madeleine and Caitlin.

Dedicated to the women and men struggling to reclaim their lives after being raped, to those helping them, and to those struggling to eradicate sexual violence from our world.

FOREWORD

On an October evening in 1978, 5,000 Irish women marched through the centre of Dublin to protest about rape. The 'reclaim the night' march was organised by a small group of feminists who went on, the following year, to establish the Dublin Rape Crisis Centre (DRCC). Their primary aim was to help and support women who had suffered the degradation of sexual violence. But they also challenged many myths about rape – myths that often left women feeling ashamed and guilty, as if they were to blame for their own violation.

Seventy women contacted the DRCC in its first year. Twenty-five years later, in 2004, over 15,000 people called its 24-hour helpline. The centre started with a telephone answering machine in the corner of another organisation – now it needs more space than it has in its rented premises on Leeson Street and an outreach centre in Coolock. There are plans for other outreach centres in Tallaght and in Dochas, the women's prison. Recognising that many victims of sexual violence cannot come to a centre, the DRCC is training others in the community to be receptive to them and to have the skills to help them. It has also helped internationally, developing and running programmes for the victims of rape as a war crime in Bosnia and Kosovo.

The DRCC has been a catalyst for creating counselling services by exposing the levels of sexual violence in Irish society and the immense hurt and damage caused. It was to the DRCC that the victims of child abuse began to come in the early 1980s, some of them still children, others adults who had kept the secret their abuser imposed on them, sometimes for decades. The women who set up the DRCC found within a very short time that rape was rife, that its victims included babies and very old women and that while most were women and girls, men and boys were raped as well. They found that the vast majority of rapists were men, of all ages and classes, and that most of them were getting away with their crimes.

Over the years there were attempts to silence the DRCC and the other Rape Crisis Centres and support groups set up since 1979, but those involved refused to stop listening and speaking out. They insisted that to impose silence is in itself a form of violence. Some of the most inspiring and dignified voices heard in Ireland in recent times have been those of people like Sophia McColgan and Colm O'Gorman, who triumphed over sexual abuse.

The DRCC recognised the devastation caused by sexual violence. Its counselling and support have helped thousands of people to regain self-respect, trust and happiness in their lives. It has also campaigned for the rights of rape victims. When the Centre opened, it was not a crime for a man to rape his wife, and if another man raped her, her husband could sue him for damages. The DRCC sought to get rid of the 1861 law, which was steeped in the notion of women as men's property. When a new law introduced in 1981 proved inadequate, it kept on campaigning. In 1990, marital rape was criminalised. Crimes regarded as minor in 1979 now carry heavy penalties, and some degree of protection is offered to the rape victim in court.

Further campaigns of the DRCC were to get the Sexual Assault and Treatment Unit set up at the Rotunda Hospital, for treatment programmes for sex offenders in prison and in the community and for a register of sex offenders. It continues to campaign, for there is much to be done. Up to 70 per cent of victims of sexual crimes still do not report them to the gardaí. Ireland has the lowest rate of convictions in rape cases in the EU. Men, women and children are still being raped in Ireland and those who have been raped are still blaming themselves. But the Dublin Rape Crisis Centre, 25 years on, continues to support those who have been hurt and to fight for changes in laws and attitudes. It is now part of a vibrant network of Centres from Belfast to Letterkenny to Tralee.

This is a proud history and powerfully told by Susan McKay, a former volunteer of the DRCC, founder member of the Belfast Rape Crisis Centre and author of *Sophia's Story*. I commend her for recording this story and warmly congratulate all associated with the first 25 years of the Dublin Rape Crisis Centre.

Mary Robinson

1

Reclaim the Night

The women on the front line of the march carried a huge Women Against Violence Against Women banner, the torches and candles in the crowd flaring brightly in the darkening autumn evening. The Emerald Girls Pipe Band, in kilts and feathered caps, played as they led the way across the Liffey at O'Connell Bridge. It was 13 October 1978, and women from all over Ireland had gathered to protest against rape.

They'd come because they were frightened and because they were angry. A 16-year-old girl was recovering in a Dublin hospital after a gang of eight young men had raped her and left her traumatised and badly injured in a derelict basement in Sean Mac Dermott Street. 'It was a very brutal and savage attack. She was held all night and repeatedly raped. They were very violent, vicious young fellows,' said one of the guards who investigated the attack. 'She was fortunate to survive.'[1] It was the Dublin Rape Crisis group that had called the women out. The small group of about ten Dublin feminists had organised the march to demonstrate women's anger about rape and announce plans to start up Ireland's first Rape Crisis Centre. A statement issued in advance of the march set out its politics: 'We are told that we provoke attack by behaviour such as walking alone at night or wearing certain types of dress. The implication is that if women severely curtailed their freedom as individuals they would be safe from attack.'

The statement also said that verbal abuse of women 'is a constant reminder that we exist in the eyes of too many men predominantly as objects of their sexual fantasies'. The march would show 'that the streets are ours to walk in whenever and wherever we choose, without fear of abuse, verbal or physical'. This explicitly feminist statement was signed by politicians, including Eileen Desmond, Monica Barnes and Gemma Hussey, the late actress Maureen Potter, Patsy Lawlor of the Irish Countrywomen's Association and Molly Cranny of the Irish Housewives Association, as well as by journalists, trade unionists and feminist activists.

A leaflet advertising the march demanded: 'Are you afraid to walk alone at night?' It ridiculed the idea that women were 'asking for it' and that men were subject to uncontrollable sexual desire. Most rape was planned, it said. It also addressed the idea that a woman could always resist rape: 'As one rape victim put it, "Try keeping your legs crossed when there's a knife to your throat or your face is being pulped."' It placed rape at the extreme end of a continuum of harassment: 'Rape is a violent act which humiliates and degrades women. Its effects are as much mental as physical. It is up to you as women to come out and show that we are not prepared to tolerate these attacks and insults any longer.'

'We expected hundreds,' said one of the organisers, Anne Connolly, the founder and then director of the new Well Woman Centre. 'We got about 5,000. It was overwhelming, the sheer numbers, the spirit of the thing. It was heady and atmospheric – you could feel the emotional strength of it.'

Nell McCafferty, one of the invited speakers, recalled that when she arrived at St Stephen's Green that evening she was amazed by the size of the crowd. 'It was massive,' she said. 'A lot of that was down to the fact that Gay Byrne had given us his blessing.' Byrne had urged listeners to his hugely influential morning show on RTÉ radio to attend the march.

'I said to one of the organisers, "We should put all the

prominent women to the front,"' McCafferty recalled. 'She said, "No way. This is a march for all women – it isn't élitist." I was struck by that – how right she was. It was a very happy event. There was a great sense of power. There was a terrific sense of sweeping through the streets.'[2]

Audrey Middleton worked in Belfast Women's Aid, supporting women who had been forced to leave home because of domestic violence. 'We stood outside the Rotunda Maternity Hospital and sang, and the women came to the windows and waved and cheered us on. It was wonderful.'[3]

About £600 was collected in the buckets passed around at the march. Middleton was one of those with a collection bucket. She asked a group of men standing outside Clerys on O'Connell Street for a contribution. One of them waved a pound note at her. 'How many rapes will this buy us?' he demanded. His friends laughed. Middleton refused the money.

A song sheet was handed out, but there weren't nearly enough copies to go around. Connolly had a megaphone. 'We want the right to walk at night,' she led. 'Yes means yes/No means No/However we dress/Wherever we go.' To the tune of 'Glory, Glory, Hallelujah', women sang, 'It's we who've done your cooking, done your cleaning, kept your rules/We gave birth to your children and we taught them in your schools/We've kept this system running, now we're laying down the rules/That's why we're marching on!'

Journalist Micheline McCormick met a woman who told her that her daughter had been raped. McCormick wrote afterwards that the woman cried as she told her, 'We're afraid to let our daughters out at night ... The laws will have to change ... my daughter still gets sick many days – and the fellow that raped her is going around free.

'Another thing we need is more women judges. Men just don't understand how awful a woman feels if she has been raped, and how broken-hearted a mother feels.'[4] The placards women carried on the march included, 'Night is for women as well', 'Your daughter could be next', 'Rape – crime against women'. Others read, 'Bring back the cat of nine tails', 'Castrate rapists!' and 'Kill Saturday night rape fever'.

At Parnell Square, just a few streets away from Sean Mac Dermott Street, Monica Barnes was the first to speak from the platform on the back of a lorry. 'I rejoice in tonight,' she said. 'This is a historic night. We are showing our fear and also our anger at the way women are treated. Rape is the extreme expression of the fundamental attitude towards women in society.'

Barnes, from the Council for the Status of Women, said women were exploited throughout society, in the workplace and in the home. The solidarity demonstrated on the march would lead to revolution, she said.[5] Barnes remembered the euphoria and the solidarity: 'It frightened the hell out of a lot of men,' she recalled.[6]

The crowd was agitated. Some women were shouting, 'We're marching against rape, not against men!' and 'What about the rapists?' Others were shouting 'Castrate the bastards!' There was cheering and clapping. Newspaper headlines that morning had claimed men were to be banned, and Nuala Fennell was quoted as opposing this. 'We'd put this out as a women's march,' said Anne Connolly. 'Then the issue came up about whether it would be women only. We had a series of meetings about it and we came up with a compromise. It would be a women's march but men could support us by marching at the back. Nuala Fennell was at that meeting. When we saw the papers the following morning, we felt very betrayed.'

Fennell laughed as she remembered the row. 'Yes, I messed up all their plans,' she said. 'In women's lib generally there were anti-man undertones. I'm a practical person. They were saying men shouldn't be there – and my husband was the most wonderful feminist man! There was a hysterical attitude among the organisers of that march.'[7] Nell McCafferty remembers feeling she needed to calm things down as she got up to speak at the march. 'The crowd was quite hysterical about the young woman raped on Sean Mac Dermott Street,' she said. 'I wanted to move things on. I felt the calls for castration were anti-man, not feminist.'[8]

The speech McCafferty went on to make that night would go down in feminist history. 'There isn't a woman on this march who hasn't been abused physically or mentally. Every woman has been raped in thought, word or deed ... Women are raped, not because they walk on certain streets at certain times, but because men walk on those streets ...' she said. 'Sisters, tonight the streets are ours. We are not looking for jail for men. We are not looking for castration for men. We are not looking for men at all!' There was wild cheering, but McCafferty was not finished. 'There were no men on this march tonight,' she said, 'and that is why there was nobody raped!'

Some of the crowd loved it. Some of them hated it. McCafferty recalled it as a speech of which she is still proud. Fennell commented that 'Nell was always shooting herself in the foot.' Connolly remembered it as a 'blistering attack on men'. Looking back, she said, 'It left me open-mouthed, thinking, "This is the last thing on earth we need."'[9]

McCafferty was followed by a spokeswoman for the Rape Crisis Centre group. At that stage, the group's policy was not to publicise their names, for reasons of personal safety, a policy they had adopted from the London Rape Crisis Centre. 'As women who have been raped know all too well, when a rape case comes to trial it is unfortunately not the man who is on trial for rape, it is the woman,' she said. 'What we want is a change in the law.'

She said the Rape Crisis Centre would provide a 24-hour phone service offering counselling and support, and an education programme for school children. She said the Centre would open in a fortnight. The crowd roared approval. The final speaker was identified only as Lillian, a young woman from the inner city. 'I am not anti-man,' she began. 'I like men as much as anyone here. But we have situations now where a man can plead guilty to rape and get 15 months in prison while girls end up dying or in mental hospitals. I am not anti-man, but it is not men who get raped. It is women.'

Derek Speirs, the photographer who for decades was rarely absent from any political demonstration, climbed onto the platform with his camera. 'It was suggested to me that I shouldn't be there as a man,' he recalled. 'I could understand that point of view, but all I was concerned with was that there should be a photographic record. No one tried to force me to leave.'[10] He was amused and gratified when the publishers of the Irish feminist calendar subsequently asked him for photographs of the event.

After the speeches, the crowd drifted away, but a small group of women marched as far as the Grand Canal to show solidarity with the prostitutes who worked there. A young woman who had given up prostitution two years previously, and had been living on the streets, had recently been raped and murdered. Teresa Maguire's attacker beat her so badly with an iron bar, she was unrecognisable, then left her to die with the bar pushed up her rectum.

Lyn Madden, then a prostitute and a woman who had experienced a great deal of rape and battering, was at the march. When she went down to the canal to work the following night, the prostitutes gave out to her about the 'bunch of fuckin' feminists coming down here and queering up business'. They'd told the prostitutes they were 'reclaiming the night'. Madden asked a woman called Annie what had happened next. 'We ran 'em, didn't we?' she replied.[11]

The newspaper reports the morning after the march were mostly focused on the impressive turnout. But the backlash was swift. Gay Byrne voiced his disapproval. Anne Connolly said she was 'sent for' by RTÉ and 'hauled over the coals'. *Sunday Journal* columnist Micheline McCormick had written the week before the march, 'It is the duty of every woman in this city to get out and march on Friday night next. You may be complacent and say, "Oh, it could never happen to me", but the way things are going, it could.' She said women had to demonstrate to 'show how powerful they can be' and force Gerry Collins, then the Fianna Fáil Minister for Justice, to get tough on rapists. 'Then and only then, will rape stop,' she concluded. However, two days after the march her column was headlined, '"We've been used" rape marchers tell me.'

McCormick quoted two women she had met at the march who had told her their daughters had been raped. She said they were deeply upset and that they accused the organisers of the march of using them: 'You used us to talk politics and do your women's lib bit against men in general.' And, commented McCormick, 'They were right.' The Rape Crisis Centre group 'had at least 4,000 women in the palms of their hands', she wrote, 'and they blew it.' She said other women were angry that men 'hadn't been allowed take part'. Women told her they would never march again.[12]

The following Sunday, McCormick's column, headlined 'Fuming', returned to the attack. She accused the organisers of being 'extremists who ... are neurotic over the fact that women here are a downtrodden race'. She said she believed 99 per cent of the women on the march felt as she did. 'We were not the typical pro-contraception, pro-abortion type women that men automatically dismiss as "women's libbers". We were just your average modern, emancipated women. We felt our power.'

She said men should have been allowed to march. 'Men who are the fathers, husbands, boyfriends – in other words 99 per cent of men in this city who are (and this may come as news to some of the organisers of the march) *not* rapists.' She made a point of shunning the Council for the Status of Women's submission for changes in the rape laws, presented to the Minister for Justice the week after the march. 'All I can say is that if it was anyway as neurotic, as biased, as out of touch as the speeches we heard from the organisers of the rape march, Gerry Collins will turn a deaf ear. And I wouldn't blame him.'

On the same page, however, Eamonn McCann declared that James Connolly had been right when he described Irish women as the 'slaves of slaves'. The claim that the marchers had been used was 'pathetic'. 'They are used day in and day out by a male establishment which is, arguably, the most chauvinist and sexually bigoted on earth and which has at its back an all-powerful Church which admits men only to its priesthood and regards all women as mere lays.' If the speeches from the platform went further than many in the audience would have liked, 'they will at least have planted a flag way out in front, to be focused on in the future', he wrote.

The battle continued in the letters page of *The Irish Times*.

The Irish Federation of Women's Clubs said it supported the march but objected to the event being 'turned into an extremist women's lib anti-male protest'.[13] Others claimed the speakers had 'alienated' the marchers. A man wrote that he had 'objected strongly' when an 'official' on the march had asked him to leave and he had declined to do so. 'Do the organisers not realise that one does not need to be black to be anti-apartheid … nor to be abused to be against abuse?' he demanded.[14] Kevin Myers protested that 'men were not allowed' on the march and concluded that 'if men are not allowed to carry their greater share of the responsibility for ending rape, then we may rest assured that the blight will continue'.[15]

Five women from the Labour Women's National Council wrote explaining that, because of capitalism, women lacked control over their lives. However: 'Destructive and violent women can emasculate men … the psychological consequences of inequality between the sexes work both ways … men who rape women are in a tiny minority,' they declared.

McCafferty replied that if Gay Byrne and other journalists who had expressed disapproval of her speech wanted 'to organise a march against rape, based on the slogan "We love men", they are welcome to hold their public meeting in the back seat of my mini'.[16]

The Rape Crisis Centre group fought back, too. One member wrote that the point of the march was to show that women had the right 'to go out unaccompanied by a male who is presumed to be able to defend them from attacks by other males'. Would trade unionists welcome employers on their marches, she asked. 'It is always difficult to accept that one is a member of an oppressing group, especially when there is no escape from it in this society,' she wrote. 'But then there is no escape from the threat of rape either and that is much more difficult to live with.' She described the march as 'a first and a great step in the right direction'.

Anne O'Donnell wrote of the 'spirit and atmosphere' of the march, which was of 'a new found strength among so many women in protest about rape'. She objected to the use of the term 'women's lib' instead of women's liberation. 'It trivialises a very socially significant women's movement,' she wrote. 'Women who have the experience, potential and drive to organise a large protest must be very involved in the subject of their protest – rape,' she wrote. 'Let's not forget that certain women's liberationists are among those fighting most strongly and consistently for the rights of Irish women.'

The most furious response came from feminist Anne Speed, who said some of the letters *The Irish Times* had published were 'enough to make the blood boil'. She was tired of 'patronising declarations of support' from men who aggressively and antagonistically refused even to accept that women had the right to march alone and 'to begin to build solidarity', the 'starting point for resistance'. It was 'downright hyprocrisy' and the product of embarrassment and guilt. 'Why is it that only when women take up the issue do we have men wanting to march against rape?' she demanded. Besides, she pointed out, men *hadn't* been barred.[17]

Two men wrote to support the organisers. Men could have marched against rape at any time, they wrote. 'They (we) didn't. As it is, very few of us even have the sense or the guts to voice our objections to the sexist jokes we hear every other day.'[18] Another said the real outrage was 'the oppression of women by male violence'.[19]

In her report in the *Galway Advertiser*, Veronica McDermott returned to the spirit of the march. 'It was as lovely as it was rare to feel so safe, so unthreatened in the streets at night.' Paraphrasing Barnes, she wrote: 'the way forward for women was not to meet violence with violence, blindness and cruelty with more blindness and cruelty ... women, by just being themselves, by not adopting male values or male reactions, can work out their own solutions.'[20]

Feminists in Britain were impressed at what the Rape Crisis Centre group had achieved. Reclaim the Night marches had been held in London, Manchester, Leeds, Newcastle and in other British cities during 1978. Their organisers were inspired by similar demonstrations in Germany, reported in the feminist monthly *Spare Rib* and by discussions at a 'Revolutionary Feminist' conference in Edinburgh in 1976.

The impetus came from feminists in Leeds spurred on by the early murders carried out by the 'Yorkshire Ripper' (see chapter three). *Spare Rib* reported that the Dublin march was 'far bigger than any women-only march we've ever had in Britain' and 'an immense show of potential, and very significant as a consciousness raiser in building the women's movement in Ireland'.[21] *Spare Rib* had been banned in Ireland as indecent.

Looking back, one of the founders of the Rape Crisis Centre group, writer Evelyn Conlon, said the march and the controversy that surrounded it epitomised the struggle the group had embarked on. 'Violence against women was fundamental. There was no point talking about any other rights while women were being battered and raped,' she said. 'And yet, when you mentioned you were involved in the group in those early days, more often than not, people would make a joke. "You should be so lucky," or "I should be so lucky." I don't know which was worse. The biggest difficulty we faced was changing attitudes, and that is the biggest thing we've achieved.'[22]

Anne O'Donnell agreed. 'We were considered off the wall. People say to me now in 2005, "Your views have moderated." But they haven't. What has happened is that society has caught up with us – almost. But back in the dark days of 1978, Ireland was completely not ready for us.'

2

THE CAMPAIGN AGAINST RAPE (CAR)

'I'd always been vaguely political,' said Anne O'Donnell. She'd joined the anti-apartheid movement as a schoolgirl, and the youth branch of the Labour Party. As a student she was 'always' on marches and pickets. 'I was motivated by a sense of injustice,' she said. In 1975, International Women's Year, she got involved in Irish Women United, which emerged that year out of the ashes of the Irish Women's Liberation Movement. Many IWU members came from left-wing political groups.

June Levine, a veteran of the IWLM, described the women in the new group as 'young, brilliant, bursting with energy and commitment, and they brought home to me that the women's movement here had reached a stage where change was inevitable'.[1]

'We used to meet on Sundays in Pembroke Street, in the same house that would later become the temporary premises of the Rape Crisis Centre,' said O'Donnell, who was then a primary school teacher. 'It was run as a collective. The loudest voices prevailed. I never opened my mouth most of the time.'

The IWU occupied the Federated Union of Employers over equal pay, invaded the all-male swimming preserve – the 40 Foot – on Dublin Bay, protested outside the all-male Fitzwilliam Tennis Club and went on 'the *Spare Rib* train'.

This action was in the tradition of the famous Contraceptive train of 1971, when women travelled by train to Belfast and brought back illegal contraceptives. This time, the booty was copies of the illegal feminist magazine. The Emergency Powers Act was invoked against the protesting women.

The IWU agreed on its charter at a public meeting in Dublin's Mansion House in June 1975. Based on the Irish Transport and General Workers Union charter, it pledged to 'fight sexism in all forms and oppose all forms of exploitation of women which keep them oppressed'. Its demands included the right to divorce. Consciousness raising was a feature of feminism of this period. The personal was political. Issues were intensely debated and documented in discussion papers. One of these, on 'Feminism and Socialism', noted that 'feminist organisation is necessary to allow women to co-operate with men on issues of mutual concern without being co-opted by them. We cannot liberate ourselves as a ladies auxiliary; nor will women overthrow imperialism and capitalism alone.'[2]

'There were the republicans and the radical lesbians. Then there were the women in the middle,' recalled O'Donnell. 'I was one of those. There were constant rows and in the end the people who weren't aligned decided there were two important areas to work in: women in the media and violence against women. There was a Women's Aid, but there was no Rape Crisis Centre. So a few of us decided we'd set one up.' The evidence from Women's Aid was that services dealing with violence against women were urgently needed. Set up in 1974, its hostel was constantly packed. At one point, 117 women and children were taking refuge in a four-bedroom house.

The first meeting of the provisionally named Campaign Against Rape (CAR) was held in a room in the Students' Union building in Trinity College at 6.30 p.m. on 26 July 1977. The first item on the agenda was a discussion about Noreen Winchester. The young Belfast woman was serving seven years in jail for murdering her father after enduring years of incestuous rape at his hands. It was agreed to find out more about her situation – this would be the first campaign in which the new group involved itself.

The minutes record that 'after a long discussion, it was agreed the group would be autonomous, small at first, and keeping a feminist perspective, and that possibly later on a legal campaign might broaden it out'. There was talk about premises and it was agreed 'a house would eventually have to be got'. The group decided that it would hold a public meeting 'on the lines of the one held by the Battered Wives'. The meeting ended at 10.30. The Dublin Rape Crisis Centre was on its way.

Noreen Winchester was in Armagh prison. In 1977, the 20-year-old from Belfast's Sandy Row had been convicted of the manslaughter of her father, Norman. She admitted stabbing him 21 times with a breadknife at their Hunter Street home, on a Saturday night in 1976. She and her younger brother and sister then dragged his body onto the street. They cleaned up the house and, when the police came, denied they knew anything.

Police at first assumed Winchester had been murdered by paramilitaries, but soon suspicion turned on the family. Questioned again, Noreen confessed. She also admitted Norman Winchester had been asleep when she killed him. Her sister, Tina, was also arrested. Noreen was charged with murder and appeared in court in February 1977. She pleaded not guilty.

Defence counsel then suggested that she plead guilty to manslaughter, and she did so. Although her 13-year-old brother gave evidence that their father had been harsh, little emerged in court about the reality of life with Norman Winchester. Neither Noreen, her mother, Annie, nor her Aunt Nessie were called to give evidence. There was no independent psychiatric report. Although Noreen had made a statement to the police giving harrowing details of rapes and violence she had been subjected to by her father, there was only the briefest plea of mitigation.

Audrey Middleton, then the chairwoman of Belfast Women's Aid, heard about Noreen from journalist Sarah Nelson. The women decided to investigate and soon uncovered enough of the horrific facts to convince them that Noreen should never have gone to prison.

Noreen was the eldest daughter in a family of eight. Her father, a heavy drinker, started beating his wife, Annie, early in the marriage and gradually cut her off from the outside world. She became violent towards the children herself and also became an alcoholic. The family lived in poverty.

Winchester began to rape Noreen when she was 11. Annie called Noreen her husband's 'wee fancy bit', though she did, at times, make efforts to protect her. In 1974, she left and ended up in a mental hospital. Winchester kept Noreen, Tina and a younger brother. He made a prisoner of Noreen. He forced her to leave her job as a stitcher in a factory, keep house on a pittance, look after the younger children and submit to his violence.

Welfare workers who occasionally called were sometimes turned away and never allowed to be alone with the children. Neighbours would later claim they had no inkling that there was anything wrong. They noted that Noreen took the other children to the public baths, kept the house clean and tidy, and kept herself to herself. Winchester dressed well and was known as a singer in local pubs. Some members of his family denied Winchester was a violent man.

Audrey Middleton began to visit Noreen in prison, and they became close. Noreen said she hadn't understood what was happening during the trial and didn't realise she could appeal. Middleton and Women's Aid launched a campaign, at first behind the scenes. 'Noreen and her aunt and others around them felt it should be private,' recalled Middleton. 'They felt it was shameful.' The Campaign Against Rape was one of the groups which got involved at this stage. 'We had a brilliant network,' said Middleton.[3] One of those centrally involved was a young solicitor called Padraigin Drinan, who would later lend her support to the Belfast Rape Crisis Centre. 'One day, I was with Noreen and I thought, "I'll break all the rules and ask her, why didn't you do anything sooner?"' she said. 'I was stunned by her reply. She said, "I didn't know it was wrong."'[4]

The campaign brought over British barrister Barbara Calvert to lead an appeal, but in April 1978, Lord Chief

Justice Lowry refused it. However, the court accepted that the nature of the provocation was not sudden but gradual, consisting of 'a lengthy and ultimately intolerable course of conduct including frequent beatings, most of which were administered … in order to make the applicant submit to her father's degrading and horrifying advances.'[5]

Lowry indicated, however, that justice could be tempered by mercy under the 'Royal Prerogative'. It was a clear signal to the then British secretary of state for Northern Ireland, Roy Mason. It was time for the campaign to go public. The morning after the judgment, the walls of Belfast were plastered with 'Free Noreen Now' graffiti. Drinan recalled being stopped by a British army foot patrol a few days later. 'The soldiers were wearing "Free Noreen" badges!' she said. 'I think it was the only time in the history of the troubles they were allowed to do such a thing.' On 21 April 1978, the headline on the front page of the *Belfast Telegraph* announced 'Noreen freed from jail'. She had served just over a year.

Noreen Winchester's case was enormously educational for the women in CAR. Sarah Nelson wrote extensively about it. She said there was no point in scapegoating individuals, but the attitudes of the professionals needed to be examined. 'What was most lacking in those involved with the Winchester children after the killing was the capacity for "sympathetic imagination", the ability to understand what life was like in that family,' she wrote.[6]

The killing had been premeditated, unprovoked – in the normally understood sense of the word, since the victim was asleep – and brutal. Nor was Noreen insane. However, Nelson argued, 'No one began from the other end and asked why.' Then, she said, the crime might have been recognised for what it was: 'an uncontrollable explosion of her real feelings for her father'.

Nelson described the class prejudices displayed by the lawyers, judges and social workers involved in the case. 'The Winchesters were a family close to the bottom of the social pile. By and large, they were treated accordingly.' One social worker expressed the view that incest was extremely common in 'these areas' and was accepted as a cultural practice. The fact that Noreen hadn't left home was seen as evidence of a degree of collusion with her father. Her mother was judged harshly, without regard for the fact that she too had been brutalised.

Nelson went on to write a ground-breaking book on incest in which she contended that it was widespread, hugely damaging to its victims and that its cause was neither complex nor mysterious. 'Instead, it is a simple and straightforward form of sexual abuse and exploitation of female children by adult men, for the selfish purpose of sexual gratification,' she wrote.[7]

CAR celebrated the freeing of Noreen Winchester, well aware that in all likelihood they would soon be hearing from other women trapped in similarly appalling family situations. The family's tragedy was not over. In 1993, the body of Noreen's younger sister, Tina, was found near the scene of her father's murder. She had been raped and strangled. No one has been convicted of her murder.

Just two weeks after its inaugural meeting, CAR was confronted with another legal situation. This time, it involved the trial of John Shaw for the abduction, rape and murder of a young Mayo woman, Mary Duffy. Women in Ireland had only just won the right to sit on juries in 1976, after two feminists took a case in the Supreme Court (*de Burca* v. *Attorney General* IR 38). They had established that they had a right to be tried by a jury of their peers and that this must therefore include women. However, when the court assembled for the Shaw trial, the first act of both the defence lawyers and the prosecution was to reject the eight women who had been selected for the jury.

Anne O'Donnell and Evelyn Conlon for CAR wrote in protest to the papers. They said the women had been rejected 'solely on the grounds of their sex, because it was believed that the facts in this case were too emotionally disturbing for women and might result in a bias against the defendant'. They added, 'What a comment on our society! Should not such horrific facts be as disturbing to men as they are to women? We don't believe that justice is more likely to be reached by an all male jury than by one which includes women.' They said they were disturbed that the case could establish a precedent.

One detective told journalist Stephen Rae that Shaw and his accomplice, Geoffrey Evans, were 'really the first serial killers. If it had not been for luck on our part they would have left a trail of bodies around Ireland.'[8] Both were jailed for life.

Throughout the summer of 1977, while the women in CAR were educating themselves on rape and preparing to open the Rape Crisis Centre, the details emerging from the Shaw trial at the Central Criminal Court were a horrific reminder of the brutal extremes to which rapists might go.

On the night of 28 August 1976, 23-year-old Elizabeth Plunkett left a pub in Co. Wicklow. She had come down from Dublin for the weekend with her boyfriend. Evans and Shaw spotted her and followed. They had been 'looking for a bird'. Evans said of Elizabeth, 'She will do.' He dropped Shaw off, then turned back and offered Elizabeth a lift. She accepted. Evans then picked up Shaw, and they took Elizabeth Plunkett to Castletimon forest.

The two men, on the run from rape charges in England, first tied their victim up, then battered her, then raped her repeatedly through the night. Afterwards Shaw throttled her with a shirt. In the morning they weighted her body with a stolen lawnmower, then stole a boat and rowed out into the Irish Sea, where they dumped her.

Back on shore, while the murderers were burning her clothes, gardaí, alerted by a report that the men were trespassing, arrived and questioned them. The pair then set off on a spree of burglaries across Ireland. Elizabeth's family reported her disappearance to the gardaí on 30 August. Following a widespread search, one of her shoes was found at the forest. The two Englishmen became murder suspects. The pair had already picked up a young nurse who was hitching a lift in Co. Galway. She became frightened, got them to stop at a pub and made her escape.

On 22 September, in Castlebar, Co. Mayo, 24-year-old Mary Duffy was trying to organise a lift home from the café where she worked. It was after 11 p.m. She used a payphone near the café to ring the garage where her brother worked. She left a message that she would set off walking and that he should pick her up on the way. Shaw and Evans spotted her. Shaw got out, followed her, grabbed her and dragged her to the car. Afterwards, local people said they heard screams.

Mary struggled, but she was a small woman and she suffered from back problems. Her assailant was a former coal miner. In the car he tied her hands behind her back. The men took it in turns to drive and to rape the young woman. They brought her to woods near Ballinahinch Castle. There they continued to rape and beat her. They also left her tied to a tree for several hours and assaulted her throughout the following day. Her family had assumed she had stayed in Castlebar overnight and gone to work in the morning. In fact, she had the day off, so her employers didn't know that she was missing either. That night, Shaw suffocated and strangled her. Then the two men brought her body out on a boat into Lough Inagh in the Connemara mountains, tied her to a concrete block and a sledgehammer and threw her into the lake.

Shaw and Evans then headed for Galway to hunt down a 'small bird'. After rejecting about a dozen, they had just identified the woman they intended to target near a hotel in Salthill when gardaí moved in on them, and they were arrested. Two days later, Elizabeth Plunkett's body was washed ashore at Duncormack, on the Wexford coast. Twelve days after that, divers found the body of Mary Duffy at the bottom of Lough Inagh.[9]

'The more knowledgeable you became, the more incensed you got,' said Evelyn Conlon, recalling the education the women in CAR embarked upon in 1977. 'We decided very early on that we weren't going to open the Rape Crisis Centre until we were ready, however long that took, because we wanted it to last.'

Rape was supposedly regarded in law as second only to murder, yet non-custodial sentences were common in cases which CAR saw as rape, though the law defined them differently. In the summer of 1977, for example, a Dublin man who 'had unlawful carnal knowledge of' a 19-year-old girl and sexually assaulted a 16-year-old girl at knifepoint was given a suspended 12-month sentence. The Circuit Criminal Court was told that the man's actions resulted from the 'mental and nervous strain of marital problems'. The older girl, in her statement, 'admitted' that she had, in the past, had sexual intercourse. CAR recognised that the use of a woman's past sexual history in court was going to be a central issue.

The group devised its own training, inviting a different expert to speak at its weekly meeting. One of the first visitors was from the London Rape Crisis Centre, which had been set up in 1976 by a group of feminists who believed that 'it is difficult for women to speak about experiences of sexual violence … society perpetuates a hostile silence which denies reality for women who have been raped … in the Women's Liberation Movement we have learnt that talking and working together to break this silence can be enormously strengthening.'[10]

Some of the group visited the London RCC to find out more about the service it offered and the type of contacts it was getting from women. It rejected the word 'victim' because it implied powerlessness 'and contributes to the idea that it is right and natural for men to "prey" on us.'[11] The Dublin women were also influenced by the radical London-based Women Against Rape (WAR) group. WAR engaged in direct action – invading courtrooms to protest against decisions which proved in WAR's view that 'judges are encouraging rape and the government is prepared to stand by and watch it happen'.[12]

CAR discussed fierce documents like one presented to the Women's Liberation Conference in London in 1977 by a London anti-rape group. This declared that, 'feminism must begin to fight for the total eradication of rape and not just the mere containment of it by legislation' and that 'sexism is how male power operates against women … rape is the inevitable brutal expression of that power … we must start to expose the patriarchy's most blatant forms of intimidation by making an attack on rape.'[13]

Another 'Manifesto Against Rape' by French radical feminists attacked men of the left and men of the right for distorting the truth about rape: 'On the left, they tell us that rape is the result of sexual, so-called capitalist, impoverishment – a new ploy to silence women before the law and justice. On the right, they tell us rape is an accident, that it is committed by alcoholics, psychopaths, immigrants, deviants and sex maniacs – a lie. Every man is a potential rapist ... Rape is the physical and cultural act on which patriarchal society is founded.'[14] However, the Irish women also discussed the possibility that a raped woman might want to talk to a priest, and CAR drew up a list of suitable ones.

One of the first Irish experts invited to speak to CAR was Maire Butterly of the Irish Society for the Prevention of Cruelty to Children (ISPCC). Conlon remembered that Butterly told the group that her work was bringing her into contact with significant numbers of children who had been subjected to incestuous rape. 'I remember not believing her,' said Conlon. 'Not being able, at that time, to believe her.'

Garda Brid Wymes told the group about police procedures. She explained that since hearsay evidence was admissible in rape cases – in particular circumstances, under the doctrine of 'recent complaint' – a rape crisis counsellor might be called to give evidence if a woman had come to the Centre first, before going to the gardaí. The minutes of that meeting noted that, given her encouraging attitude, 'it looked as though we may well be able to avoid the bad relations with the police that had so hampered the London group'.[15]

Mary McAleese, now the president of Ireland, then a young lawyer, talked to the group about the law on rape and explained the implications of the Morgan case in the UK. This case allowed for the acquittal of a man on a rape charge if he could persuade the court that he had believed the woman was consenting to sex – however unreasonable that belief. However, she also pointed out that if he was reckless as to whether she consented, then that was rape. McAleese said that, although a husband could not be convicted of raping his wife, there was precedent in the UK for accusing a husband where the couple was separated by court order. She suggested CAR submit recommendations to the Law Reform Commission.

Monica Barnes offered the group the support of the Council for the Status of Women, with which she was then involved. She invited them to sit on its subcommittee, which was preparing to make a submission on rape to the Law Reform Commission. The submission was presented in September 1978.

The late Dr Hazel Boland, who went on to become a Fianna Fáil politician, told the group that the doctor who examined a woman after rape would be an important witness in court. She told of her horror when she discovered that medical students were given lectures on rape that emphasised false allegations.

Nuala Fennell, who had set up the AIM family-law group, talked to CAR about 'the need for a good image, to be able to co-operate with the bureaucracy'. She advised the group to speak to as many women's clubs around the country as possible.

Other speakers included Maureen Gaffney, then a psychologist with the Eastern Health Board, psychologist John Cullen, social workers, the Samaritans and therapist Nicola Quinn, who provided more intensive training later. Gaye Cunningham, one of the original members of CAR, said the training was 'very thorough'. She felt O'Donnell was a driving force from the start. 'She was very passionate – very determined that we were going to do the thing right.'[16]

CAR experienced at an early stage one of the least acrimonious splits in Irish feminist history. 'It was more a parting of the ways,' recalled Betty Purcell, now a senior editor at RTÉ.[17] Purcell and some others felt the most important issue was to expose 'the use of rape as a method of intimidating all women'. In an internal paper presented to the group, she proposed that an upsurge in rapes was the result of gains made for women by feminism. 'This rise in brutality probably stems from the resentment felt by many men against the threats being made to their supremacy ... attacks against women individually occur in the social context of the attempt to drive women out of their barely found freedoms and back into the home.' Purcell felt that the fact that CAR was a closed group – necessarily, because of the training – meant that other women who were willing to campaign were unable to do so. However, while her analysis of rape was not disputed, a majority of CAR decided the priority was to start up the Rape Crisis Centre. The name was changed to the Rape Crisis Centre Group (RCCG) in September 1977.

'We were very intense,' said Conlon. An early policy document proves it. Members were to attend the weekly meeting without fail. 'When I was about to have a baby, I remember phoning in to say I couldn't get to the meeting because my waters had broken!' recalled Conlon. The minutes duly recorded 'Evelyn's confinement'. She would probably miss several meetings 'unless they could be held at her house'.

Commitments to other groups had to be abandoned. The RCCG was not a matter of 'filling up spare time'. Members were obliged to take part in ongoing training, including 'participation in encounter groups, attendance at public speaking lessons, role playing sessions etc.' Considerable amounts of time were to be spent reading about rape and studying. One instruction sounds more like something from a convent: 'Members must be prepared to make a big effort to get on with everyone in the group, making a special effort not to form individual friendships.' During counselling, members 'must be prepared to offer a non-directive and non-judgemental approach to the raped woman, making sure the counselling is never used for "crusading" purposes for any particular religious, political or feminist viewpoint'. The public image of the centre was to be 'a dignified one where appearances and manner can never be used to alienate public or bureaucracy opinion.'[18] The march of October 1978 would prove how difficult it could be to realise this last ambition.

3

Taking on 'the Ancient Atmosphere of Rape'

'We had Ireland's first telephone answering machine,' said Evelyn Conlon, with real pride still in her voice. 'Well, one of the first, anyway.'[1] At a press conference in Dublin on 19 February 1979, the Dublin Rape Crisis Centre announced its opening. The service would be run by the 19 volunteers. Some of the original group had left by this stage, and new volunteers had been trained.

The answering machine was installed in an office in Women's Aid, then based in a dilapidated building on Harcourt Street that was owned by the Legion of Mary. The message on the machine gave the phone number of whichever volunteer counsellor was on call that night or over the weekend.

The press conference also saw the launch of the DRCC's First Report: 'A female definition of rape can be obtained in a single sentence,' it began. 'If a woman chooses not to have sex with a specific man and that man chooses to proceed against her will, that is a criminal act of rape.' However, it went on, rape had entered the law as a property crime of man against man, with woman as the property. This had led to a 'whole ideology of rape fuelled by cultural values ... and it is only by exposing and attacking these values that rape can be eradicated ... Rape is to women as lynching was to blacks, the ultimate physical threat by which women are kept in a state of psychological intimidation. That some men rape provides a sufficient threat to keep all women in "their place".'

The report pointed out that rape in marriage was not illegal. 'The historic price of women's protection by man against man was the imposition of chastity and monogamy ... sex is seen as part of the marriage contract, her duty, his right.' It referred to the use of rape by men who battered their wives and to the fact that a man could sue another man who raped his wife for compensation under the law of criminal conversation.

The use of rape in war was described as revealing 'the male psyche in its boldest form without the veneer of chivalry and civilization ... the act of the conqueror ... on the bodies of the defeated enemies' women'. Gang rape was 'one of the most brutal expressions of the power and dominance of men' and rape was used to torture women political prisoners.

According to the section on 'Social Acceptance and Myths', rape was the logical conclusion of propaganda based on the social model of aggressive man and passive woman. Men used rape to take a woman 'down a peg or two'. Myths about rape covered up the fact that it was socially acceptable 'except in the most extreme cases'. The most widely accepted myth was that rape was a result of a woman provoking a man's sexual urges so much that he lost control. In fact, rape was a violent act meant to humiliate and was often accompanied by 'savage acts of degradation'. Most rape was planned. Women had internalised the myth that they were to blame and agonised over how they had provoked the attack.

Catholic morality permeated social thinking, the report said, with women divided into virgins and temptresses. 'The church's glorification of Maria Goretti displays an inhuman approach towards women.' Goretti was a young Italian girl who died rather than surrender her virginity to her would-be rapist. 'The church is seldom seen to take the rapist and the male rape mentality to task.'

Another widely held belief was that women cried rape after

having sex and then changing their mind. In reality: 'If a woman reports a rape she will have to go through a lengthy police interrogation, an internal medical examination, an appearance at court, and a possible nine-month wait before attending the trial where she will have to face the distress and humiliation of intimate cross-examination on the details of the rape and about her previous sexual history.' Any woman could be the victim, young or old.

Women were asked to censor themselves in the company of men, to control their own sexual urges as well as those of their boyfriends and dancing partners, the report asserted. This was certainly the view of sexuality promoted by the legendary *Sunday Press* agony aunt Angela MacNamara, who warned in 1969 that 'it is in the nature of a man to be the aggressor – the one who initiates' and that if a girl allowed a man to 'fondle and embrace her and give prolonged open-mouthed kisses ... she cannot then blame him if his nature propels him in passion to seek the ultimate closeness of sexual intercourse.'[2]

According to the DRCC report, 'while traditional attitudes about the role of women in society prevail, the crime of rape will continue. Women will continue to be terrorised by the possibility of sexual attack. To use the words of Susan Brownmiller, "Rape is a conscious process of intimidation by which *all* men keep *all* women in a state of fear."'[3]

These were fierce claims and this was 1979, the year Pope John Paul II came to Ireland and more than a million people flocked to listen to him telling women that their 'vocation' was to be mothers in traditional families. Mná na hÉireann, a group which promoted traditional Irish Catholic values, was not impressed by the politics of the Rape Crisis Centre. In a statement, it said it took 'strong exception' to remarks made by one of the DRCC women during an RTÉ interview. 'She implied that the men of this nation, our husbands, our brothers, our sons, are guilty on a national scale of incest and child molestation,' said Mná na hÉireann. 'This is a down-right lie.'[4]

The report described the type of support the DRCC

intended to offer. 'The purpose of our work is to help raped women to regain their confidence and self-determination,' it said. 'The help which can be given to a woman who has been raped … is what we mean by counselling … We believe in the need to encourage the raped woman to come to terms with and solve her own problems. We think this can best be achieved by the support and advice which unprofessional but committed and sympathetic feminists can provide.'

The report summarised the law on rape and other sexual offences, and outlined the procedures a woman would have to go through if she decided to report to the gardaí. A counsellor would offer to accompany the woman to doctors, to the gardaí and to court, if required. There would be a campaign to change the law. The DRCC had the full support of the gardaí, who would be referring women to the centre. The DRCC would also embark on a programme of public speaking, educating the community about rape and encouraging other people to help the centre, or start up new centres. The First Report outlined a very ambitious programme of work. It stated that the aim was to operate a 24-hour-a-day, seven-day-a-week service.

'We were shocked to find that women were contacting us who had been raped maybe 10 or 20 years previously,' said Evelyn Conlon. 'A lot of them would say they had never, ever spoken about it before, to anyone. We were an organisation that believed people. We didn't at first really understand how monumental it was that these women had been given this right, by us, to speak. And it was hard, at times, to listen to what you had to listen to.' In the first year, the Centre dealt with 70 cases of rape.

'We cannot and do not wish to offer ourselves as professional counsellors,' the DRCC stated in an early document called 'Peer Counselling'. 'We believe that for many raped women the understanding and sympathy of a committed woman may be more beneficial than counselling from professionals, since in many cases her problem is social rather than classifiable in any particular counselling discipline.' Women with 'severe psychological problems' might need to be referred to a professional. However, the DRCC counsellor was more than a 'concerned friend'. She had to know the facts about rape and the myths. She had to have 'worked through' her own feelings so as not to pass on her own problems and hangups. Counsellors were, after all, 'to some extent products of repression', brought about by 'oppressive attitudes' transmitted through the Catholic Church and Irish education.[5]

The centre used a counselling model devised by British social scientist John Heron, called 'six category intervention analysis'. The categories were 'authoritative' and 'facilitative'. The first group included being prescriptive – giving advice, seeking to direct the client's behaviour; being informative; confronting – challenging the client about an attitude or way of behaving. The second group included: being cathartic – releasing tensions so that the client can 'abreact painful emotion'; being catalytic – helping the client to reflect and develop by self-direction; and being supportive – affirming the worth and value of the client.[6]

Terri Morrissey, now the director of a consultancy company and chairwoman of the Aoibhneas women's refuge in Dublin, joined the DRCC at this stage and stayed until the early 1980s. She remembered the first case she dealt with as a volunteer counsellor. 'A woman from the North West rang me in the middle of the night. She was suicidal and there was nothing I could do except talk to her and try to persuade her not to kill herself. She came to Dublin to meet me soon after that, and I went up to see her.

'Her case had come to court and the man who raped her had got off. He sneered at her on the way out of the courthouse. She was terrified and she tried to kill herself a couple of times. After a while, she stopped calling. We had a policy of not following people up if they dropped contact. Her mother rang once in despair, but after that I heard nothing more,' she said.

'We were a very political group of women, and we debated everything. We refused a grant from one company that made tights because they had horrible ads of women's legs. We had a ferocious argument with a leading barrister because he defended rapists in court. We were in your face.'

Author June Levine, who had been involved in the Irish women's movement since the earliest days of Irish Women United, also joined the Rape Crisis Centre at this time. 'It was Anne O'Donnell who inspired me to join,' she said.[7] During the training course, she remembered an incident from her life as a young married woman in Canada. Levine recounted the episode in her book *Sisters*. As she got in her car, after an appointment, a group of young men getting into another car said something to her. She responded politely, then set off to drive the 40 miles to her home.

After a few miles on the road, she realised they had followed her and were trying to shunt her off the road. In a sweat of terror, her bowels opened and her nose bled. When she got home, she washed her clothes, didn't tell her husband and privately blamed the high-heeled shoes she was wearing. When, later, she told a psychiatrist about the episode, he remarked: 'Yes, but nothing actually happened, did it?'[8]

During a discussion about how rape affects women, as part of the 1979 training course, the episode came back to her. 'I remembered that fear in my car that afternoon. It had been a fear like no other, yet familiar, sickeningly recognisable, making other fears trivial,' she wrote. 'It had a life of its own. It dwelled as a race memory, poised in the pit of my stomach, prepared to grow in relation to one signal, the ancient atmosphere of rape.'

Levine said she had never driven a car since the incident. Looking back, she said, 'I was very angry about rape and very sympathetic towards women who had experienced it. I was comfortable with my anger – I knew where it came from and that it was totally justifiable. The attitude in those days was that the woman who said she'd been raped was guilty until proved innocent, and then she was marked.'

She found, however, that she couldn't handle the counselling. 'On nights when I was on call, I'd lie awake hoping no one would ring,' she said.[9] Levine was able to help the DRCC in another way. She was a friend of a friend of the then Taoiseach, Charles Haughey, and encouraged him to support the new service. In August 1980, the Department of Health, through the Eastern Health Board, gave the DRCC a grant of £5,000. The centre immediately appointed Anne O'Donnell as its administrator. She started work in the Centre's first proper premises, a shabby bedsit in a big house on Pembroke Road in Dublin 4. After years in borrowed rooms, the Dublin Rape Crisis Centre had its own front door, and with the appointment of O'Donnell, it was finally able to offer the full-time service it had promised during the long years of preparation.

'I was terrified out of my wits,' said Gemma Hussey, recalling the day in April 1979 that she brought her proposed bill on rape to the senate. 'I was going to have to stand up in the Oireachtas and use words like penis and penetration and vagina. In those days women just didn't talk about those things. You were regarded with terrible suspicion. What you were up against was a strange hostility that gave you a shock each time you encountered it. What I did was, I got all the sisters to come in to the senate and they sat in the little public gallery sending out supportive vibes.'[10]

Among the sisters was Anne O'Donnell, who had greatly impressed the young senator. 'She was a very inspiring person, quite evangelical – and fearless. I had been moved almost to tears by speeches I'd heard her give. I began to work closely with her on the rape issue.' Hussey moved a motion that the senate should note the report presented to the government the previous year by the Council for the Status of Women (CSW).

Anne Connolly of the Rape Crisis Centre had advised the Council during the 18 months it spent preparing the detailed and thorough report, which it presented to the Minister for Justice, Gerry Collins, a few days after the 1978 march against rape. In the furore over whether or not men should have been allowed on the march, the document got little attention in the media at the time. The CSW said there was a 'crying need' for reform.

The Minister had promised to study it carefully. However,

in the six months that followed, there was no further response. The report called for a broadening of the definition of rape, training for gardaí and health professionals and new measures to ensure that at least four women would be jurists in any rape trial.

The committee that produced the report, chaired by Dr Hazel Boland, had described as 'intolerable' the fact that Irish politicians had not discussed rape. It said the prevailing 1861 law 'reflects the fact that women are socially and legally the property of ... their husbands and fathers'. The CSW 'utterly rejects' this view, according to its report. 'We believe the law ... should reflect contemporary ideas.'

The CSW document quoted the 1736 British source for the law that a husband could not be found guilty of raping his wife 'for by their mutual matrimonial consent and contract, the wife hath given up herself in this kind unto her husband, which she cannot retract'.[11] However, the CSW stopped short of demanding that marital rape be made criminal. Instead, it called for a 'modification' such as had been introduced in Britain. If, 'in reality the marriage is no longer a going concern, then the possibility of rape should be recognised', according to the CSW.[12] It noted that while the law stated that intercourse with a girl under 15 was statutory rape, girls could legally marry at 14.

'Attitudes to a woman who alleges she has been raped are often harsh and uncomprehending,' the CSW complained. 'It has long been the law that, just as the defence can call evidence to establish that a woman is of "notoriously bad character", so she herself can be cross-examined to the same effect.' The document said cross-examination as to a woman's past sexual history should be distinguished from that as to 'notorious bad character', the latter being an allegation of prostitution. 'In Ireland sexual relationships outside marriage are still likely to be viewed by a jury as indicative ... of a general willingness to consent,' the report stated. It called for a ban on questions about the 'chastity or general sexual disposition of the complainant'. The CSW report called for anonymity for rape complainants and for special training in taking forensic evidence for doctors. It suggested the setting up of 'a comprehensive medico-legal centre' where rape victims could be taken for medical examination.

Hussey overcame her nerves and spoke at length about rape that day. She went further than the CSW on the issue of marital rape. It was a crime and should be recognised as such in the law, she said. In the debate that followed, Senator Ken Whitaker opposed this. For married people living together, he said, there should be a 'virtually impregnable presumption of consent'. One senator said many women 'upset the biological balance of a man and then claim they were raped'. The then Minister for State at the Department of Justice, David Andrews, said the CSW document was being 'sympathetically considered' by the government. Mary Robinson, then a senator and barrister, said the whole approach to rape was based on 'values and concepts that are no longer acceptable'. She praised the women's movement for highlighting 'an area that causes great injustice and suffering' and said she was 'really impressed' by the First Report of the Dublin Rape Crisis Centre. She appealed for it to be given financial support.[13]

In a scathing news report on the debate in *The Irish Times*, Dick Walsh noted that for the most part the senate 'heard the "predominantly male" view of rape from people who admitted they were appalled by their own ignorance of the subject until the publication of its first report by the [Dublin Rape] Crisis Centre'. Walsh quoted Labour's Justin Keating: 'Rape is not about sex, but about domination, power, humiliation.' Keating had compared rape to lynching and terrorism, intended to have an effect not just on the victim but also on her peers. He said he was appalled by 'the gradations in morality according to which it was impossible to rape one's own wife, an offence to rape the wife of another man, and virtually ok to rape a prostitute'. He said incest, involving rape, was widespread in Ireland but 'virtually unmentionable'.[14]

Fianna Fáil's Eoin Ryan told the senate that preparation for the government's own rape bill was at a 'late stage'. He opposed Hussey's motion, which was defeated by 21 votes to 16.

'I knew my bill wouldn't get through,' said Hussey. 'But it

was important that we got the issue talked about. There was a picture of me in one of the papers the next day wreathed in cheroot smoke and looking as tough as old boots. I was thrilled at the support I got from independents and from the Labour Party. I wrote in my diary, "For this I got elected and it makes it all worth it."' As for the government's intentions: 'I remember Charlie Haughey passing behind me around that time and he tweaked my bra strap,' Hussey recalled. 'I wheeled round and he said to me, "Don't worry now about your bill. We'll get that through." However, on the anniversary of its submission on rape in Ireland, the Council for the Status of Women issued a strong statement denouncing 'a very negative response and a total lack of progress'.

In 1980 Mary McAleese and Mary Robinson were interviewed by Betty Purcell in the journal *Crane Bag*. Purcell asked them about the 'insulting' existence of the law on criminal conversation. Robinson noted that since this law allowed a man to sue for damages for the enticement away of his wife, thereby clearly seeing her in terms of her property value to him, a woman would have a 'very good action before the Commission and Court of Human Rights' since 'this is cruel and degrading treatment'. In fact, this clearly sexist legal principle was the subject of the first major Law Reform Commission report in 1981 and was abolished that year in the Family Law Act.

Purcell referred to the fact that the Law Reform Commission was looking at the CSW's proposals for rape law reform. McAleese replied: 'I have no faith at all in the Law Reform Commission. Their reports are usually shelved and their methods of approaching matters of urgency leads me to believe that they're not going to be challengers.' Robinson agreed that their reports lacked political significance. McAleese said it was significant that Fianna Fáil had 'dropped' the only woman who had been on the Commission. 'The law of rape does certainly need to be reformed ... Rape trials, at the moment, tend to become a trial within a trial where the woman finds herself answering very personal and traumatic questions about her sexual life not only with the person who is accused of rape but with x, y or z. It is a terrible indictment of our Court system that this should happen, and often, instead of establishing the truth of whether the accused committed the crime, it only succeeds in casting her in the role of a whore or a bad woman, thereby attacking her credibility as a woman and as a witness.'[15]

The Rape Crisis Centre meanwhile lobbied for a meeting with the Minister for Justice. It finally got a meeting with the then Minister for State at the department, Seán Doherty, in September 1980. An account of the meeting was included in the DRCC's 1981 annual report. Doherty said he agreed with the demand for anonymity for rape victims, but not that the woman's sexual history with men other than the accused should be deemed irrelevant. He told the women it was probably unconstitutional to legislate to ensure that there were always at least four women on any rape jury. He rejected their demand for the definition of rape to be extended to include rape by objects and oral and anal rape.

The DRCC demanded that women be assured 'proper access to adequate legal advice'. Doherty was 'unforthcoming' on this. The women were left in no doubt as to the government's position on marital rape: 'Absolute rejection of this proposal. No way will this be in the new legislation.'[16]

In October 1980 Gerry Collins finally introduced the Criminal Law Rape Bill in the Dáil. Although it included some of the measures the DRCC had recommended, and increased the penalty for indecent assault from two to ten years, it fell far short of the Hussey bill. The Rape Crisis Centre expressed acute disappointment.

'The bill doesn't go nearly as far as it should and it isn't a well drafted piece of legislation,' said Anne O'Donnell. 'There are very many sexually degrading and harmful acts which are still not technically regarded as rape but cause even greater suffering and distress, including violation of the genital area with bottles and sticks.' These would continue to be defined as indecent assault. Boys under 14 would continue to be presumed incapable of rape and, crucially, rape in marriage would not be recognised, even though, as O'Donnell pointed out, it was a fact of life for many women in the Women's Aid refuge.

Nor did the bill go far enough, O'Donnell said, in protecting the woman from questions about her sexual history. She said certain omissions in the new law could be remedied by updating garda regulations on the taking of evidence, and the introduction of briefings of rape complainants by state lawyers bringing the case on their behalf. O'Donnell argued for the fast-tracking of rape cases, because delays of nine months or so can have 'the most traumatic consequences for the woman who has the case hanging over her so long'.[17]

Supporting O'Donnell, Hussey spoke of the 'glaring omission' of marital rape. 'A husband can sexually attack his wife, tie her up, abuse her body to his heart's content in the most savage ways possible and it isn't rape,' she said. 'Because they are married there is no such thing, even if it happens on the kitchen floor with her children looking on, after a woman has been beaten into submission.'

At a packed public meeting organised by the Rape Crisis Centre in Liberty Hall on 25 November 1980, Hussey described the exclusion of marital rape from the bill as 'an extraordinary admission of cowardice and unwillingness to face reality'. Miriam Logan, a worker from Women's Aid, told the meeting that the majority of women who came to the refuge had been raped by their husbands and that recently two women had required medical attention because of objects placed in their vaginas during such rapes. Women raped in marriage didn't associate sex with love or tenderness, she said, adding that their daughters were sometimes left with an attitude of abhorrence towards sex. Anne O'Donnell told the meeting that the major problem in dealing with rape in Ireland was the attitude of society, which was reflected in the attitude of juries, making it difficult to get convictions. She quoted statistics from the London Rape Crisis Centre which showed that women were more at risk in their own homes than on the streets at night.

In the months that followed, women picketed the Dáil in support of the DRCC's demands for amendments to the new law. A spokeswoman at one such picket, Molly O'Duffy, said the reluctance of the government to agree to the changes was due to 'a basic distrust of women'.[18] A support group, Action Against Rape, was set up. At one picket a small girl held a placard which said, 'Even I can be raped. Please protect me.'

During Dáil debates on the new bill, Seán Doherty continued to resist demands for changes. He said it was not possible to extend the definition of rape. It was important to realise that the crime of rape carried the possibility of pregnancy so that 'natural intercourse' was an essential ingredient. Women's groups were calling for marital rape to be included, he said, but they had failed to indicate the extent of such rape. Some of those calling for rape in marriage to be criminalised were, in fact, in the Fianna Fáil party. Eileen Lemass called for a comprehensive overhaul of the bill to include many of the provisions called for by the DRCC. She also criticised judges for lenient sentencing.

Labour's John Horgan said that when a woman entered into marriage she did so to acquire rights, not to sign them away, and Noël Browne of the Socialist Labour Party said it was strange that marriage, which was referred to by the Church as a sacrament, deprived a woman of her constitutional right.

When the bill reached the senate in 1981 Mary Robinson said it 'dodged the key issues'. She said the Minister seemed to be 'hung up on a Victorian definition of rape'. Mary Harney criticised the bill for failing to extend the definition of rape and for excluding rape in marriage. Rape was not just a crime against a victim, she said. It was a crime against society.

However, the Fine Gael former Minister for Justice, Paddy Cooney, denounced the bill for entirely different reasons. 'There is a reaction here to the emotionalism of a campaign mounted for understandable reasons against the crime of rape,' he said. 'The emotionalism assumes that the complainants are all innocent and the rapists are all guilty.'[19] It might be 'distasteful' for the defence to attack the complainant on the basis of her sexual history, he said, but it was relevant to know if the complainant was promiscuous or a prostitute, he asserted. Doherty said that if it were possible for wives to bring charges of rape against their husbands, the problems that could arise from hasty allegations should be obvious to everyone.

The debate continued in the newspapers. Pat McCartan, now a judge, was a criminal lawyer at the time. He questioned the ability of any rape bill to deal with rape as a social problem. 'Rape is a crime based on the myth of male supremacy and domination fundamental to our social values and it is in education, social attitudes and the position of women generally that changes are essential,' he said.[20]

McCartan alleged that the provision for anonymity for the rape complainant in the new bill was an infringement of the concept of an open court and set a dangerous precedent. He also opposed the restrictions on questions about a woman's sexual history, regarding this as potentially infringing the right of the accused to explore all relevant matters. The new bill defined the law on consent and would lead to judges directing juries that they were to have regard as to the presence or absence of reasonable grounds for the accused to believe the complainant was consenting. The DRCC opposed this because it was 'too subjective a test'. McCartan said it was 'unwarranted, unprecedented and possibly a breach of the constitutional concept of a separation of powers between legislature and judiciary'.

The Prisoners' Rights Organisation (PRO) raised the fact that prisons had no facilities to treat sex offenders, an issue which would come to preoccupy the DRCC in the years to come. The PRO also objected to the restrictions placed on the defence's right to use evidence of a woman's sexual history. Spokesman Joe Costello said this interfered with the accused man's rights. It was unconstitutional and would be challenged in the courts.

The Criminal Law Rape Act was passed in June 1981. Anne O'Donnell gave the Rape Crisis Centre's verdict. The new law would let the government off the hook on rape, she said. It was an inadequate law and a bad one.

4

ANGER

In 1980 19-year-old Deborah Robinson from Belfast was raped and murdered, her body dumped in a ditch in Co. Kildare. Newspapers reported that police were hunting a 'fiend'. It was one of several murders of women that year.

A 17-year-old girl was raped by a man who dragged her down a laneway as she walked home from her grandmother's house in Dublin's northside. She screamed, but passers-by who came to her rescue left after the rapist said, 'Go away; she's my girlfriend.' The judge sentenced the 23-year-old rapist from Co. Mayo to seven years' penal servitude and described rape as 'a most revolting crime that strikes the foundation of civilised society'.[1]

Two teenage girls from Drogheda were sexually assaulted after they accepted a lift from three men, mistakenly believing they knew them. The father of one of the girls told the court she was 'not the same since the incident and would never be the same again'. A six-year-old girl was sexually assaulted, beaten and left naked in a field in Co. Down. Two young children were sexually assaulted by an 80-year-old man in Co. Wexford. The judge described the attacker, in whose home pornography was found, as a 'lonely old man' and gave him a two-year suspended sentence.

A young woman was raped after she left a dance in Co. Donegal with a 29-year-old man. The judge said the man had set out 'to ravage this girl', first charming her, then luring her off and terrorising her. The judge remarked that 'this type of offence is so prevalent in Ireland today' and sent the rapist to prison for ten years. A 66-year-old woman from Co. Mayo was indecently assaulted by a man to whom she opened her door. A 13-year-old girl was raped by a 17-year-old boy who then killed a priest who disturbed him during the attack at a presbytery in Dublin.

A 17-year-old girl was sexually assaulted by a 19-year-old Kilkenny man. She ran away from him and hid overnight in an outhouse. A 20-year-old woman had to have her arm amputated after she was raped and beaten up by an 18-year-old Waterford man who hit her with a typewriter and a hurley stick. He broke into her home and raped her while her four-month-old baby lay beside her.

A 12-year-old girl became pregnant and had a baby after a 26-year-old Cork man had 'unlawful carnal knowledge' of her. His wife was also pregnant with her third child at the same time. The judge gave him a six-year suspended sentence.

Another 12-year-old girl was raped by a 23-year-old Cork man who threatened her he would kill her brother. He got a two-year suspended sentence. The Rape Crisis Centre issued a statement in which it said it was 'extremely disturbed' by the outcome of this last case and described the sentence as 'degrading' to the status of the child. 'If this is what happens when the accused pleads guilty, what hope is there for women where the case is contested? We are sorry and depressed,' the statement said.

There were many other cases. Women were being raped all over Ireland. Before the Rape Crisis Centre was set up, no one had drawn attention to this horrific fact of Irish life.

From 1975 to 1981, women in the North of England were terrorised by a man who became known as the Yorkshire Ripper. This was a serial killer who used hammers, knives and screwrivers to inflict horrific injuries on the women he attacked. He murdered 13 women, striking in towns and cities right across Yorkshire. At least seven other women survived attacks by him.

The women in the Dublin Rape Crisis Centre followed these dreadful events, not least because of their links with the Rape Crisis movement in Britain, where, throughout this period, feminists organised Reclaim the Night marches and demonstrations against 'sex shops'. Police in Yorkshire advised women not to go out alone – *Spare Rib* carried articles about women who had been raped by men whom they had trusted to accompany them. Women who opted for self-defence were convicted of carrying knives.

In January 1981 Peter Sutcliffe was arrested, apparently on the verge of killing another woman. Three months later, he pleaded guilty to the manslaughter of 13 women and the attempted murder of seven more. His plea of diminished responsibility was accepted, and he was sent to Broadmoor Hospital to serve his 20 life sentences, though there was clear evidence that his madness was contrived to avoid prison.

Disturbing evidence emerged that the police had botched the hunt for the killer, not least by disregarding the evidence given by women who had survived attacks. One woman had helped police prepare a photofit picture which, it turned out, bore a remarkable resemblance to Sutcliffe. Instead, police were led off the trail by hoax tapes in which a man boasted that he was the Ripper. It emerged that Sutcliffe had first been arrested in 1969, armed with a hammer in the red light district of Bradford. He had been questioned several times during the hunt for the Ripper and should have been identified as a chief suspect long before his final capture.

The story was extensively covered in the Irish media. In its Second Report, published in 1981, the DRCC included a furious letter that it had sent to the editors of all the national papers. The letter condemned the 'hysterical and sensationalist tone' of reports on the Ripper case in the Irish as well as the British press. It described as 'voyeuristic' and 'pornographic' headlines such as 'Ripper's Gruesome Gallery' over photographs of the murder victims. It said descriptions of the women conveyed prejudice – reports stated that, while the first five victims were prostitutes, 'in June 1977 he struck down innocent shop girl Jayne MacDonald, 16'. Other victims who were not prostitutes were referred to in reports as 'respectable'. According to the DRCC, 'the implication inherent in such commentary is clearly that the murdered women described as prostitutes had in some way deserved their fate'.

The letter agreed with the suggestion by feminists in Leeds that if there was to be a curfew, it should be imposed on 'the aggressors – men' and not on women. It pointed out that while one Irish paper said women in Yorkshire were taking to the streets again 'because for them the danger is past', the same report revealed that the killer of another woman in the area was still at large. 'The assaults and murders attributed to the Yorkshire Ripper are of a particularly brutal nature, but the hatred of women manifested by their perpetrator must be recognised as an underlying factor in all sexually violent crime.'

It accused the papers of dressing up coverage of such crime as serious news 'while treating them as "page three" type sex features'. Sexual violence had a social context – the media should 'investigate seriously its sources and effects rather than falsify its reality by sensational exploitation of its particular manifestations'; the letter concluded: 'If the Yorkshire Ripper is a monster, he is a monster which our society has produced.'[2] Meanwhile rock group Thin Lizzy had released a single in 1980 called 'Killer on the Loose'. It included the line 'I'm a mad, sexual rapist ...'

Among British feminists, there were fierce debates about 'heterosexism' and 'political lesbianism', with the Leeds Revolutionary Feminist Group declaring that 'men are the enemy' and 'serious feminists have no choice but to abandon heterosexuality'. The heterosexual couple 'is the basic unit of the political structure of male supremacy' and women within such couples were 'collaborators'.[3]

Increasing numbers of women working in British Rape Crisis Centres and women's refuges were lesbian separatists who saw themselves as the frontline of the feminist army. Anne O'Donnell recalled attending a conference in the North of England during this period. 'We were called half sisters,' she said. Margaret Martin, then a volunteer in the DRCC, now director of Women's Aid, said she was startled by the militancy of some of the British women. 'I'd never encountered so many varieties of extreme feminism,' she said. 'It made me realise that in Ireland the women's movement made a very easy bedfellow with other radical groups.'

On the other hand, Martin was dismayed to find that British feminists seemed to believe that the most important issue for women in Ireland was the national question. 'They were inclined to support republicanism in what I saw as a simplistic way,' she said. 'At the same time, in Ireland, women I felt should be supporting the likes of the Rape Crisis Centre were putting all their energy into organising republican marches around the H blocks and the Hunger Strikes.'

The Dublin Rape Crisis Centre never subscribed to separatism. It did, however, continue to insist on supporting American author Susan Brownmiller's statement that 'all men are potential rapists'. It was considered essential that any woman joining the collective should 'accept it or the essential meaning of it'.[4] It was introduced for discussion during training courses. Mary Quinlan, who was a volunteer at the Centre from 1981 to 1984, said she had 'believed passionately' in the statement. 'I remember discussing it with my partner, and only recently he told me that he never walked behind a woman on the street after that, in case she'd be afraid,' she said. Brownmiller's ground-breaking book, *Against Our Will – Men, Women and Rape*, was obligatory reading for volunteers at the Rape Crisis Centre.

'I used to be very angry in those days,' said Mary Quinlan. 'A friend of mine said to me recently that she was scared to death of me back then. She said I'd have bitten the head off anyone.' Quinlan said it was necessary to be radical and vigilant in those early years of the DRCC. 'We were the vanguard,' she said. 'We kept on talking about the myths of rape and the reality of rape. We used every opportunity, and it was very powerful. We took a lot of shit and abuse for it, but we did change the way rape was seen.'

Liz Sherry, a DRCC volunteer who later represented the centre on the Council for the Status of Women (CSW), said the Centre had to be provocative. 'We needed to rattle cages and to get people to accept that something was going on that needed attention. You had to be extreme to get some balance.'[5]

Terri Morrissey remembered the anger, too, and the lure of the extreme. 'I felt so extremely angry about rape, and looking back, I can see I was very aggressive,' she said. 'I read all the feminist books, Germaine Greer, Marilyn French, and I bought into the whole militant thing. I remember telling someone I supported SCUM, the Society for Cutting Up Men.' While she was proud of her involvement, she felt the work damaged her. 'At first, we didn't really look after ourselves. We didn't consider the effect this exposure to rape was having. It turned me off sex. I was impossible to live with.

'I decided to go. I believe you can only do that sort of work for a certain amount of time. You lose perspective. I remember I was reading an Andrea Dworkin book and I ended up throwing it across the floor. I felt the images I was getting in my head were going to kill me. If I'd stayed any longer in rape crisis work I felt it was going to destroy me.' Twenty-five years later, Morrissey said that she has changed. 'I work in a more conciliatory way now, but I still respect the anger of those days. We had to be extreme because of what we were up against.'[6]

Barbara Egan joined the DRCC as a volunteer in 1981. 'I'd worked in child psychiatry and I felt I wanted to work with women who had been wronged,' she recalled. 'The training really made me open my mind and question everything. I loved belonging to a campaigning organisation and I loved that we were bucking the system. I was articulate and I liked lecturing, so I did a lot of that. We thought we could make a huge difference to society. Almost to a woman, rape victims felt shame. I remember just one woman who was only angry. She was quite a woman. She reported the attack on her to the gardaí and they didn't take it seriously. She rode a motorbike, and she searched the pubs for weeks, wearing her helmet, until she spotted this man and then she had him prosecuted.'

Egan was employed as a fundraiser in 1982. She said she

had never agreed with statements like Brownmiller's about rape as a conscious process of intimidation. 'It was a wild statement and it never served us well,' she said. 'I remember a Reclaim the Night march in the early eighties. Some men came to it to show support, including men who were partners of women working in the Rape Crisis Centre. Some women on the march behaved badly, jeering at them, and I felt ashamed. Men weren't the enemy – men who raped were. I was selling T-shirts I'd had made for the occasion from the boot of my car. They had the moon and stars on them and they were gorgeous. There were all sorts of rabble-rousing speeches and I was glad I could keep my head down behind the car. Afterwards, we had a disco which was for women only. A bunch of very angry lesbian-feminist-separatist-type women arrived along very aggressive and drunk. First they tried to get in without paying and then they caused fights on the dancefloor. I thought to myself, I have far less in common with these than with most men.'[7]

The Centre's Second Report contained its first set of statistics. Counsellors at the Centre saw 126 women, most in the 16 to 35 age-group, though they were contacted on behalf of two children under the age of nine and a further seven aged under 15. Most women rang the Centre primarily for emotional support, but many also needed medical and legal advice.

Out of a sample of 95, 40 per cent were raped by a stranger, 22 per cent by an acquaintance or colleague, 16 per cent by a friend or neighbour, 9 per cent by a relation, including fathers and brothers, and almost 12 per cent by a lover or husband. Almost 40 per cent of women were raped in their own home and 12 per cent in the rapist's home, while 42 per cent of rapes occurred outside, in streets, laneways or fields. One of the most striking statistics revealed that almost 70 per cent of the women hadn't reported the rape to the police. The report noted that some women said they were too disturbed and upset to report the attack, while others feared retaliation from the assailant or members of his circle. Some women said they were afraid the police wouldn't be sympathetic, wouldn't believe them or would consider they had been 'foolish' or 'asking for it'.

Three women had dropped charges because they couldn't endure the lengthy delays in reaching court. Out of eight cases which the Centre had seen through legal proceedings, there were four convictions for rape, one for attempted rape and one for indecent assault – in both these cases the initial charge was rape, but this was reduced when the defendant agreed to plead guilty to the lesser charge. In two cases, the defendant was acquitted.

The Second Report carried (with the consent of the women) three 'case histories' of women who had contacted the Centre. The first concerned a 43-year-old woman and her 11-year-old daughter who were raped at knifepoint in their home. The man was a 24-year-old married acquaintance of the woman's ex-husband. He broke into their house at 3 a.m., came into the woman's bedroom and tied and gagged her. When the child came into the room, the rapist tied her up. He then raped the woman, continually threatening her about the safety of her children. He then raped the child. After he left, the woman alerted neighbours and the police were called.

A police doctor examined both mother and child for forensic evidence. The following day, statements were taken and the day after that the assailant was arrested and charged. He was held in custody until the hearing in the Central Criminal Court, seven months later. About two months after being raped, the woman contacted the Rape Crisis Centre and both she and her daughter came regularly for counselling. Both were, the report said, 'extremely upset and disturbed … and terrified of the impending court case'.

The police co-operated in every way with the woman and girl who were raped, and also with the Rape Crisis Centre. Two weeks before the court case, as a result of a meeting between the Rape Crisis counsellor and the Director of Public Prosecutions, two consultations and a visit to the courts were organised for the mother and daughter. 'They found it extremely helpful to have an opportunity to speak with the counsel for the state and actually see a courtroom before the case.'

The case was held in camera. Both mother and daughter were called to give evidence. Counsel for the defence attempted to have the rape crisis counsellor removed from the court, despite the fact that the woman who had been raped and her daughter were very dependent on her for moral support, since neither wanted to be present for the other's evidence. After some wrangling, the judge decided the relationship between the counsellor and the two witnesses was important and invited her to remain.

The case lasted two days. The rapist was found guilty of raping both witnesses and sentenced to 12 years' penal servitude.

In the second case, a young woman went to a disco in a neighbouring town and took a lift home with a man who claimed to know her family. On the way home he stopped the car and told her he was going to rape her. When she struggled, he hit her head and face off the steering wheel and ripped her clothes. He then raped her.

Afterwards, she told her sister what had happened and her sister took her to the local doctor. The woman was distraught and tried to slash her wrists. The doctor sent her to the county hospital to be examined. Then she reported the rape to the police. Six months later she was informed that the case was to be heard in the local Circuit Court. The woman had not seen or spoken to the person who was to represent the state on her behalf, nor had she any idea what was to happen in court. She did not realise she would be cross-examined but thought they would simply read out her statement. She was extremely upset prior to the case.

When she was called into the witness box, she was on tranquillisers. 'She was aware of the accused staring at her and, as she stated, "chewing gum and smirking" at her,' the report said. 'In the witness box the judge asked her to define what she meant by rape. She could not answer. He repeated the question a number of times and she broke down and would not answer. The judge dismissed the case.'

Since the court case, the woman was in and out of the county psychiatric hospital, suicidally depressed. She gave up work. She found it extremely difficult living in the town, because she felt people were talking about her. She had to have surgery on her nose as a result of the beating during the rape. 'She feels cheated and angry,' the report said. 'She wants justice.'

In the third case, a teenage girl was offered a lift by her friend's neighbour. He drove her up a laneway and raped her, using force and threats. Then he picked up a friend who also brutally raped her. They dumped her on the road and a passing motorist brought her to the police. She had to attend an identification parade and pick out the two rapists.

Contact was made with the Rape Crisis Centre the morning after the rape and her counsellor made sure she received a copy of her police statement. She came for counselling for many months and was extremely upset by the rape. She was afraid to go out alone by day or by night. Details of the rape were constantly running through her mind. After some months, she began to improve and started to go out again on rare occasions. She was still terrified of the prospect of the court hearing.

The projected date for the court case was to be approximately nine months after the rape. As the month of the court case approached, nightmares returned, the details of the rape again began to dominate her mind and she became frightened of going out.

Suddenly, she was informed that the case had been deferred for another seven to eight months. There would then be the possibility of two court cases, as one of the assailants had skipped the country. A separate trial would have to be held for him at some unknown date in the future. The woman would have to give evidence at both cases. 'At this stage,' the report said, 'she decided she had endured enough, and she informed the police that she would not be prepared to give evidence.' The police were forced to drop the charges. The woman was angry that the men were 'getting away with their crime'.[8]

5

MEDDLING WITH THE MORAL LAW

Mrs Valerie Riches came to Ireland in March 1980 with a dire warning. The secretary of the British Responsible Society group said that, 'In Britain today, the family as an institution is under very serious threat indeed.' The slide towards moral depravity had started with the legalisation of contraception. It would go on, inexorably, she said.

She was speaking at a meeting on 'The Permissive Society – its implications for Ireland.' It marked the launch of an Irish branch of the Responsible Society. Bernadette Bonar became chairperson, while John O'Reilly became secretary. Bonar was a member of the Eastern Health Board. O'Reilly's view of the Rape Crisis Centre was stark. It was an example of how 'ultra permissive forces can fasten onto what appears to be a compassionate or charitable cause'.[1]

The reality of pregnancy arising from rape was central to the concerns of those determined to maintain traditional moral values in Ireland. In 1939, in the Bourne case, an English doctor had been prosecuted under the 1861 Offences Against the Person Act for performing an abortion on a 14-year-old girl who had been gang-raped by soldiers. The maximum penalty under the act was life imprisonment. Bourne said that if the girl had been forced to go through with the pregnancy, she would have been a psychological wreck. The judge in the case ruled that abortion was lawful if a doctor felt that continuation of pregnancy would endanger a woman's life or seriously disturb her mentally or physically. This led, finally, to the 1967 Abortion Act in Britain.

At the Responsible Society launch, Riches outlined a conspiracy theory. There was a network of organisations campaigning for liberal reforms, including, most insidiously, sex education for children. Manipulating it all was the International Planned Parenthood Federation, whose members included the Irish Family Planning Association. Those concerned about the imminent demise of traditional values in Irish society should beware of the clamour for 'laws relating to the status of women'.[2]

The Society for the Protection of the Unborn Child was founded in the same year, and a variety of ultra-Catholic groups began to organise against those advocating the sort of reforms Riches had described. In January 1981, the honorary secretary of the Irish Family League, Mary Kennedy, took on the subject of 'Family Law, i.e. contraception, rape and criminal conversation'. She berated the government for having 'meddled' with contraception, thereby ignoring 'the moral law of God'. One thing would lead to another: 'it is a hard fact that anti birth policy and abortion is a package deal; you cannot buy one without the other', she wrote.[3] It was 'rather extraordinary' that Senator Hussey and the AIM group were campaigning for marital rape to be included in the law. 'This, too, is part of the general attack on marriage, and the relationship between the spouses.'

According to the Family League, the law of criminal conversation (which feminists were fighting to overthrow) 'operates to defend and protect marriage'. It should be extended 'to enable the wife to recover damages from the adultress'. To say this law made the wife a 'chattel' of her husband was 'just a piece of mendacious semantics'. The 'divorce lobby' wanted to legalise adultery: 'Let wives be warned.'

In the same month, Fine Gael TD Oliver J. Flanagan stood up in the Dáil and asked the Fianna Fáil Minister for Health,

Michael Woods, if he was aware that the Rape Crisis Centre was part of a pro-abortion alliance. Was the Minister sure the grant of £5,000 he had given the DRCC the previous year hadn't been used to subsidise abortion referral and propaganda? Woods replied that he had received detailed information about the centre before making the decision to fund it.

Back in July 1980, when the Minister had announced that he had instructed the Eastern Health Board to make the grant, he told RTÉ that the government expected that the funding would be ongoing. 'I expect we'll give them continuing support not just in money terms but in maintaining a relationship and giving them whatever help we can,' he said.[4] However, in June 1981, the Rape Crisis Centre revealed that since it had applied for a grant of £20,000 in October 1980, it had heard nothing from the Eastern Health Board.

At the launch of the Second Report, Anne O'Donnell said the Centre had £600 in hand and debts of over £2,000. There was no money for wages, no money for advertising, no money for research, no money to pay the rent. Pointing out that Cherish, the organisation for unmarried parents, and Women's Aid were also in dire financial straits, O'Donnell said, 'It seems to us that women in distress come last in the priorities of Ireland's concerns.'[5] She was scathing about 'paltry' amounts given to the Centre by banks, drinks companies and other businesses. 'A £50 cheque from an organisation that makes millions in profits is almost insulting,' she said. It was not support, it was 'more like conscience money'.[6] 'Most sectors of society cry out against violence, but is anyone prepared to put their money where their mouth is?' she demanded. The Centre needed £40,000 a year, it estimated. 'We do not beg for financial aid – we have a right to be supported by the community which creates this problem in the first place.'[7]

A general election was pending. Gemma Hussey, who had joined Fine Gael, said on the groundbreaking (and short-lived) RTÉ radio programme *Women Today* that Fine Gael, in government, would make sure that the Rape Crisis Centre and other voluntary women's groups got the help they needed. Shortly after the election of a Fine Gael and Labour coalition, Anne O'Donnell said that under the last Fianna Fáil government closure had seemed inevitable. It was a 'great relief' that the coalition was now in power, given promises made. It would be a 'real sellout' if they failed to deliver.

In an article in *Status* in late 1981, Nell McCafferty recounted a revealing anecdote involving the late TV personality Eamon Andrews, who had recently 'regaled' a Dublin Chamber of Commerce gathering with behind the scenes stories about the making of the TV series, *This is Your Life*. 'When he sprang a surprise on the late Lord Mountbatten, Mr Andrews chortled, Mountbatten remarked that this invasion of his private life was akin to rape – if it's inevitable you might as well lie back and enjoy it.'[8]

'That such an attitude to rape might still cause male chuckles in Ireland in 1981 is no surprise given the government's attitude to the Rape Crisis Centre,' she wrote. Following Fine Gael's electoral success, the organisation had received what McCafferty called 'a paltry £600 increase in its annual grant from the Eastern Health Board'. McCafferty pointed out that not only was the grant of £5,600 completely inadequate, there was also no guarantee that it would be made again the following year.

O'Donnell said at this time that she was sick of fighting for a shoestring budget. 'We need a fixed annual sum, index-linked, to end all this insecurity,' she said. 'It is time we were free to get on with our work.'[9] A lot of energy was wasted, she said, not just on fundraising, but also on the perpetual battle with conservative groups which were trying to have the Rape Crisis Centre closed down.

In a 1981 newsletter, the Responsible Society boasted of its struggle against the renewal of the government's grant to the Centre that year. 'It is our belief that in funding the Rape Crisis Centre the state is funding and lending respectability to promoters of abortion,' it stated, adding, in what was an extraordinary admission, 'even though the amount is small and it cannot be proved that the Rape Crisis Centre as such is in any way connected with abortion or with abortion referral.'

The author went on: 'After a long fight, the grant was paid to the Centre at the same rate as for 1980 which was well below the expectations of the Centre and this represented a victory of sorts. It will be opposed again in 1982.'[10]

Abortion was prohibited in Ireland under the 1861 Offences Against the Person Act. In April 1981, the Pro-Life Amendment Campaign (PLAC) was launched. Its aim was to amend Article 40 of the Constitution, on the right to life, to include the amendment: 'The State recognises the absolute right to life of every unborn child from conception and accordingly guarantees to respect and protect such life by law.'[11] At a time of political instability, it was able to manipulate the political parties with ease. Fine Gael leader Garret FitzGerald jumped to support it, though it was clearly contrary to the spirit of his 'constitutional crusade' to make Ireland non-sectarian. Fianna Fáil leader Charlie Haughey was equally enthusiastic about the PLAC proposal, as was his Health and Social Welfare Minister, Michael Woods. Labour leader Frank Cluskey prevaricated.

The PLAC included among its affiliates two groups that had already declared their opposition to the values they ascribed to the Rape Crisis Centre. These were the Irish Family League and the Responsible Society. Journalist Fintan O'Toole attended a meeting of the PLAC in Kildare in July 1982 and wrote about it in *In Dublin*. After showing a gruesome film about abortion, Bernadette Bonar addressed the audience. She had a specific warning about rape. 'I know of one TD who has spoken out against abortion, and every week coming to his clinic there's a couple of seemingly respectable little women giving him sob stories about 12-year-olds being raped and getting pregnant and the like,' she said.

Loreto Browne of the Society for the Protection of the Unborn Child (SPUC) also addressed the rape issue. She said the abortion lobby used 'soft cases' as a basis for its arguments. 'Rape is very horrible, but most women who are raped don't conceive,' she said. 'Men that go in for rape are not usually fertile – they tend to be impotent.' In any case, even if a woman did become pregnant, it was no excuse for abortion:

'A woman who has been raped can have a washout,' she asserted. 'It may not be very successful but it can be tried.' According to O'Toole's account of the meeting, she then surveyed the audience. 'How many people here know how they were conceived? Do they know they weren't conceived as a result of rape? That is worth pondering.'

The Catholic Church's position was that pregnancy resulting from rape meant there was now an 'innocent third party'. O'Toole described the attitude of Professor John Bonar, professor of obstetrics and gynaecology at Trinity College, Dublin, towards raped women. Bonar said if a raped woman came to him, he would make a 'personal decision' as to how to proceed. If he thought she hadn't yet ovulated and therefore could not be pregnant, he would give her the morning-after pill to prevent her from conceiving. However, if he thought she might have conceived as a result of the rape, he would not give her the pills.

The Rape Crisis Centre asked for and was given space to reply to the allegations made in the *In Dublin* article. It began by refuting Browne's claim that rapists tended to be infertile and impotent. Many of the women coming to the DRCC had been raped by married men who had children. The assertion that women who were raped didn't conceive was one of the myths – they frequently did. As for the 'washout' suggestion: 'There is no hospital in Ireland which provides a D and C or any other means of preventing pregnancy to a woman who has been raped.' Anyway, it would be ineffective, whereas the insertion of an intra uterine device (IUD) or use of the morning-after pill might be successful. The Centre took issue with Bonar for assuming that it was his right to decide for a woman, that 'the professor's opinion ... is perceived by himself to be fundamentally more weighty than the conscience of the woman involved'. It was also 'hypocritical' to discriminate against a woman just because of the stage of her menstrual cycle when she was raped. The decision should be the woman's. 'The physical act of rape was inflicted on her by her assailant,' said the DRCC. 'It is odious that the doctor should also seek to impose his will on her.'[12] As for the idea that pregnancy arising from rape was exceptional: 'Rape is no longer exceptional and pregnancy is common,' said the DRCC.

The Centre then dealt with the boast that the Responsible Society had fought and would continue to fight to stop the Rape Crisis Centre from getting public funding. 'We find it both incomprehensible and repugnant that organisations that claim to be pro-life are using their time and energy to discredit and financially debilitate the Rape Crisis Centre,' it said. 'The Responsible Society's concern for life does not appear to extend to those who have been raped, but solely to the unborn foetus.' It added that Eastern Health Board (EHB) personnel who had visited the Centre had expressed 'admiration and respect'. The Centre provided a 'unique service, which could not be provided by a statutory agency'.

The article explained that the counselling offered by the DRCC was 'non directive and non-judgemental'. Information was given about 'all the agencies which deal with problem/ unwanted pregnancies', but the Centre felt that the most successful means of helping raped women was to 'provide them with time and space to make their own decisions'. Gardaí, social workers, doctors, voluntary and statutory bodies with whom the DRCC had contact all had good relationships with the Centre: 'The Responsible Society and "pro-life" organisations are alone in their condemnation of the Centre and its work. Their attempts to blacken our name and have our funding withdrawn are totally unforgiveable considering that we are here to help women who are usually in a state of severe distress after one of the most humiliating and frightening human experiences – rape.'

Anticipating a movement against the amendment, John O'Reilly had written in 1981: 'the strategy, no doubt, would be to spread confusion by arguing for abortion in cases of rape, incest, alleged "life and death" situations, and in the case of foetal abnormality.' It would be 'highly emotive and libertarian'. To counter it, 'emotion will have to be made to serve the unborn'.[13] It most certainly was. The PLAC set about creating a climate in which people were persuaded that abortion was 'simply another name for genocide' and that in supporting the amendment, they were, to use Fine Gael deputy Alice Glenn's words, opposing a 'slaughter of the innocents'.[14]

In March 1982, Judge Frank Martin took the step of expelling a counsellor from the Limerick Rape Crisis Centre from the courtroom. 'More injustice is done in these cases by do-gooders from Rape Crisis Centres,' he said. The Limerick Centre had been set up in 1980 with the help and support of the Dublin Centre.

The Dublin Rape Crisis Centre canvassed and got the support of groups, including the Council for the Status of Women, the Free Legal Aid Centres and the Irish Council for Civil Liberties, and some female TDs. In a statement, it pointed out that rape victims were in a completely different situation in court than state witnesses in any other sort of trial.

'In no other criminal case is the first witness for the state subjected to the type of cross questioning and humiliation prevalent in rape cases,' it said. 'She is clearly placed in a greatly more upsetting role as a witness since she must prove her lack of consent to the rape, and therefore deserves to be prepared for the experience.' The statement said that since the state did not recognise its duty in this respect, the DRCC saw the preparation of a woman for court as one of its functions: 'In our experience the majority of women are terrified at the prospect of appearing in court and request that their Rape Crisis counsellor be present.'

Two trials that took place during this period highlighted the truly horrific extremes to which sexual violence could be brought. In March 1982 a 28-year-old former soldier was convicted of the murder of Deborah Robinson. The young Belfast woman had been raped before she was strangled. Her genital area was bruised and torn. Her killer claimed that she had consented to have sex with him. The murdered woman's parents were so distressed by the implications in court about their daughter's sexual behaviour that they vowed to 'clear her name'. Her mother, a doctor, also felt that it had been implied in court that because she worked she didn't have a good relationship with her daughter. After the conviction, her family issued a statement in which they said, 'We wish to establish once and for all … that Deborah was a respectable, normal, healthy girl who was not promiscuous nor even sexually experienced. The pathologist in his evidence established that she was a virgin.'[15] The murderer of Deborah Robinson got life imprisonment.

A few weeks later, the rapist and killer of another Irish woman got a very different sentence. Molly Daly, who was 61, ran a bakery business in Co. Monaghan. She lived alone. On 21 July 1981 a 55-year-old local man told a doctor's receptionist that Molly Daly was dead. When gardaí went to her home, they found her body. She was lying naked on her bed, which was covered in blood. A battery from a transistor radio had been forced into her vagina. The state pathologist told the court he had identified 120 bruises on the dead woman's body, and a large amount of hair had been torn from her head. There was blood and hair in every room of the house, indicating a high level of violence.

The man who had reported her death admitted having a 'tussle' with Molly Daly. Later, he admitted killing her. He said they had been friends, and that he had been 'naturally jealous' when he heard that she had 'other boyfriends'. Initially, he claimed their relationship was not sexual. Later, he claimed it was. A garda superintendent accepted the assertion by defence counsel Seamus Sorohan that the man's initial denial had been 'to protect her honour'. He also agreed that he was known as a quiet, inoffensive man, 'except when he had drink taken'. Sorohan told the court that what caused the accused most anguish was that Miss Daly died without a priest. The accused's conscience 'cried out for punishment' and he had not taken bail because of the shame he felt at causing her death, he said.

Mr Justice Barrington said he was satisfied that the accused had 'a genuine affection' for Molly Daly. 'If it was not for drink you would never have laid a hand on her,' he said. He adjourned sentencing for a year and gave the man bail on condition that he submit to treatment for alcoholism.

The DRCC was 'shocked and horrified' at the judgment. In a statement, it said the guilty man's reputed affection for the woman he had killed and his inebriated state should have been irrelevant. 'Killing a woman is always a crime of violence, regardless of the circumstances,' it said.[16] The AIM family law reform group expressed 'extreme concern'.

Monica Barnes and Gemma Hussey tried to raise the case in the Dáil. Hussey challenged the Fianna Fáil Minister for Justice, Seán Doherty, to say whether he felt the public was being properly protected 'by allowing out on bail someone who murdered someone after grievous sexual assault on the ground that he was unfit because he had taken drink'. She described the judge's decision in the case as 'extraordinary'. She got no answer.[17] There were just 11 women deputies in Dáil Eireann at this time to 155 men. It was the largest representation of women there had ever been in the house. Barnes said it was a lonely time to be a woman deputy: 'It was wall to wall men,' she said. 'Women had no power.'[18]

'The Rape Crisis Centre has decided to come out ...' When Anne O'Donnell announced at the launch of the anti-amendment campaign in June 1982 that the Rape Crisis Centre was to back the campaign, Liberty Hall erupted into applause and she received a standing ovation. The support of the Rape Crisis Centre was of huge moral significance for the campaign. Those promoting the amendment had dismissed the issue of pregnancy arising as a result of rape – the Rape Crisis Centre was in the best possible position to speak about the reality.

Back in 1978, the founding group had discussed the issue of pregnancy arising from rape. Anne Connolly had outlined the situation prevailing for women who wanted to have an abortion, and the group had decided that 'the policy of the DRCC is non-directive counselling and to give full support and information (including abortion referral and advice if necessary)'.[19] They had also written to the London Rape Crisis Centre asking the women there if they would be able to meet and give support to raped women travelling from Ireland to England for abortions. The DRCC's policy was that it would be equally supportive of a woman who chose to continue with her pregnancy. Its list of supportive persons and agencies included Catholic priests.

By April 1982 it was obvious that the Centre would come under pressure to declare and defend its policies in relation to both abortion and the referendum. There was a long discussion at the weekly collective meeting. It was decided that 'the DRCC supports a woman's decision in any matter concerning the question of pregnancy … If the press push us and ask when we say we support a woman's decision whatever it may be, would we support her choice for abortion, our answer is yes. We support the Irish Pregnancy Counselling Centre (IPCC) and will publicly be seen to do so if asked [and] if they are threatened with closure.'[20]

It was a radical position to adopt – the IPCC was the abortion referral service set up in 1980 by the Women's Right to Choose Group, which advocated that abortion should be legalised and made available in Ireland. It was set up because 'the Well Woman was finding itself unable to keep up with the demand for its referral service and this was resulting in unacceptable delays' for women seeking abortions. It was unclear at this time whether or not abortion referral was illegal. 'So the IPCC represented, as well as a service, a political act of confrontation.'[21]

Two delegates from the collective, Margaret Martin and Collette Cullen, attended the meeting at which the Anti-Amendment Campaign was formed. They reported back to the collective that the campaign would argue that the amendment was 'undemocratic, sectarian … and no resolution to the problem of abortion'.[22] The Centre agreed with the policy adopted by the campaign – it would oppose the amendment, without taking a position for or against abortion.

The decision to support the Anti-Amendment Campaign was unanimous. 'We were being attacked, left, right and centre,' recalled Mary Quinlan. 'But when we were attacked, we were very strong. We didn't take positions lightly, so once we reached consensus on something, we were committed to it.

On the amendment, we were 100 per cent certain that we were right.' Besides which, she added, 'We had our enemies, but we also had our friends.'[23] They included Moira Woods, then a doctor at the Well Woman Centre. 'She was so knowledgeable and supportive and she fed us a lot of good information. We used to be able to bring women to her, day or night, and she'd always help. She'd test for VD or pregnancy and she'd give the morning-after pill. I remember bringing women to her house on Ailesbury Road and she'd be there with her family, but she never turned us away. She was rock solid.' Woods was one of the sponsors of the Anti-Amendment Campaign.

A statement from the Rape Crisis Centre featured prominently in the book brought out by the Anti-Amendment Campaign in 1982: 'The fear of a possible pregnancy is uppermost in a woman's mind after being raped and adds greatly to her distress and trauma. As an organisation run by women for women it is obvious to us that women are very much discriminated against in Ireland. The attempt to introduce this amendment … will do nothing to solve the problem of unwanted pregnancies in Ireland, or improve the abysmally low level of practical support for single women and their children. The money for the referendum would be better utilised in areas where it will positively reflect a concern for the problems of women with unwanted pregnancies.'[24] It was estimated that the cost of the amendment campaign would be £800,000 – at a time when the DRCC was being told that £5,600 per annum was all the state could afford to pay it to provide support for raped women.

The Anti-Amendment Campaign adopted as its slogan 'It's life that needs amending, not the Constitution', and artist Robert Ballagh used it on the campaign poster, with a drawing by Kathe Kollwitz. The campaign's first statement emphasised that one of the objections to the amendment was that it would allow for no exceptions, even for cases of rape or incest. The sponsors were an eclectic group. Along with the Rape Crisis Centre and other service providers like Cherish and the Well Woman Centre, there were the Women's Right to Choose Group and the separate Women's Right to Choose campaign, left-wing political parties and trade unions including the Union of Students of Ireland. There were also Protestant Church leaders, politicians and lawyers, including Mary Robinson, Noël Browne, Pat Rabbitte, Bernadette McAliskey, David Norris, Catherine McGuinness and Conor Cruise O'Brien, and academics, singers and artists, including Christy Moore, Neil Jordan, Camille Souter and Robert Ballagh. The medical profession was represented by, among others, Moira Woods, Dermot Hourihane, Dean of Medicine at Trinity College, and George Henry, Master of the Rotunda Hospital. A spokesperson for SPUC said the Anti-Amendment Campaign was just trying to confuse people.

O'Donnell was elected to the steering committee and soon became one of the campaign's main spokespersons. In July 1982, a letter of which she was the co-author appeared in the papers pointing out that much of the debate about the proposed amendment had centred on legal, medical, philosophical and theological arguments, while little had been said about the 'practical problems of women living in present day Ireland'. It went on: 'Rape and incest are acts of forcible sexual violence, for which the girl/woman has no responsibility. Who then has the right to insist that these victims of male violence should be forced to carry and bear an unwanted child, conceived during rape? No hospital in Ireland offers a raped woman the opportunity to terminate her pregnancy, even immediately after possible conception.' The referendum had been declared sectarian by the Protestant Church leaders and by the chief rabbi, but it was also sectarian and divisive in the way it singled women out for attack, 'the most discriminated against section of our community'.[25]

Another letter objected to the claim by the SPUC that the Anti-Amendment Campaign was a campaign for abortion, and that those involved didn't respect human life. Was SPUC accusing the Rape Crisis Centre, Cherish and AIM of not respecting life, the letter demanded? 'These organisations care for women and children who are violated and discriminated against,' it said, adding that, by contrast, SPUC's concern 'appears to begin and end with the unborn foetus'.

When the government's wording of the amendment was published by Health Minister Michael Woods in November 1982, the Anti-Amendment Campaign objected to the fact that its implications for rape victims and users of IUDs and morning-after contraceptives were unclear. The Fianna Fáil government fell soon afterwards and Garret FitzGerald became Taoiseach again. He admitted regretting that he had agreed to the amendment and was memorably depicted by *Irish Times* cartoonist Martyn Turner regretting that he had ever been 'unborn'. An attempt by Fine Gael to make the amendment more anodyne failed. The Anti-Amendment Campaign pointed out that it would merely copperfasten the existing 1861 legislation prohibiting abortion and would allow for no exceptional circumstances, including rape and incest.

Those who believed that rape rarely resulted in pregnancy were presented with shocking evidence to the contrary when the Rape Crisis Centre published its statistics. Thirteen of the 152 women who had contacted the Rape Crisis Centre during 1982 had become pregnant after they were raped. Twelve women had avoided pregnancy by taking the morning-after pill, Cathy O'Brien of the DRCC told a seminar. She said the Centre was concerned that if the amendment was passed, the morning-after pill might be outlawed. In 1983, a 32-year-old Kerryman was convicted of sexual attacks on two girls, aged 14 and 16. Both had given birth to babies as a result.[26]

The amendment debate plunged onwards. Seated beside Anne O'Donnell at an anti-amendment press conference, rebel Fine Gael TD Monica Barnes warned that the referendum on the Fianna Fáil wording would lead to the 'nastiest, most prejudiced, bigoted, divisive campaign' seen in Ireland since the setting up of the state.

The late Fr Michael Cleary soon proved her right. In his 'Reflections' column he wrote that the Rape Crisis Centre had emerged in the 1970s from Irishwomen United, one of the aims of which was to get abortion legalised. 'These are the people who are afraid to show their true colours and who confuse and deceive many decent and fair-minded people with false concern for sectarianism and other things they have hitherto shown very little interest in,' he sneered.[27]

The collective discussed the article and noted in minutes, 'babies without nappies to be deposited at his residence'. Cleary later attacked the DRCC in a TV debate which was dominated by men. Anne O'Donnell said on the programme that her experience of working in the DRCC made her very concerned about the future of certain forms of contraception if the amendment was passed. Such contraception was vital, she said, to prevent raped women becoming pregnant. Her attempt to answer Cleary was shouted down by his supporters.[28]

In the final weeks of the campaign, the DRCC released O'Donnell from her job to work full-time for the Anti-Amendment Campaign. Mary Higgins, then working with Cherish, later a leading campaigner for the rights of homeless people, was joint PRO with her. 'Actually, most of the work was done by Anne O'Donnell and Mary Holland,' she said. 'I was very taken up at the time with the campaign to end illegitimacy. Anne was a very hard-hitting spokesperson, very bossy, very focused and very businesslike and clear cut.' Monica Barnes, also prominent in the Anti-Amendment Campaign, said O'Donnell was a hugely important figure – in the campaign and as spokesperson for the Rape Crisis Centre. 'She was outspoken and she had the style and the wit and the intelligence to bring it off,' she said. 'She cut quite a dash with her cropped hair and short skirts, her little boots and her dangly earrings. And she had a great sense of humour. She was the opposite of what people expected from a tough feminist.'[29] O'Donnell and Holland, the late, brilliant and elegant journalist, made a formidable team.

A group of feminists from Belfast who came to Donegal to distribute leaflets for the Anti-Amendment Campaign met with some hostility. In Letterkenny a young man hissed at one of them, 'You should all be put up against a wall and raped and made to get pregnant.'

The full might of the Catholic Church had been mustered to urge the people to vote yes. Bishop Joseph Cassidy had warned that 'The most dangerous place in the world is in a woman's womb.'

Lawyer Breda Allen, who had become involved in the Rape Crisis Centre as a legal advisor, and went on to become the chairperson of its board, remembered the ferocity of the debate in her home town in Co. Wicklow. 'A week before the vote, people were calling to my door telling me a priest had said at mass that the Rape Crisis Centre was an abortion referral agency,' she said. 'I was outraged, and I went looking for him. I needed to find him because there was only one Sunday left. Eventually, the only way I could catch up with him was by going to confession on the Saturday.

'He started to make the sign of the cross, and I told him he needn't bother. I put it to him that he'd made this allegation, and that it was false. He said he didn't know about that, and I told him he'd have to take steps to find out the truth, and when he did so he'd have to tell his congregation the next day. We had a bit of a ding dong. I said I'd give him some phone numbers, but the light in the confession box was broken, so I had to step outside to look up the numbers and write them down. There was a huge queue outside, and when I came out, a man started struggling up from his seat to go in. I had to tell him I was not finished. I gave the priest the numbers and I said, 'I'll be at first mass tomorrow and if you don't take back what you said, I'll demonstrate and I'll ruin your mass.

'Then I walked down to the back of the church and that ghastly pro-amendment campaign poster of the baby in its nappy was pinned up. I whipped it down and threw it in the bin. The next day, I brought my totally embarrassed children with me up to the front of the church. And he did admit he'd been wrong.'[30]

All over Ireland, which had hitherto considered it indecent to discuss sexual issues or rape, men were to be heard holding forth about ectopic pregnancy, foetuses and zygotes. The AAC warned that the amendment would end up in the Supreme Court and solicitor Paul McNally warned those who intended to vote yes to rule out abortion that their vote might have the opposite effect. The amendment could be interpreted to leave the way open for abortion in certain circumstances, for example in cases of rape or incest, he argued.[31]

The DRCC was horrified to learn about the fate of Louth woman Sheila Hodgers, whose husband, Brendan, spoke out in the days before the referendum about her agonising death in a Catholic hospital. Sheila Hodgers had cancer, but when she became pregnant she was taken off all drugs and treatments, because they might potentially harm or kill the foetus she was carrying. Although she was screaming in agony, she was not given pain relief. Brendan Hodgers asked about an abortion, but got no reply. On 17 March 1983, she gave birth prematurely to a baby girl who died immediately. Sheila Hodgers died two days later.[32]

Ally, the Catholic organisation which organised family placements for pregnant women who could not stay at home, admitted that for many Catholic mothers of teenage daughters, rape cases were 'the obvious exception' to their opposition to abortion. However, Ally reaffirmed its total opposition to abortion in any circumstances.[33] Increasingly, in the days before the referendum, O'Donnell was referred to as the 'leading spokesperson against the amendment', and her photograph was widely used.

On polling day, just half of the electorate turned out to vote. The amendment was overwhelmingly passed, with 67 per cent voting for it and 33 per cent against. In urban areas, the vote was almost evenly split, but in the country 75 per cent voted against. Afterwards, O'Donnell said she was 'saddened' that those who had voted yes had been misled 'into thinking they were saving Ireland from some form of horror'. The horror was already there, she said: 'The ten women who will go to Britain for abortions today, the ten who will go tomorrow, and are not going to stop going.' She expressed anger that the debate had been dominated by men. 'I feel very sad about the way women have been used in this debate,' she said. 'As a mother, I feel totally upset by the way the debate has gone – no importance has been given to the mother as a person.'[34] However, she said she also felt 'elated'. It had been a good fight, and the DRCC had succeeded in highlighting the truth about rape and pregnancy.

The DRCC's annual report for the year states proudly that the Centre was one of the first organisations to affiliate to the campaign, which, it said, had 'raised the general level of awareness about the necessity for comprehensive morning after contraception for rape victims and the general problems associated with sexual assault'. The reference to the morning-after pill was pointed. The AAC was over – a new campaign was about to begin.

6

'WHAT SORT OF LADIES ARE WE DEALING WITH HERE?'

In January 1983 a pimp called John Cullen firebombed the home of Dolores Lynch (31), her mother and her aunt at their home in Dublin's south inner city. The three women burned to death. Dolores was a former prostitute who had given up prostitution and become a hospital worker, caring for the elderly. She had also contributed to a report on prostitution, naming 20 pimps who controlled 90 per cent of Dublin's prostitutes, and had said she would be willing to name names in court. The report had been passed to the Minister for Justice, Gerry Collins, in 1980. Dolores had expressed disappointment that the Minister would not meet her and had become well known as a speaker about prostitution, revealing much about the violence the women experienced from men who were their clients and their pimps.

Cullen was convicted of the murders after his then girl-friend, Lyn Madden, who had also worked as a prostitute, agreed to testify against him. She had been present on the night of the murders. Madden later joined forces with June Levine, a former volunteer at the Rape Crisis Centre, to write a book telling the story of her life with Cullen. *Lyn* is a powerful exposé of prostitution in Dublin. It described horrific levels of violence, including severe beatings and rapes accompanied by acts of extreme degradation. In her preface to the book, Levine described prostitution as a form of violence against women: 'women are driven into prostitution by the most negative forces, whether from the hurt sustained within their families or within society, or a mixture of both'. It was linked to poverty and women's lack of economic independence, she said. It was an issue at the heart of feminism.

Violence and rejection are contained even within the words used for prostitutes. In 1971, when Nuala Fennell announced that she was resigning from the Irish Women's Liberation movement, she said, 'Women's Lib has not only lost her virginity but has turned into a particularly nasty harlot ...'[1] Fennell incensed feminists, including the Rape Crisis Centre, again in the weeks after the Lynch murders, when, as a Fine Gael TD, she was asked if she believed that all pregnancies, including those arising from rape, should be brought to full term. 'There's not going to be any exceptions and nor should there be,' she said.[2]

In the middle of the amendment furore in 1983 Catherine McGuinness, now a Supreme Court judge, told of abuse she had received after she spoke against the amendment at a conference. In a statement she said she had received a letter which said she was 'worse even than that other moral tramp, Mary Robinson', that she was 'lower than prostitutes and vermin fattened on the innocent, but the curse of their blood would follow her'.[3]

According to Andrea Dworkin, the pioneer of feminist research into it, pornography means 'the writing of whores'. Dworkin's view was that 'pornography is the theory – rape is the practise'. When, in 1981, STOP, an organisation supported by the Knights of Columbanus and other right-wing Catholic bodies, claimed that pornography caused rape and should be banned, feminists wrote to the papers wondering why, if supporters of STOP were against rape, they were also against the Rape Crisis Centre. In February 1983, the DRCC initiated a meeting to discuss the growing problem of the 'unrestricted availability of videos containing scenes of extreme sexual violence, rape and other sexually degrading acts'.[4] After the meeting, at the offices of the Council for the Status of Women, a working group was set up to research the problem further.

On 31 January 1984 15-year-old Ann Lovett was found dying at the feet of a statue of the blessed virgin beside the Catholic Church in Granard, Co. Longford. Her newborn baby boy was lying dead beside her. She had been alone when she gave birth, and she had been alone in her pregnancy. No one in Granard admitted to having known that the schoolgirl had been pregnant, though she had gone to her full term. She had been to her family doctor twice when she was six months' pregnant. He said he hadn't noticed. The nuns who taught Ann Lovett in the local convent said they hadn't known. The Lovett family was silent. The local community reacted badly to the arrival in town of journalists asking questions. Someone blamed a traveller who had passed through the town – an outsider. Others would say nothing more than that this was a private matter. Several weeks later, Ann Lovett's sister committed suicide. The family kept their silence. Locally, the rumour went around that Ann Lovett's father was the father of her child. He has since died.

On 8 February teacher Eileen Flynn from New Ross in Co. Wexford lost her appeal against her dismissal by the Holy Faith nuns. They sacked her after finding out she was pregnant. Her partner was the man with whom she lived. He was separated but unable to get divorced because divorce was banned. Sister Anna Power told the respected young teacher to find another job and suggested she go to England. Flynn said her life was in New Ross and she was living in a family unit 'in everything but name'. Power told the employment appeals tribunal: 'She just flaunted it and did not try to hide it or to redeem herself.' Flynn appealed the case to the Circuit Court, where Judge Noel Ryan said, rejecting her appeal, 'In other places women are being condemned to death for this sort of offence.'[5] He added that he did not agree with this. The High Court also rejected a further appeal in 1985.

On 14 April 1984 a dead newborn baby was washed up on a beach at Cahirciveen, Co. Kerry. He had been stabbed 28 times and his neck was broken. A murder investigation was launched, and two weeks later Joanne Hayes, along with all her immediate family, was arrested. She told gardaí she had given birth on or around 12 April and had hidden the baby's body in a field near her home at Abbeydorney. However, she and her family also signed statements admitting that she had stabbed her baby and thrown it in the sea miles away at Dingle. Blood tests soon revealed that Joanne Hayes and the married man who was her baby's father could not have been the parents of the Cahirciveen baby. The Hayes family alleged they had been assaulted and bullied by gardaí during the taking of their statements.

Instead of abandoning the case against the young woman, gardaí came up with a theory that involved her bearing twins to two different fathers. In December, the government set up an all-male Tribunal of Inquiry under Mr Justice Kevin Lynch, during the course of which Joanne Hayes was subjected to an ordeal in the witness box, in an effort to prove that she was promiscuous and immoral and had become pregnant to two men at once. She became deeply distressed while giving evidence, was given sedatives and returned to the witness box hardly able to stand. The parliamentary committee on women's rights demanded that the Minister for Justice intervene. It said the cross-examination was harrowing, horrific and shameful. According to the account given in Nell McCafferty's powerful book on the story, the committee found that the tribunal 'showed an attitude to women's sexuality which needed to be examined. People involved in counselling rape victims had indicated to them that the "interrogation" of rape victims was similar'.[6]

The DRCC did, indeed, compare the line of questioning pursued by the barristers in the tribunal with that in rape cases. It was 'humiliating, obscene and degrading', according to Anne O'Donnell. It was also clouding the issue. 'How are the size of the clots in her miscarriage of three years ago relevant to the alleged behaviour of the gardaí?' she demanded. Women from the Dublin and Cork Rape Crisis Centres were among those who sent yellow roses to show support and concern for Joanne Hayes, and among those who demonstrated outside the court.

At one point Judge Lynch was presented with an old newspaper article alleging a case of 'super-fecundation'. He asked: 'What sort of ladies are we dealing with here?' Finally, in May 1985, a British expert was called, who said simply that Joanne Hayes could not have been pregnant by two men. As McCafferty commented, Joanne Hayes had been charged with no crime, 'but womanhood itself was on trial in Tralee'.

These were bad times for Irish women. The women in the Rape Crisis Centre were already weary from the struggle of the Anti-Amendment Campaign and dismayed by its defeat, with its implications for women's rights. The experiences of Ann Lovett, Eileen Flynn and Joanne Hayes were a chilling reminder that Ireland was still a hostile country for women whose lives took them off the narrow path of Catholic conformity.

Histories of this period tend to emphasise the gloom. Ailbhe Smyth, in her account of the women's movement from 1970 to 1990, wrote that the 'revolutionary ardour' of the 1970s had been 'well nigh quenched' by a combination of fundamentalist repression and economic recession. 'These were to be difficult and demoralising years, leading many feminist activists to a point of weary disenchantment,' she wrote. 'In retrospect, the encounters of the 1970s over contraception, rape, equal pay, appeared as mere skirmishes, a phoney war, prior to the battles of the 1980s against the serried ranks of church and state.'[7]

The Rape Crisis Centre would fight back. The mid-1980s was, in fact, an extremely productive period for the Centre. But the troubles of those times were not confined to the outside. There were internal frictions, too.

Rape Crisis women frequently refer to the 'great fun' that went along with the work. Meetings often adjourned to the pub, and there were regular parties, with each person's expected contribution of food and drink discussed and listed in the minutes. The collective even did dance routines. However, as time went on, the sense of solidarity began to be strained. 'Working in the Rape Crisis Centre back in the 1980s was mindblowing,' said Anne Roper. 'It was incredibly liberating, and extremely hard work.' Roper, now an RTÉ producer, was then a young American illegal, working as an actor and a waitress in Dublin. 'For me it started with the Reclaim the Night march in 1978. I was playing a buxom wench in a Restoration play at the time, and going out with a guy who thought women shouldn't get equal pay. I broke up with him, read Marilyn French's *The Woman's Room*, made friends with women and joined the Rape Crisis Centre.'

The demands were huge, she recalled. 'You were expected to take it very seriously and we did,' she said. 'You had to attend the Monday night collective meeting, and you had to do your rota, when you'd be on call for women phoning the Centre for help. That meant you got "cases" and you then had all the follow up from that – the counselling, the going to clinics, to police, to court – whatever came up. You had to read up on all the latest books and articles. You were expected to give talks and write articles and you would probably also be on a sub-group preparing material on some issue to be discussed or organising fundraising. We wanted to change the world, and we were sure we could do it. I think that is quite brilliant. How many 20-year-olds do you meet now who want to do that?'

Bernie Purcell, who joined in 1982, and later became the centre's director, agreed being part of the Rape Crisis Centre was exciting. 'I did the training course and I felt I had come home ... just to be sitting with women whose language was the same as my own, and not to be always in conflict. I'd always been very independent, and I'd travelled a lot as a woman alone. I'm from a very traditional male-oriented society, but I had great aspirations for myself. The one thing that frightened me was rape. It made me feel powerless. It was a very potent form of aggression. The Centre was wonderful. The decision-making process was exhausting but it was also exhilarating, and it worked. Decisions were reached and the work was done. The enemy was outside, in the courts, and in the system. We were extremely bonded in that. Anne O'Donnell was the main voice and had been for a long time. There were great things about that – she was so driven and energetic. I believed the Centre was going to go on and on fighting until rape was eliminated. I was so enamoured, I didn't see the cracks ...'

The DRCC was set up as a feminist collective, and this structure was, in itself, a political statement. 'Our society is organised in a hierarchical, bureaucratic structure – which is male dominated and controlled,' according to a position statement written in the early 1980s. Collectivism was about individuals banding together to bring about change and achieve power. 'Feminism and collectivism marry well,' according to the document. Both arose from 'feelings of powerlessness'. Each person brought different skills, but the guiding principle was that 'all are equal ... and all share responsibility'. Decisions were to be made by consensus. 'Contrary to all we have been taught, no one person has to lead ...' The document admitted though that 'consensus is not always easy, indeed it can be a constant struggle'. However, differences must be 'faced up to honestly' and the collective should 'strive to regard conflict as potential for creative problem solving'. Loyalty to the Rape Crisis Centre was to be paramount.

This was high-minded theory, and it proved extremely difficult to put into practice. Rows simmered and erupted, sometimes ending with volunteers leaving the collective feeling aggrieved and hurt. 'Meetings used to sometimes be really awful,' recalled Mary Quinlan. 'The rows were terrible. One night I remember I literally slid under the table. I just couldn't take any more of it.'[8]

Margaret Martin remembered one night when an emergency call came in from a raped woman in the middle of a fraught meeting. 'I remember volunteering to go out and take the case, even though it sounded like a very difficult situation. Afterwards I realised that was a bad comment on my feelings about the meetings.'[9] One set of minutes ends with the following: 'As minute taker I feel incapable of recording how this discussion developed except to say that the meeting ended traumatically and nothing was resolved.'[10]

Roper was often in the centre of rows. 'I was abrasive and strident and defeated my own cause a lot of the time,' she admitted, looking back. 'But I still believe it was right to have those arguments.'[11]

By 1982, a split was looming. There were rows about whether the main emphasis should be on providing counselling or on campaigning on the politics of rape. There were rows about whether or not it was always feasible to debate until consensus was reached. Some collective members felt this was crucial, but others argued that if, after 'exhaustive discussion' on an issue, consensus hadn't been reached, a vote should be taken. This was adopted as a rule in the summer of 1982.

'Once we had paid workers, the collective didn't really work,' said Roper. 'In the collective, everyone was meant to be equal, but in fact, Anne O'Donnell was a very dynamic and persuasive leader. People were sort of infatuated with her.' Some collective members chafed against this. In October 1982, a decision was taken that all letters to the papers written on behalf of the Centre were to be signed by two members of the collective, with names to be used in rotation. The following month, the collective discussed 'political endorsement'. It decided that 'in situations where we are asked for urgent comment, opinion, or support for an individual/political move, whoever is in the office is to contact a minimum of four other members of the collective to come to a decision – where possible such decisions should be deferred to the next meeting of the collective.'[12] This was reviewed in 1983 and the minimum number of collective contacts to be made was reduced to two. According to O'Donnell, this was unwieldy to the point of being unworkable.

Roper and others felt the Centre was losing its radical edge. 'Some of us wanted not to give in to the compromises that made you mainstream,' she said. 'To get government funding, you had to look normal. I wanted us to stay anarchic.' Margaret Martin was also disillusioned. 'We seemed to slip away from the sort of radical debates we used to have,' she said. 'Instead we'd spend ages discussing what sort of napkins we should have at a fundraising dinner. There didn't seem to be the same common ground any more. I felt the Centre was moving towards a softer route, more like putting a bandaid on each individual instead of trying to change things politically.'

Sheila Aherne got involved in the DRCC in 1982. 'It was one of the best things I've ever done – it was very powerful. We were constantly under siege. It was a great atmosphere to work in and I felt very happy and supported. Anne O'Donnell was a huge asset. I could see some people resented her, but I just felt she was great. We did so much work, and we learned so much. The Centre did change. It got bigger and tempered its politics. At the start, you'd have a big debate about whether it would be politically correct for the Centre to take money raised by a disco or a fashion show. Later on, the risk that our politics would compromise funding possibilities became a big issue. There began to be talk about marketing the Centre's image. By the time I left in the mid 1980s, I couldn't really identify with the Centre any more. But whereas I do think the Centre lost what it meant politically as the years went on, I don't think the service it provided for raped women was ever compromised.'[13]

Barbara Egan recalled feeling frustrated by the 'vetting for political correctness' which was applied to her fundraising proposals. 'My thinking was that the best people to target for fundraising are those who are well-got,' she said. 'My brother was Lord Mayor of Dublin at one stage and he opened the Mansion House to us. We had the rock band Hurricane Johnny and the Jets. These guys were wealthy themselves – one of them was Count John McCormack, a descendant of the tenor. A lot of very well-heeled people came. I remember being really tickled to get a cheque from Lord Ardee, the Earl of Meath. We made a lot of money but some of the angrier feminists in the collective objected to those sort of events. They always wanted tickets to be available at low cost for those who couldn't afford the full amount. I couldn't see why we should be taking money from those we were there to support.

'And then, of course, full-time workers needed to take decisions without consulting volunteers. It didn't make sense any longer for volunteers to have the same decision-making rights. There was a lot of pain in letting the collective go. Later on in the eighties we tried different structures. We evolved a management structure whereby staff had responsibility for different areas like administration, volunteers, counselling, press and information and fundraising,' she said.[14] The managers would report to the weekly collective meeting on Monday nights.

'There were people who resented the power Barbara and I had because we worked there,' said O'Donnell. 'They didn't seem to grasp that if something is your career and your life it takes on a different meaning.' She has become cynical about some aspects of the Rape Crisis Centre. 'The whole collective idea just can't co-exist with people working in a paid capacity,' she said. 'People have responsibilities towards workers but no one would think of that.'[15]

Margaret Martin, now, as director of Women's Aid, a full-time worker in a feminist organisation herself, and responsible for a sizeable staff, admits that she and others in the collective 'didn't see ourselves as employers' and that this was a flaw. 'It was an uneasy transition,' she said. 'Nowadays, organisations know you have to work at these things. I also understand now that the zealous, early people in an organisation don't necessarily stay. At the time, though, I was angry and in the end I lost heart and left, and afterwards felt quite bitter.'[16]

Mary Quinlan had no difficulty accepting that the role of the paid workers was different. 'When I'd be listening to the radio and I'd hear someone making some outrageous or offensive comment, I'd be hoping Anne would be on the phone immediately to respond. And when she did respond, she was great and I'd be saying, "Good on you." Others in the group would be giving out that she should have consulted the collective first. My attitude was, we have entrusted Anne with this position – let her get on with it.

'There is no doubt but that she was the face of the collective, and some people were jealous of that. She was very engaging and vivacious and committed and she had great foresight. She was very good at meeting all sorts of establishment figures like judges and gardaí. Above all, she always had the raped women at the forefront of her mind. She always acted in their best interests. I think some of the collective lost sight of that at times. Those big discussions we went through used to drive me crazy. I just wanted to get on with the work. I saw Anne as the motivator, and I saw Barbara as the counsellor. She was great – you would turn to her if you had a difficult case.'

The work was demanding, for paid workers and volunteers alike, and the lack of proper funding was a constant problem. Monday night meetings included a brief discussion of new cases, and sometimes there would be ten or more in a week. The paid workers were taking calls all day from women in distress, and O'Donnell admitted that it could get depressing. 'It's very draining work because to me counselling for rape is different to any other sort of counselling because rape is a subject all women fear,' she told a reporter in 1983. 'I leave here [the DRCC] every day knowing that it's there and that it could happen to me.'[17]

The surroundings didn't help. 'The Centre was really grotty,' recalled Roper. 'We didn't even have enough chairs, so people had to sit on the floor. It was in a big, old house, and it used to be quite spooky being in there on your own at night. I remember being in there one night and a man rang with a crazy call, weird and sicko ...' She shuddered at the memory. 'When you were on the rota at home, you'd sometimes get obscene calls in the middle of the night. There was no vehicle for us to disperse all that anger and aggression.

'You'd go anywhere to help a woman. I remember cycling through the city at all hours to meet someone at a phone box on South Great Georges Street. She was not there. Once I was accompanying a woman to court down the country. I stayed in a hotel room with her and during the night the guy's family came banging on the door to try and frighten her out of taking the case. She lost the case – she was a big fat woman and he was a little skinny guy and the logic was, how could he have done it? Sometimes we were out of our depth, but I wouldn't be too critical – we were doing the best we could and no one else was doing anything.'

Quinlan, too, recalled feeling out of her depth at times, but, like Roper, she is disposed not to be too critical in retrospect. 'When I look back, and compare then and now, I feel we were the vanguard. Only for the likes of us nothing would have changed.'

During 1983, the Centre received funds from the Health Education Bureau to produce a booklet simply called 'Rape'. This was aimed at health professionals, social and community workers and the gardaí, who might come into contact with raped women. It is a glossy little document, a lot sleeker than the Centre's earlier publications. However, the analysis it contains is still radical and feminist. Rape is still defined as 'a crime of violence using sex as a weapon'. Women, the booklet said, 'should be free to behave as they like without the threat of rape'. However, the booklet concludes that the presence of the rape threat means that 'women must be vigilant', adding that, 'rarely is the absurdity of women having to protect themselves from men questioned'. [18]

It started gradually, with a few cases from time to time, always disturbing, often leaving counsellors feeling unsure about their skills. The numbers grew inexorably, and between 1983 and 1984, it became a steady flow. The Rape Crisis Centre had opened a door. Increasingly, those coming through were the victims of incestuous rape. In 1983, the Centre dealt with 196 cases of rape and sexual assault. In 28 cases, the rapist was a relative and the victim was under 15.[19] The following year, out of a total of 426 cases, 152 were defined as child sexual abuse. It was not easy for the women working in the Centre to source training materials or the support and advice of experts – incest was a taboo subject in a society that insisted on the sanctity of the family and the authority of the father.

A 1978 article about incest described a case in which a father had raped his three daughters over a period of many years. Their mother died. One of the girls had a baby when she was just 14. Eventually, a doctor alerted gardaí and the abuser admitted the incest. He was released on bail on the under-taking that he would stay away from the family home and seek psychiatric help. He continued to live with his second wife and their young child. The case was adjourned for two years, during which 'his behaviour was perfect'.[20] He got a suspended sentence. Few cases were reported to the gardaí.

In April 1982, two speakers from a clinic at a Dublin hospital were invited to talk to the DRCC collective. According to the minutes taken of the meeting, they admitted that their experience of incest was limited. However, it mostly took place between fathers and daughters, and, according to what they had read: 'for some children it may be the only time they will receive any affection or closeness with the parent'. They didn't condone it, but said they had dealt with cases 'where it was very acceptable for the father to have sex with his daughter and it seems to be a widely held theory that the mother *colludes* in almost all cases'. They said it was important for the child to deal with the problem 'within the family situation' since it could be worse for the child if she was taken from her parents or her father was jailed. They felt it was important 'to make the parents more effective'.[21] In a discussion the following week, some women in the collective expressed unhappiness about some of these theories, particularly maternal collusion and the emphasis on keeping the family together.

The collective had an important decision to make. Would it deal with incest itself or would it refer cases to other agencies? Some members said they didn't think the peer counselling model used with adult women was appropriate for work with children. It was agreed that the group would consult the London Rape Crisis Centre and continue to research the subject.

The situation was becoming urgent, and the Rape Crisis Centre became involved with the Irish Council for Civil Liberties (ICCL) in setting up a working party on child sexual abuse. The group applied for funding in September 1983. In July 1984, members of the DRCC collective attended a seminar organised by the working party. Solicitor Paula Scully spoke on the legal situation. Incest was a misdemeanour if full penetration was proved; otherwise it was indecent assault or buggery. The maximum sentence was seven years. She said corroborative evidence was required. The wife of the assailant was not considered a competent witness. If a prosecution was proceeding, a protection order could be sought, but a barring order would be given only for persistent physical violence, and barring orders didn't apply to common-law families.

Scully said she believed the corroborative evidence requirement should be dropped. She also said there was a problem over judges giving suspended sentences. She said prison sentences, complete with treatment, and to be followed by treatment on probation, were required. She also said the Children's Bill, then before the Dáil, should be implemented urgently. Social workers at the seminar gave case histories and asked for advice, while a 34-year-old woman described her own experience of being abused from the age of eight, and how it had affected her life. 'A very harrowing tale,' the DRCC minutes recorded. 'She is still in therapy.'[22]

Barbara Egan said she remembered in detail many of the cases she dealt with back then, especially those involving children. 'I remember all their names. I remember the first call we got concerning a child. I took the call. A doctor rang from one of the hospitals. He had a little 12-year-old girl there who said she'd been raped by her father and so had some of her siblings. He was disinclined to believe her, and she was, in fact, discharged and sent home. I remember devastating things.

'There was one woman who came to us with her children because they had been abused. Then she found that her own really horrific abuse surfaced in her memory. I remember a little girl having to give evidence in court. She was only about five or six – she was hardly tall enough to see over the edge of the witness box. The barrister asked her what had happened. She said, "He put his bone in me." The barrister demanded, "In your vagina?" She said, and I remember the poignancy of this, "In my Mary."

'I remember one barrister who is today a judge, and he had a very lordly accent and vocabulary. He said to a ten-year-old child, "Am I right in thinking he had intercourse with you?" She didn't know what he was talking about. Then he said, "Did he insert his penis into your va-geen-a?" That was how he pronounced it, with a hard "g".

'I remember a 14-year-old girl who had accused her 18-

year-old cousin of raping her. He cried during the trial. The judge said what had happened was typical teenage experimentation and that no harm had been done except that the boy was upset. The girl got up and started shouting. The judge had her physically removed from court by gardaí. The boy was acquitted. It was unbelievable the things that went on in court. You felt completely helpless. The best I could do was to fight like a tiger to get people a decent award from the Criminal Injuries Compensation tribunal.'

In October 1984, the collective decided to ask the Health Board for funding for an incest counsellor to work with teenagers and adults. The Centre would not counsel children. In November 1984, there was an important breakthrough when the Labour Minister for Health, Barry Desmond, gave the working group a grant of £25,000 and it formally set about researching incest and child abuse in institutions. The first task was to produce an information pack. ICCL member Clodagh Corcoran chaired the group, and Mary Robinson chaired a subcommittee on legal issues. At a press conference to launch the research, Robinson said sexual abuse in childhood had been a neglected matter. The law was inadequate and outdated. Anne O'Donnell said the Rape Crisis Centre had seen more than 60 young women already in 1984, a six-fold increase over 1983. She and Bernie Purcell from the Centre were both on the working group. O'Donnell said that since a recent Gay Byrne radio programme on the subject, to which the DRCC had contributed, the Centre had been inundated.

A press statement pointed out that, 'it is unlikely that the generations of past and present children who have suffered sexual abuse and a betrayal of their trust are persuaded that the family is the cornerstone of their childhood. In these circumstances, family life is not a support structure for the journey from childhood to adulthood.' It was Dr Moira Woods who made the statement that most clearly showed that the project would potentially attract the hostility of the traditional values brigades. It may well be, she told the press conference, that the solution in some cases would be to break up the family in which the incest was occurring.

Meanwhile, in Sligo, a young social worker called Val O'Kelly had written an urgent report on a local family. 'It is my opinion that I am dealing with a very pathological family,' she wrote. 'Joseph McColgan is an extremely sick man ... and seriously perverted sexually. I feel he has everyone terrorised and keeps control by terrorising. His personality is such that he could not be considered a fit parent. His sexual activities regarding the children can only be called criminal.'[23] Within weeks of O'Kelly's 1984 report, the North Western Health Board (NWHB) in Sligo closed the file on the McColgan family. It would stay closed until June 1993, when Michelle McColgan, then 21, revealed that her father had raped, beaten and attempted to kill her repeatedly for approximately 15 years.

Michelle, her sister Sophia and her brothers, Gerard and Keith, went on to have their father convicted for a litany of violent sexual crimes against them. They also took the health board and their family doctor to court for allegedly failing to protect them. The case was settled out of court. An inquiry found that despite repeated disclosures of abuse, the McColgans had been 'trapped in a system which was not responsive to their needs'.[24]

The NWHB took an early decision in the McColgan case, after Sophia presented with physical injuries, that Joseph McColgan needed to have more authority in his family. Patsy McColgan, the children's mother, told social workers in 1979 that her husband was violent. She also told a priest, who told her that marriage was for life. The senior social worker at the NWHB, Denis Duffy, cited paternal rights and the importance of keeping the family together as reasons for the inaction of the authorities. In 1998, he said he still believed that 'the biggest penalty was to deprive a child of its parents'. In 1997, Sophia McColgan, her siblings and her mother travelled to Limerick to go to the Rape Crisis Centre there, where they saw Dorothy Morrissey: 'For the first time in my life, I found somebody who believed me and who understood,' Sophia said.[25]

7

Lifting the Veil of Silence

According to Mary Kennedy of the Irish Family League, 'Sex education outside the home is undesirable ... what young people need to be taught today, more than ever before, is to value purity and chastity and how to attain these virtues.'[1] Anne O'Donnell, speaking at a seminar on child sex abuse in Waterford in January 1984, had a very different view: 'Primary schools are the focus of where one could intervene to save young children from going through years of abuse.'

The DRCC's work was changing. In 1984, Anne O'Donnell said the Centre was seeing many young women in early adulthood who needed to talk about childhood abuse that had gone on for years. She said it was dealing with an increasing number of cases of child abuse. 'There must be thousands of people out there who haven't had the courage to come forward, who are still being abused or feel too frightened or guilty to talk about it,' she said.[2] Speaking about the launch of the 1984 Annual Report, she said: 'We can't say rape or incest is increasing. What we can say is that the more talk there is, the more the veil of silence is lifted, the more comfortable women are about coming forward.'[3]

The Oireachtas Committee on Women's Rights, to which the DRCC had made a submission, recommended in October

1984 that all schools should have comprehensive sex education programmes, while also criticising the use of schoolbooks in which there was 'blatant sex stereotyping'. The main teachers' unions welcomed the recommendation, and the coalition government's Ministers for Health and Education, Barry Desmond and Gemma Hussey, set up a steering committee to develop policies and programmes for sex and relationships education in secondary schools. The DRCC and Cherish wrote an open letter to the Ministers welcoming the move, but expressing disappointment that they were not represented on the committee, and neither was the Irish Family Planning Association, which had 'pioneered much excellent work in these areas'.

They had worked, they wrote, with women and girls who had been given no opportunity during their education to explore attitudes to sexuality, sexual violence, sex roles or their relationships with men and boys. 'It is precisely because of the lack of such education and because of the negative and repressive attitudes prevalent both in society and in many schools that our clients experience such acute difficulties.'

They referred to 'the horror of many people's lives'. Many of the pupils for whom the courses would be designed 'may be victims of incest or other forms of sexual violence, may be pregnant, or may be living in families in which they view sexual or physical violence on a daily basis'. They added that they were already used by many professionals and agencies as 'specialists in the general area of sexual attitudes in Ireland today'.[4]

There were those, however, who totally rejected the DRCC's views. Some of the groups that had united to fight for the abortion amendment had formed themselves into a new Catholic lay organisation called Family Solidarity. In its efforts to retain 'the traditional Christian Irish way of life', it had its sights set on plans to liberalise contraception law and a campaign to remove the constitutional ban on divorce. It was also totally opposed to sex education. During a protest meeting organised by Family Solidarity against the Minister for Health's proposed new Family Planning Bill in 1985,

Bernadette Bonar of the Responsible Society said she wanted to 'warn the audience very carefully against sex education in schools'. She said that suicide and anything else you could call bad were always to be found in countries where you got sex education. It taught adolescents that it was normal to sleep with your boyfriend or to be 'a homosexual or a lesbian'.[5]

The Irish Family League had also warned that liberal groups were keen to get into schools to provide sex education, because they wished to promote the 'perversion' of homosexuality. In March 1983, the Rape Crisis Centre was among the groups which marched in protest after Mr Justice Seán Gannon gave suspended sentences to four Dublin youths. He found them guilty of the manslaughter of Declan Flynn in Fairview Park. The four beat the young man to death. They admitted they had been out looking for gay men and claimed they were 'queer bashing'. The Rape Crisis Centre expressed 'horror' and called for the removal of 'unsuitable judges'. A letter from Jean Forbes of the DRCC said that, while prison wouldn't eradicate rape and murder, 'prison sentences should reflect the severity of the crime' rather than the 'whim' of the judge. At the march, one of the placards read 'Rapists and queer bashers – same male violence'. One of the four killers was in later years convicted of raping a woman.

The ICCL working group on incest and child abuse presented a series of advice sheets in 1985. 'In Ireland we have neither questioned our attitudes to incest nor to the sexual abuse of children by those in positions of trust,' it said. Children who had cried for help had been ignored because adults didn't know what to do. 'Consequently there are many adults today who still carry their childhood secret with them, and who suffer depression, repeated suicide attempts, guilt, shame, low self-esteem, an inability to socialise and an inability to maintain a loving relationship.' We had to admit that child sexual abuse happens and then 'the healing process will at last begin'. The document quoted Sarah Nelson's book on incest and her finding that professional attitudes had been 'heavily biased and ill founded'. The document also quoted

US and UK research which showed that incest and child abuse were rife and were contributing to a wide range of social ills. One study showed that one out of four women are sexually abused as children, and one out of eight men are sexually abused as children.[6] Another showed that 70 per cent of young prostitutes had been sexually assaulted in childhood by a family member.[7]

Figures produced by the Incest Crisis Link (UK) were particularly shocking. They were 'taken as a mean average from surveys done worldwide over the past 15 years' and included the following findings:

90 per cent of rapists were abused children
30 per cent of rape victims were abused children
40 per cent of alcoholics and drug addicts were abused children
75 per cent of prostitutes were abused children
30 per cent of children in care were abused children.

The guidelines included specialist notes for professionals. They were advised to be aware that child abuse was far more prevalent 'than you think' and to accept that 'childhood fantasies do not normally involve sexual abuse'. An NSPCC report of 1984 was quoted: 'Any allegation of sexual abuse by a child should be believed and investigated thoroughly.' Doctors were urged to be alert to families in which there was an excess of 'accidents' and to be suspicious of a father who consistently accompanied his daughter on medical visits. They were asked to encourage patients to talk to them, since British evidence showed 'many victims of rape or incest are unwilling to go to their family practitioner because of fear, guilt or shame'.[8]

The ICCL working group suffered internal disagreements, which delayed publication of its report until 1988. Its recommendations included public education campaigns, a preventative education programme 'to teach self-protection' to schoolchildren, treatment programmes for abusers, an interdisciplinary response from professionals and mandatory reporting, along with structural changes to the child protection system to make such reporting effective.[9]

The DRCC, which had helped compile the ICCL report, was worried about not just the attitude of doctors to child victims of incest, but also their attitude to adult women who had been raped. Writing in the *Medical Monthly* in 1984, Dr Percy Patton stated that 'the fear of parental rebuke and the fear of pregnancy are the two outstanding reasons why so many willing partners, later on reflection, decide to report their case as one of rape'.[10]

Patton had been one of the speakers invited to address the founding group of the Rape Crisis Centre back in 1978. They were uneasy about some of what he said. This was the man who had carried out most of the medical examinations of women in Dublin who had come to the gardaí alleging rape. Yet he had seemed to suggest that many allegations of rape were likely to be false. The DRCC was to find that he was far from being alone in this attitude. Dr Hazel Boland wrote in 1979 that many doctors 'willingly admit that they just would not know what to do if suddenly presented with a case of rape'. The stigma was still put on the victim, she wrote. 'She is assumed to be partially responsible, and in a reversal of the normal procedures of justice, she is the one who appears guilty until proven innocent.'[11]

In 1982, a young medical student wrote that the textbooks from which she had been taught ranged in attitude from 'benevolent condescension to blatant misogyny'.[12] Orla Hardiman quoted one: 'Many allegations of rape are false, possibly as many as 11 out of 12. Such allegations may be from spite, jealousy, in order to precipitate marriage, etc ... the man's story may accord better with the facts than the girl's.' She pointed out that this dismissed as false the claims of 91.67 per cent of women who said they had been raped. 'Strangely, the Federal Bureau of Investigation in America attributes a modest two per cent of rape allegations to fabrications,' she commented.[13] The book suggested, she said, that women should be hysterical and tearful after rape, and doctors should be wary of those who were logical and coherent.

The medical student quoted another book: 'no difficulty is experienced in singling out the chaste from the wanton, or the shy and bewildered from the brazen and affectedly hurt'. Some books had accounts of women making false allegations and none of women making true ones. Others stressed that physical injuries didn't necessarily indicate rape, and that the doctor should concentrate on establishing whether or not the woman seemed to be telling the truth. Only women who had been murdered, she said, escaped the notion of contributory guilt. 'Medical textbooks have a long road to travel before they become satisfactory guides for prospective doctors to the complexities of rape,' she concluded. 'They help to entrench … feelings of guilt … which constitutes a major hurdle to be overcome in rape crisis counselling.'

The Rape Crisis Centre believed the doctor's role was to carry out a series of procedures with a view to collecting potential forensic evidence, not deciding whether or not the woman was telling the truth. There were other issues, too. The then state pathologist, Dr John Harbison, wrote in the same issue of the *Medical Monthly* as Dr Patton that women doctors should be trained to deal with rape victims. He said garda stations were not equipped for gynaecological examinations and that a hospital setting was far more appropriate anyway. 'Dr Harbison was great,' said Barbara Egan. 'I did several talks along with him to medical students. He gave us a lot of support in trying to make things better for rape victims. He always criticised the fact that doctors got so little training on how to deal with rape. We used to get a lot of calls from doctors who were flustered when faced by a rape victim. Others were very patronising.'

The DRCC informed women that they had a right to request a female doctor or to ask for a particular doctor to examine them. In practice, however, women often had little choice. In January 1984, it emerged during a rape trial that a 17-year-old girl who had been brought by gardaí to Galway Regional Hospital for a forensic examination after she was raped had been turned away. It emerged that this was hospital policy. The then Minister of State for Women's Affairs and Justice, Nuala Fennell, said she was gravely concerned.

The Dublin Rape Crisis Centre said it was shocked and

horrified. 'In this country there are no police doctors and the police are therefore dependent upon the hospitals and individual medical practitioners to carry out such examinations,' said Anne O'Donnell. The Medical Union blamed the government for failing to appoint police doctors and said casualty doctors had neither the time nor the expertise to provide such a service. O'Donnell revealed that the DRCC was to meet with the masters of maternity hospitals and senior casualty staff in order to discuss the best arrangements for rape victims. In the short term, she said, casualty departments must continue to carry out the examinations, 'until another system is set up'.[14]

The DRCC had already had talks which would lead to setting up a new system. Dr Moira Woods was working at the Well Woman Centre when she was approached by the DRCC and asked if she would see women who had come to the Centre in the immediate aftermath of being raped. She was soon providing a regular service for the DRCC, both at the Well Woman and at home. 'In those days, apart from the Rape Crisis Centre, hardly anyone was telling women they could get pregnant or get a sexually transmitted disease as a result of rape,' Woods recalled. 'There was a pack for doctors doing a forensic examination for a woman who was making a complaint of rape to the gardaí – it contained a list of all the swabs that should be taken. But I said, "You have to take the whole person into account. You have to offer tests for sexually transmitted diseases and pregnancy tests, and you have to offer emergency contraception."'

The Rape Crisis Centre wanted a place where a raped woman was not at risk of further trauma. 'We all felt a garda station was completely wrong and that a hospital accident and emergency department was most unsuitable also, not least because of Saturday night drunkenness,' said Woods. 'On the other hand, you sometimes needed a hospital setting – for example, if someone needed to be examined under anaesthetic. We needed access to somewhere 24 hours a day. The only other hospital departments which were open all the time were the maternity hospitals. It turned out the Master of the Rotunda,

George Henry, had just come back from Australia, where he had seen a centre such as we envisaged. The idea was we would train doctors to take forensic evidence for the police, and they would be women doctors with an interest in sexual abuse and family planning, who would feel easy about talking about sex and who would have basic psychological training regarding the acute stage of rape. If the raped woman hadn't been referred to us by the Rape Crisis Centre, we would refer her to it. George [Henry] was very interested.'

The DRCC, Woods and others lobbied Health Minister Barry Desmond, who set up a committee to look into the idea and then provided a grant of £12,000. 'We were very lucky that Desmond was Health Minister,' said Woods. 'He funded us for a six-month pilot programme, and we drew up a training programme in consultation with people like Fred Lowe, who had done psychosexual medicine. Alice Swann came as well.' Swann, based in Belfast, had been carrying out pioneering work with sexually abused children in the North during this period. Although the unit was set up for adults, Woods could see the trend. 'I said to George, "We are going to be inundated with children,"' she said.[15]

With 12 women doctors trained to provide its services, the Sexual Assault and Treatment Unit (SATU) opened in January 1985. All garda stations and health agencies in the Eastern Health Board region were notified. It was quickly to be embroiled in controversy. During the run up to the abortion referendum in 1983, the DRCC had said it was 'very frightened that even the current limited availability of the morning-after pill will be threatened'.[16] Some of those urging a yes vote, including Fianna Fáil's health spokesman, Michael Woods, gave assurances that the morning-after pill and the IUD would not be outlawed if the amendment was passed.

However, having secured a huge majority in favour of the amendment, its champions moved on to attempt to outlaw contraception, including emergency contraception for women and girls who had been raped. 'Rape is the most horrible of human crimes,' wrote one doctor. 'One of the proposed treatments for victims … is to kill a new human which they may have conceived as a result of the dastardly attack. The fact that conception following rape is quite rare is neither here nor there ... The morning-after pill has been produced with only one end, to kill a human life ...' For the DRCC, what was at issue was the crucial matter of giving a woman back control over her own life and body.

The SATU was strongly defended by journalist Ann Harris, who wrote: 'The doctors at the Rotunda have finally grasped the nettle and made a stand for compassion.'[17] She accused those who opposed the use of the morning-after pill (MAP) of having a 'Kitty the Hare, rural midwife view of modern sexual ethical problems' and described an 'abyss which hides the dark monsters of Irish gynaeco-sexual politics'. Catholic control of hospitals was part of the problem.

The Rape Crisis Centre had 'raised a great rumpus about the prevalence of rape' according to Family Solidarity; 'If one were to fully believe all the propaganda, one would believe that Irish society is rife with incest and that rape is as common as parking tickets.' In an extraordinary article in the *Irish Catholic*, Family Solidarity claimed that the DRCC used 'public aversion to rape as a lever to serve [its] own ideologies', which may be 'radical feminist and anti-life', and used figures on rapes reported to the police to show that there had been 'no significant escalation' in the previous 20 years. 'Why the great sudden need for the Rape Crisis Centre and the Rotunda unit?' it demanded. A unit for 'genuine bona fide rape victims' would be a good idea, but not one which existed 'simply to pass out abortifacients to women who allege they have been raped'.[18] The DRCC discussed this article and decided to try to get 'someone influential and sympathetic' to reply.[19]

At this time, hard-pressed staff at the Centre were receiving 'millions' of calls about abortion. 'We're being tested ...' the minutes record. The response was to ask the caller if they had been raped, and if they said no to refer them to a Family Planning Clinic. 'If they have been raped, ask them to come in and discuss it – never discuss anything like that over the phone. Ditto for MAP inquiries. Except of course for rape victims ... direct them to SATU.'[20]

Several correspondants to the newspapers reasserted the myth that pregnancy rarely resulted from rape. One demanded: 'Why is it that when taxpayers' money was being allotted for the treatment of rape victims it couldn't have been given to people who do not employ abortifacient procedures?'[21] He didn't suggest any names. A doctor wrote that rape should be dealt with by medical and legal experts, without input from 'non-professional' groups like the 'self-styled Rape Crisis Centre'. This was, he or she said, an off-shoot of the 'Women with right to choose' group and had 'no expertise in rape'. The DRCC's data on rape were 'worthless' and 'suspect' since the group had an 'axe to grind'.[22] The DRCC replied, pointing out that rape victims had received no adequate help before the Centre was set up.[23]

By this stage, the Centre had an accepted role in the mainstream of the health services. Its expertise was valued by doctors, social workers, gardaí and teachers, and it had been centrally involved in providing training for those staffing the new SATU. Its statistics were analysed at Trinity College, with funds from the Health Education Bureau.

One young woman who had been raped at the age of 12, and had been counselled at the DRCC years later, wrote to defend it. She said the DRCC and SATU were both 'desperately needed' and asked, 'How is it that so many people who are so supposedly pro-life can have such inhuman attitudes to women?'[24]

In March, the Catholic bishops issued their 'Love is for life' pastoral letter, which said artificial contraception was morally wrong. Rape victims could take post-coital contraception to prevent fertilisation, but not to prevent implantation. They did not spell out how the rape victim should establish the facts required for this decision.[25] Undeterred, the Minister for Health said at the official opening of the SATU that it was the single most important advance in the country in the treatment of rape victims since the opening of the Rape Crisis Centre in 1979.

'It was way ahead of its time,' said Maud McKee, who joined the SATU's panel of doctors soon after it was set up and later joined the board of the DRCC. 'Its whole approach was very innovative. The idea was that the first contact the woman had was very important. You gave her time and a sense of control. You had to make her aware that your duty was to her but that you also had to record things. Sometimes women would think you were the judge and jury. Sometimes a woman would already have told her story to the guards and then it might be a bit of an ordeal for her to tell it again. The Rape Crisis Centre was great. It was really supportive. We referred all our raped women on. The work was very difficult and I was shocked by it. Just when you thought you'd seen it all, you saw something worse.'[26]

'The Rape Crisis Centre was incredibly important,' said Moira Woods. 'Far more so than us. The best we could do was try to normalise an awful situation, try to reassure the person. But we couldn't deal with long term effects. We had weekly meetings with the Rape Crisis Centre, and they were involved in all the training courses we did. At parties you'd hear people giving out about "that bunch of lesbian feminists at the Rape Crisis Centre, putting ideas into people's heads". If I had to pick an institution that has done the most for women, it would be the Rape Crisis Centre. They were so consistent in everything they did, whether it was pressurising the government or warning about the incidence of child abuse.'

'It's a Pandora's box,' said Anne O'Donnell in a 1985 press interview. 'Sometimes we sit in here in the office at the end of the day and ask ourselves, "What in God's name is going on out there?"'[27] She was commenting, in October 1985, on the fact that in the first eight months of the year the centre had been contacted by 318 people in need of help as a result of child sexual abuse or incest. The previous year there had been 152 cases. In 1983 there were just 21. There had also a huge rise in the number of cases of adult rape in 1985. Already the centre had seen 300 women, compared with 274 for the whole of 1984. O'Donnell said that since the figures had been made public, the Centre had been inundated. 'We are all like washed out dishrags here. The phone hasn't stopped ringing.'[28]

In one week in 1985 there were 29 new incest cases and 10

new rape cases. In November the collective discussed the fact that the full-time counsellors, Bernie Purcell and Barbara Egan, had 'more than full appointment lists' and didn't know what to do. Their caseloads were huge and it was hard even to find time to keep the detailed records required for proper statistical analysis. After 'much heart searching' it was decided to try to do more counselling by phone rather than encouraging new clients to come in to the Centre, to increase volunteer counselling and to publicise the fact that 'we may be forced for the first time in seven years to turn away clients'.[29]

The Minister for Health had allocated £10,000 to the DRCC for advertising in 1984, but the Centre had decided to wait to use it until the SATU was up and running. Already overstretched, it needed the backup of the Rotunda centre to cope with any new influx. In 1985, it launched an advertising campaign. It had also been given a weekly advice and information column in the *Sunday World*. As Nell McCafferty commented, 'It is an open secret that the DRCC bit its fingernails to the quick at the thought of reaching out to people who have never heard of the centre by appearing in public and in print alongside page three photographs.' The response, she said, was salutary, with an increase of about 20 calls a week.[30]

Awareness about the abuse of children had also been raised by the shocking recent deaths of several little girls in England. One was starved to death by her stepfather, one was raped and murdered by an unknown attacker, one was neglected and murdered by her stepfather and one was bitten to death by her father. However, as Justine McCarthy pointed out in the *Irish Independent*, Ireland had its own share of extreme violence towards children. She referred to the finding, in 1981, of the battered body of a three-year-old girl in Ballymun and the 'non-accidental' deaths of two other children in the same year.

The Centre revealed that it had dealt with one case of a mentally handicapped girl who was repeatedly raped by her father, and a number of 15- and 16-year-old girls who had become pregnant as a result of incest. Debunking the myth that incest happened only in certain poor and extremely marginal families, the DRCC said its cases were drawn from urban and rural areas and from all social classes. Most abusers continued to be male relatives, but the DRCC also drew attention to the fact that a significant number of the child abuse cases involved abuse by male babysitters, some of whom were themselves as young as 13. O'Donnell warned that the women and girls coming to the Centre were increasingly revealing abuse by people in positions of trust, such as priests and youth club leaders.

In the week after the figures were released, the Centre got 35 new cases. Olive Braiden, who had been appointed as the Centre's crisis counsellor in 1984, said some of these cases also involved babysitters, and some were horrifying. 'Babysitters have conducted what amounts to a reign of fear over the children they were looking after,' she said. She too said the deluge of child abuse cases was taking its toll on the workers at the DRCC. 'There are times we leave the office, walk along the street and find it difficult to believe that there are any nice people in the world,' she said.[31]

Although its detractors tried to write off the DRCC's statistics by calling them propaganda, its findings were backed by other groups. Child abuse had reached 'massive proportions', according to the Aid for Parents Under Stress group. The ISPCC said it was 'inundated'. And, at the SATU, one new case of child abuse a day was being reported.

This, warned Moira Woods, was certainly just the tip of the iceberg. There was no reason to suppose that Ireland would prove different to anywhere else, she told a seminar in Dublin. This meant that somewhere between one in four and one in ten children could expect to be abused before they reached their late teens. She made an impassioned appeal to Education Minister Gemma Hussey, who was in the audience, to instigate a sex education programme in schools as a matter of urgency. Consultant psychiatrist Nollaig Byrne used the same ratio of one in four when addressing a symposium on child abuse held around the same time by the Irish College of General Practitioners. A senior registrar in psychiatry told the symposium that child abuse was not restricted to any population group. 'It applies to people you play golf with, and your bank manager,' Dr Jackie Benbow told the assembled medics. She said the problem was more easily missed in middle-class families.

The Rape Crisis Centre collective had decided in early 1985 to make a real effort to return to its earlier practice of having in-depth discussions about relevant issues. During a 'long and complex' discussion about incest, it was decided that the Centre should seek every opportunity to educate the public about the fact that children were at risk within the family, as well as outside it. 'We agreed that the closer the relationship the more severe the hurt and disturbance felt by the victim. We felt that it was more difficult for a victim to get help when rape or assault was taking place within the family.'[32]

The DRCC called for training programmes for doctors, social workers, teachers, psychiatrists and judges. 'Right across the board, the lack of training, the lack of information and maybe the fear of the whole subject affect the way the problem is being handled,' said O'Donnell. She said the DRCC regarded child abuse as child rape and that the effects were similar. 'What kind of society do we live in which creates an environment in which someone who has been horribly abused, degraded and sexually violated, experiences such guilt and self-hatred?'[33]

The DRCC was cautious in dealing with requests from journalists to do interviews with rape victims. However, after careful discussion with the woman, it did sometimes facilitate such interviews, to powerful effect.

'The first time I went, I was a bundle of nerves. I just sat there trembling – I couldn't open my mouth. I had such great defences about the whole thing for such a long time, that it took ages to break them down. When I finally began to speak about it, I wanted to tell everyone. But I don't think people want to know …' This is how one young woman, Laura, talking to journalist Mary Kerrigan, described her first counselling session at the DRCC in 1984.

Laura's father first sexually abused her when she was seven. 'Even though I was very young, I always knew there was something wrong with what my father was doing to me,' she told Kerrigan. 'When I did mention something about it to one of my school friends, she just laughed. She didn't believe me.' Laura became very withdrawn and silent. Looking back, she said she couldn't cope and just 'shut it all out'. The abuse went on for eight years, then stopped. She pushed the memories to the back of her mind, until 'Something snapped inside me. I just couldn't keep it in any more,' she said. 'I decided to confront my father.'

He denied everything and said she was mad. If he had done such a thing, he'd kill himself. Laura, Kerrigan reported, 'went to pieces after that'. She left home and moved into a flat. 'The realisation of the whole thing hit me,' she said. 'I couldn't sleep. I had nightmares. I'd lie in bed and everything would be replayed to me. It was like watching a film. I couldn't stop thinking about it.'

Laura told Kerrigan she had few friends. She was nervous and edgy all the time, she said, and depressed. 'Any time I have tried to talk about it or confide in someone, they'll be sympathetic, say "that's terrible", and move on to the next subject. I don't think people understand really – I just can't seem to stop thinking about it. It's not so much the actual act, but the whole invasion, the injustice and the betrayal. I feel so angry. I really hate my father.'[34]

The explosion in clients coming to the Rape Crisis Centre to talk about child sexual abuse and incestuous rape presented the counsellors there with a huge challenge. 'The counselling we'd been trained in just was not adequate,' admitted Bernie Purcell, who, along with Olive Braiden, became a full-time worker in the Centre in 1984. 'People were needing to come for longer, and needing more help. We were seeing more victims of gang rapes. Men who had been raped were beginning to come to the Centre. We were seeing people who had been raped in childhood, and we were seeing people who, having been raped as adults, were remembering experiences they'd had of abuse when they were children. By 1986, we were beginning to meet people who had been abused in institutions, too. We began to feel overwhelmed.'

It was not just the women at the DRCC. 'I remember

meeting doctors and social workers who were just terrified. They didn't know what to do. A very different picture of Irish society was emerging in the mid-1980s. We were being challenged all the time by something new that we hadn't envisaged. We were realising how pervasive sexual abuse had been in Irish culture,' Purcell said.

'Every case was terrible and it preyed on your mind. They were depicting a debauchery of society and there was no way of resolving it in yourself. Most people didn't believe this was happening. My full day was that view of the world, and that had an effect on your own mental world. I remember being out socialising and people would tell jokes and I'd sit, stone faced. Sometimes someone would make a *faux pas* and then they'd get your whole week's rage ...'

Anne Roper, who was deputed to see many of the younger clients during her time in the DRCC in its early years, recalled that with one, a young woman who had been incestuously raped, she relied on her intuition. 'The basic principles of peer counselling and six category intervention [see page 27] were fine, but I knew I was not getting close to what the woman wanted to talk about. Eventually, I intuited that maybe what she was feeling so bad about was that she had experienced physical pleasure during the abuse.'

However, in another case, Roper said she realised too late that an adult was silencing a young client. 'This girl had rung the Centre and had talked to me in great detail about being abused by her father. We arranged that she would come in, but when she came her mother was with her, and the girl was very quiet and eventually said it was not true, she'd made it up. I hadn't the experience at the time to see why the mother insisted on staying. I sometimes felt very exposed. There was the fear that you could do damage.'

The DRCC sent Bernie Purcell out in search of expertise. 'I spent time with people like Susie Orbach in the Women's Therapy Centre in London getting ideas,' she said. 'We didn't want to go the psychological or psychiatric way which put a distance between the counsellor and the client, but it seemed there were no feminist models.' In 1986, the DRCC published a booklet by Purcell on 'Counselling Adolescents and Adults Who Have Suffered Sexual Abuse'.

Defining herself as a feminist psychotherapist, she described pervasive social attitudes which blamed women for rape. Victims of abuse had internalised these, and they needed to be addressed in counselling. 'Rape and sexual abuse are an integral part of our society and thereby frequently part of the dynamics that operate within families,' she wrote. Therapy must take place in 'an atmosphere of equality and respect', and therapies based on sexist ideas were intrinsically damaging. Purcell said many women who turned to the DRCC 'have experienced a reluctance or denial on the part of a previous therapist to accept the reality of sexual abuse'. [35]

She blamed Sigmund Freud for making respectable the idea that children were 'seductive'. Children were sensual, Purcell wrote. They might want love and affection and might learn through abuse to equate sex with love, but 'children do not want abuse'. The 'incest taboo' didn't prevent incest occurring – it merely prevented its disclosure. Purcell surveyed theories on child sexual abuse, rejecting those which implicated the victim. Sarah Nelson was quoted, warning about certain types of family therapy: 'incest cannot be prevented by re-creating patriarchal families'.

Purcell was influenced by Susan Forward and Lucy Berliner, both advocates of group therapy. The DRCC had always offered one to one therapy – and once it had large numbers of clients and a full-time counsellor it set up groups. 'We had groups for women who had been raped or abused, and groups for partners and friends,' said Purcell. 'And we had groups for mothers, many of whom felt terribly to blame. The groups were an effort to break down the isolation,' she recalled. 'It was quite incredible what emerged. Women who had been raped would listen to someone describing how guilty they felt and they'd express real sympathy and strongly encourage the woman not to blame herself. Then they'd talk about their own experience and they, too, would blame themselves.'

Purcell wrote that many adolescents disclosed abuse because the conflict between normal adolescent issues and the demands of the abuse situation became intolerable, or because of the fear that the abuser had started preying on a younger sibling. She said clients sometimes described having cut themselves off from their feelings. She quoted Suzanne Sgroi (the US expert who would, in 1997, give evidence in the McColgan case), who identified a number of issues for the therapist. The abused person might feel that they were 'damaged goods'. They might feel guilt – including guilt about the disruption in the family caused by disclosure. They might feel fear, depression, low self-esteem. They might experience repressed anger and hostility – towards the perpetrator and possibly also the mother or other family members for not protecting them. They might feel unable to trust anyone, especially men.

Purcell wrote that clients sometimes initially said that they felt numb or had no emotions about what had happened. However, after the counsellor spent time exploring the actual events of the abuse, other feelings emerged. Feelings changed in the course of the therapy – guilt and shame frequently turned to anger, for example, including overwhelming, explosive anger. There might be nightmares. The counsellor needed to recognise and respect the limits to which a client was willing or able to go. She described helping clients to regain control of their lives, exploring destructive myths, validating their strengths and recognising 'that people resolve their difficulties up to their age and level of ability'.

In counselling adults, the DRCC found that sometimes an event in adult life might 'trigger' a reaction to abuse experienced many years previously. These events included marriage, childbirth or the death of a parent, a marital crisis or finding out that someone else in the family has been abused. Sometimes, Purcell wrote, a woman would come to the DRCC to talk about feeling overprotective of their child – and would go on to disclose that she herself had been abused in childhood. One woman came for therapy because her experience of being abused was adversely affecting her relationship with her young sons.

The Rape Crisis Centre recognised that for a woman to take the step of coming to the Centre was brave and momentous. 'It is important to remember all through therapy that women who have been abused from an early age and are now seeking help are perhaps for the first time in their lives confronting the possibility of having a fulfilled satisfying life,' Purcell concluded. 'While on the one hand this can be exciting, it can also be terrifying.'

Maeve Lewis, then a teacher, now a therapist, joined the DRCC as a volunteer in 1985. 'I had a political interest in it as a feminist, with a great sense of the injustice of sexual violence. I thought the training course was very good, but it was geared towards intervention in cases of adult rape. Increasingly, it seemed the actual work was all about victims of child abuse. Nowadays, the idea of letting a volunteer with only that level of training loose on clients would be unheard of, and I did sometimes feel ill equipped. But there was nowhere else for people to go, so we did what we could, and we learned from wherever and whoever we could.'

Lewis did a psychology degree at University College Dublin and followed it with a diploma in psychotherapy, while continuing to work at the DRCC. 'It was hard work, but at the time we had almost a siege mentality,' she said. 'Looking back at old diaries, I find I was doing a night duty a week, and I had the Monday night collective meeting to go to, and then I was maybe seeing 10 or 12 clients a week.' She was also increasingly involved in the Centre's education and training programme and became a paid employee of the Centre in 1989.

The academic and professional training at UCD re-inforced her feminist perspective on the work. 'The political analysis fitted. After I left the DRCC I worked with women who had been raped during the genocide in Rwanda, and even in those circumstances, the victims tended to internalise it and feel shame and guilt. Putting rape into the context of gender-power dynamics really helps to deconstruct that framework. As far as I'm concerned, things the DRCC said in its First Report 25 years ago were brilliant and still need to be said today.'[36]

8

Moving On

'We thought we were in heaven,' said Bernie Purcell, recalling the difference the move to Leeson Street made to the women in the Rape Crisis Centre. 'We had our own front door, a hall and plenty of big, bright rooms. It was wonderful. Never mind that the nightclub in the basement was called Fanny Hill's! We used to go down there sometimes after work for a drink.'

By 1986, the two rooms the DRCC was renting above Cherish in Pembroke Street had become completely inadequate for its workload. The Centre had dealt with 1,000 cases in 1985, and by the middle of 1986 the numbers were already up by 35 per cent. In the first three months of 1986 there were 363 new cases, of which 249 were child abuse. The work generated by these was added to work going on with people receiving long-term help. 'We just had to move,' Anne O'Donnell said as they prepared to go. 'In our present offices, clients often have to sit out on a landing and phone calls can be overheard. These people are often in distress and find the situation very embarrassing.'

It was Olive Braiden who found the new premises, after a long search. 'Some landlords were keen to rent until they found out who we were,' she said. Some landlords said other tenants might complain. One said he didn't want 'the building full of screaming women'.[1]

Braiden said the move was essential. 'By that stage there were eight workers in the office and volunteers and clients coming and going. It was impossible. You'd be trying to counsel someone, and someone else would be talking on the phone. We were always running up and down the stairs to answer the doorbell and there would be women in distress on the stairs. The rent in the Leeson Street building was £11,000 a year. My view was – we'll find it. It was the least of our worries.' Speaking at the time, O'Donnell expressed the same view. 'We will get further into the red because we have to,' she said. 'Somebody will bail us out.'[2]

The DRCC applied for a £28,000 grant to refurbish the offices and got £20,000, presented to them by the Minister for Social Welfare, Gemma Hussey. In an interview on the Gay Byrne radio show, Braiden appealed for volunteers to help paint and decorate. There were plenty of offers, the best of which came from Tom Lundy, president of the Irish National Painters' and Decorators' Trade Union. So professional painters took on the job, giving up their weekends for months to get it done. The union's general secretary, Gerry Fleming, painted the front door. Graduate art student Paula Erraught painted murals of trees which curved up the walls and over the ceiling of the waiting room. Architect Ken Tiernan supervised the work. As Mary Maher wrote in her Irishwoman's Diary in *The Irish Times*, 'The results are wonderful ... the DRCC now has a full Georgian house, glowing in pale serene colours, with five counselling rooms, two kitchens, several small offices and a large meeting room for training sessions.' She quoted O'Donnell: 'The difference it will make is unimaginable.'[3]

'You can't stop living. If you do that you are giving in to people like this rapist.' This was Anne O'Donnell's advice to the 300 or so people who packed the Virgin Mary School Hall in the north Dublin suburb of Ballymun on a dark November afternoon in 1986. The Rape Crisis Centre had been asked to speak at the meeting, organised by a local women's group, because a serial rapist was believed to be at large.

Gardaí said they had reports of three rapes, but local women said at least seven women had been raped over a period of two months. Others had been attacked. The sexual abuse and rape of children had been making the headlines, but the rape of adult women hadn't stopped. The end of 1985 and early 1986 had also seen the rapes and murders of 61-year-old Margaret Nolan and her daughter Anne at their home in Wicklow and the murders of Maureen Stack in Sandycove, Co. Dublin, and Linda Sheedy in Clondalkin, in west Dublin. Adrienne Murray, a young woman from Kinsale, Co. Cork, had been murdered. A witness had heard her screaming 'Rape!' Gardaí were warning schoolgirls in one south Dublin suburb not to walk home alone because of a series of attacks.

November nights come down early, and Ballymun was full of dark places, including the entrances to the towerblocks of the flats where many of the residents lived and the big, bleak open spaces around them. Local people had long been concerned about bad lighting in the area. The lifts were un-attended and often, in any case, broken, so that residents had to climb up long, lonely stairwells. One woman was attacked in Poppintree Park, a large, unlit green area. Another was attacked at two in the afternoon. Gardaí issued a photofit picture of a tall blond man with stained teeth.

One woman described her anxiety: 'The other day I thought I was being followed by a man who fitted the description,' she told reporter Joan Brady. 'I met a priest and the man went off. Maybe he was harmless. I don't know. I suppose any fellow who's six foot and blond should be pitied really, because people will think he's the rapist.'[4]

One of the organisers of the public meeting was the late Kathleen Maher, a tireless campaigner for working-class women for several decades. She urged women to report any attacks to the gardaí, who had extra patrols in the area. A spokesperson for the Holy Faith convent in Glasnevin, the suburb adjacent to Ballymun, said the school had to strike a balance between alarming the students and protecting them. 'They were issued with a warning before and became very frightened as a result,' she said. 'Announcements are regularly made over the intercom telling the girls not to speak to strangers.'[5] Local men organised vigilante patrols.

The All-Ireland heavyweight and lightweight black belt karate champion of the time, David Wilson, was from Ballymun and spoke from the platform with O'Donnell. He offered free self-defence classes for local women. O'Donnell urged women to be vigilant and to take careful note of the gardaí description. She said children shouldn't be let play alone outdoors, and parents should make sure they always knew where they were and when they'd be home.

Acknowledging that women must be very frightened, she suggested that women should try to live as normally as possible. She suggested they should band together for support and travel in groups of two or three, advice reiterated by Marian Earley, the co-ordinator of the Ballymun Women's Centre. 'Ask a friend or even a strange woman going in the same direction to walk home with you,' she said.

O'Donnell slated the gardaí for not sending a speaker to the meeting. 'How can they expect residents to co-operate and to report sexual assaults if they are not prepared to speak to the people on their own ground?'

One young woman told journalist Joan Brady she had been viciously attacked but had refused to make a statement. 'The police wanted me to charge him,' she said. They told her he had been pulled in for 'this sort of thing' before. She refused. 'It would be my word against his. They'd probably say I led him on or something. Anyway, he'd only get three months, or maybe the probation act – 12 months suspended sentence or something. I wouldn't go to court for that.' She said she had been walking home from the shops and crossing an area of waste ground in Ballymun when a man had approached her and walked alongside her. He told her it was not safe for her to walk alone. She became uneasy. She told him she was on her way to meet her boyfriend and headed off towards a house where she knew her friend was baby-sitting. He said, 'Aren't you going to shake hands?' When she went to do so, he put his hand over her mouth and dragged her off by the hair. He beat her about the face, threw her on the ground and put his knees on her stomach. 'He was hurting me. He went to kiss me and I just locked my teeth into his lower lip. I could feel the blood in my mouth but I wouldn't stop till he swore he'd let me go,' she said. When she did let go, he walked off.

She did report the attack to the gardaí, but didn't find them sympathetic. 'They just said yeah, yeah, yeah, and what happened then?' A month later, she saw her attacker in a local pub and was persuaded by a girlfriend to tell the police. 'I thought, maybe he'll do it to other girls,' she said. 'So I did.' She identified him and felt frightened by the fact that he recognised her, too.[6]

In October 1987 a 19-year-old man pleaded guilty to the indecent assault of a 15-year-old girl in February that year and to the rape of a 19-year-old woman a week later. Nine further charges including rape, indecent assault and buggery on four different women were dropped by the state when he made his guilty plea. The court heard that the man, wearing a balaclava, had grabbed the 15-year-old in the early afternoon in a laneway. He put his hand over her mouth and a black leather belt around her neck and dragged her into the bushes and across a field. He then ordered her to take her skirt off, but passers-by saw what was happening, and he ran away.

It heard that a week later, at seven in the morning, a 19-year-old woman was walking across the park near her home in Ballymun on her way to work. The same man emerged from the bushes and asked her the time, then clamped his hand over her mouth and trapped her head under his arm. He dragged her down a hill and across a river. He ordered her to take off her clothes and tried to rape her. Then he made her get dressed and brought her over several barbed-wire fences to a garden. There he raped her. He tried to choke her with a scarf but she managed to free herself and knock him down. After a fierce struggle, he threatened that if the woman told anyone, he would kill her. He ran off. His defence counsel, Patrick McEntee, said the rape had been a handbag snatch that had escalated. The crimes were acts of lunacy, for which the man was sorry. He was sent to jail for eight years.

'Politicians streamed after each other into the launching party,' wrote Mary Maher of the opening at Leeson Street. 'The Minister for Social Welfare, Mrs Hussey, was there to say the few appropriate words ... Ms Fennell, the Minister for Women's Affairs was there, and so was Mr Charles Haughey, and Mary O'Rourke. The Labour Party and the Worker's Party had sent representatives and Michael Keating was there for the Progressive Democrats.

'All of which must mean,' she continued, 'that the current campaign to change the laws on rape is going to get somewhere in the new Dáil – doesn't it? Because, just occasionally in the general merriment and chat, someone from the DRCC staff would suddenly gently remind a guest or two that the whole thing is actually in aid of victims of brutal violence, most of whom are too afraid to take legal action in the present system.'[7]

Speaking at the launch, Hussey described rape as a 'grotesque wart on the face of society' and acknowledged that many cases of child abuse were never reported. 'Is it not a strange and cruel legal system which permits the victim of one of the most horrible crimes – rape – to be treated so badly and with such a lack of respect in court?' she asked. Rape was a 'trauma and a tragedy' for women, but the 'care and support' offered by the DRCC would ensure that victims would feel less isolated and better able to resume a positive role in society. Those who blamed women for inciting rape wanted to sweep social problems under the carpet, she said. 'That response demeans all women and trivialises their role in society.'[8] Anne O'Donnell recalled that, as he left the building, Haughey pressed a £50 note into her hand. 'He said it wasn't for the centre – it was for us, the women who worked there, to have a drink. And we did. It was a really nice gesture.'

In 1984, the DRCC had dealt with 426 cases of rape or sexual assault. Of these, 97 had been reported to the police and just 15 proceeded to court. In 1985, out of 73 rapes reported to the police, three led to convictions for rape.

The Rape Crisis Centre had, in fact, been campaigning for the repeal of the Criminal Law Rape Act since it was enacted in 1981. Every Minister for Justice had been lobbied. Meetings had been held during which women from the Centre made Ministers and their aides go through the law line by line. However, it was in 1986 that the Centre decided the time was right for the big push. In April it got the support of the Council for the Status of Women. At its first policy-making conference, one DRCC volunteer said that to say that penetration by a penis was rape while penetration by a broken bottle was not was 'like saying it's a lesser offence if someone breaks into a house by picking a lock rather than by breaking a window'.[9] In May, it made a submission to the Oireachtas Joint Committee on Women's Rights. Drafted in close consultation with Breda Allen, it was a typically hard-hitting DRCC document. 'The Act fails,' it stated, 'to criminalise rape within marriage, to adequately define rape, to protect the anonymity of the victim, to restrict evidence on the victim's sexual history, and to protect the victim from feeling that she is "on trial".'

According to the DRCC, 'We would go so far as to say the majority of rapes probably occur within marriage.' This was a controversial claim and was bound to incense the DRCC's traditional enemies, many of whom were at this time involved in fighting to stop divorce being introduced to Ireland. It was based on the experience of the DRCC and of Family Aid and other organisations working with 'battered wives'. The DRCC said rape was no less abhorrent when it was committed by a woman's husband. 'It would be unthinkable to refuse to prosecute a man who murdered his wife, on the grounds that she was married to him,' it reasoned. Many other countries had already criminalised marital rape.

One woman told journalist Deirdre McQuillan the story of how her husband had raped her. He was a violent bully who kept his family terrorised until Mary, his wife, finally obtained a barring order to exclude him from their home. He broke into the house and raped her in front of their children. She became pregnant and told McQuillan she would be going to England for an abortion. She didn't want the baby and said her husband would 'beat it out of me' anyway. 'I always thought rape had to do with dark laneways and strangers,' she said.

That night had taught her differently. 'It was not about satisfaction, or pleasure, but sheer aggression. He said he was going to "get me" whether I liked it or not.'[10]

The DRCC had welcomed the call by the Law Reform Commission in its report of January 1986 for the law to be changed on spouses giving evidence against an accused person to whom they were married. The existing law meant that a woman couldn't testify against her husband if he raped her or if he sexually abused their children. In the former case, she might well be the only witness. (The law on marital rape doubly debarred her and protected the rapist husband.) In the latter, she might be the only adult witness. The law meant that many cases of rape were unable to go to court. 'It is all very well to say that the family is important and should be protected,' said O'Donnell. 'But what sort of family is it where its members are being abused?'

The definition of rape – 'unlawful sexual intercourse without a woman's consent' – was too narrow, the DRCC said. It should be extended to include the use of objects, including the man's fingers, to penetrate the woman's vagina, as well as oral sex and buggery. 'In seven years working with victims of rape and sexual assault, we can find no evidence that penile penetration is any more disturbing than other forms of vaginal penetration or violation,' the submission stated. 'Many women found oral sex to be the most degrading form of sexual attack, while others found forced anal intercourse more debasing.' Rape was a crime of violence using sex as a weapon. Many of the crimes defined as indecent assault in the 1981 act should be redefined as rape. The new definition would allow for the prosecution of rapists of men and boys.

Under the 1981 law, boys under the age of 14 were assumed to be incapable of rape. The DRCC pointed out that several cases in which the assailants were under 14 had been through the courts in recent years, and that the assumption was clearly false. The submission added that it appeared that many young rapists had themselves been the victims of sexual abuse as children. 'To re-victimise another younger or more vulnerable person is a classic psychological coping mechanism adopted by boys and men who have themselves been victimised,' it noted. The DRCC called for prison sentences for boys who raped, with 'appropriate' treatment during their sentence. 'There is absolutely no doubt that sexual offenders do not "grow out" of the behaviour, but rather "grow into it",' the submission warned.

The DRCC called for the removal of the right of a judge to relax or remove the rape complainant's right to anonymity. Under the 1981 act, the judge could allow the woman to be named 'in the public interest'. The DRCC also called for rape cases to be heard 'in camera' (i.e. in the absence of members of the public and press), if the complainant requests this.

The 1981 law restricted the right of a man accused of rape to bring in evidence relating the woman's sexual history with anyone other than himself. However, the DRCC objected to the fact that such evidence could still be used at the judge's discretion. Nor, it argued, was the woman's previous relationship with her attacker relevant either. 'In any other criminal case if the accused introduced evidence about the complainant's character, it would lose him the protection of the court and would open the way for the prosecution to introduce evidence about his previous convictions (if any) or his general character.'

Juries in rape trials conducted under the 1981 act were instructed that if the accused believed the woman was consenting to the alleged rape, then that was a defence, even if he did not have reasonable grounds for this belief. The DRCC believed that this was deeply unjust since it meant that the motives and actions of the accused were assessed subjectively, whereas the woman complaining of rape had to prove objectively, backed up by forensic evidence and beyond all reasonable doubt, that she did not consent to rape. The man could use this clause of the act as a defence even after it was proved that he raped the woman against her will. The DRCC called for objective proof of the motives and actions of the accused.

'Many of our clients experienced the court case as being worse than the actual rape, describing it as "like being raped again in public", in a hostile and frightening environment,' said the submission. 'In no other criminal case would the complainant be subjected to the type of cross-examination and humiliation prevalent in rape cases ...' The DRCC pointed out that a woman alleging rape was in a different position to a person who had witnessed a robbery or other criminal act – yet the law treated her the same. She had no access to discussion or consultation with the state prosecutors, and the state saw its role as presenting, rather than fighting, the case. Given the frequently aggressive cross-examination engaged in by lawyers representing the accused, the state should continue to present its case against the accused, but rape complainants should also have their own legal representation 'fighting the case on her behalf'. This was the 'cornerstone' of the DRCC's submission, O'Donnell said.

At a public meeting held to promote the campaign, Sergeant Derek Nally, garda co-ordinator of the Irish Association of Victim Support, supported the DRCC's claims that rape complainants felt intimidated in court. However, defence lawyer Paddy McEntee argued that, while 'ordinary humanity' must be shown to any witness, sometimes men were falsely accused of rape, 'and sadly one of the few ways of testing the veracity of a witness is by cross-examination which is sometimes vigorous'. The DRCC claimed that its counsellors had frequently witnessed other criminal lawyers using 'abusive, degrading and patronising tactics'.[11]

The submission returned to the issue of all-male juries in rape cases and recommended that rape juries should be balanced: six women and six men. It said the practice of hearing rape cases in the District Court, where the maximum penalty that could be imposed was 12 months in jail, should be stopped. Rape was a serious crime – cases should be heard in the criminal courts.

The submission also dealt with investigative procedures. It said gardaí should inform the rape complainant of her right to be examined by a doctor of her choice, and that they should explain that the state would be taking the case and why her statement was needed. She should be given the phone number of her nearest Rape Crisis Centre. She should be sent a copy of her statement and she, or her legal representative, should be kept informed of the progress of the case. In particular, she should be told if the accused has been apprehended, is out on bail or is in remand.

'We have dealt with a number of women and girls who first heard of the fact that their assailants had been tried and sentenced when they read of it in the newspapers,' the submission revealed. She should not be left in a state of ignorance; 'after all, *she* is the person who has been irrevocably brutalised and who is suffering the after-effects of rape'.

The work of the SATU was praised and the DRCC recommended that further such units should be set up around the country. In the meantime, its practices and attitudes should be adopted. The DRCC should be invited to contribute to the training of medical personnel. Rape cases should be given priority listing, since a woman couldn't get over a rape while a trial was ahead of her and most cases took at least a year to come to court. Judges should be directed that if a woman wanted her Rape Crisis Centre counsellor to attend court with her, she should have a right to be there 'without question'. Women often preferred a counsellor to be with them than a family member 'because of their embarassment or feeling of humiliation in front of those they love' or because the details would be too upsetting for them. Very often, the submission tellingly added, the counsellor might be the only other woman in the courtroom, apart from the stenographer.

A week before the DRCC presented its submission, a 22-year-old man was sentenced to eight years in jail after he raped a 50-year-old woman whom he had attempted to rape on two previous occasions. He had been jailed for the previous attacks but was released early. The Department of Justice had given assurances that its early release and temporary release scheme wouldn't apply to prisoners convicted of rape or sexual offences. The DRCC said it had several clients who had been raped by men released under such provisions. The practice should stop.

The submission described as 'astounding' the inconsistency

in sentences given for sexual offences, ranging from a three-month suspended sentence for a man who raped a 13-year-old girl in Wexford, to a 15-year penal-servitude sentence for a man convicted of rape in Dublin. The DRCC was 'appalled and outraged' when senior counsel Seamus Sorohan appealed to a judge to be lenient in sentencing a convicted rapist. His client had 'given way to a human sexual urge', he said, and if he were a practising Catholic 'it would mean 23 minutes in confession to wipe the slate clean'. The DRCC said the remarks 'stepped outside the bounds of acceptable pleading' and trivialised the crime of rape which a woman experienced as a 'total invasion of her body, her mind and her privacy'.[12] The rapist got a three-year sentence.

The campaign to change the 1982 law was formally launched in October 1986. The DRCC's proposals were backed by the Rape Crisis Centres in Galway, Limerick, Cork and Waterford. These had been set up in 1984, 1980, 1983 and 1984 respectively, with advice, training and support from the Dublin Centre. Politicians from all the main political parties were on the platform. They included Monica Barnes of Fine Gael, Mary O'Rourke of Fianna Fáil, Mary Harney of the Progressive Democrats, Proinsias De Rossa of the Workers' Party and Eithne Fitzgerald of the Labour Party.

'Irish women are completely and utterly disillusioned with the Irish laws on rape as they stand,' said O'Donnell. She said that it was because most rape victims were women that it was given so little attention. After all, most of the legislature and most of the lawyers and judges were men. 'We in the Rape Crisis Centre know more about this than anybody else,' she said. Journalist Anne Marie Hourihane described the campaign, based on the submission, as 'the most comprehensive examination of rape ever undertaken in this country'. She commented that it was a 'sign of the DRCC's success that it is now in a position to command a respectful hearing from the politicians'.[13]

Kieran McGrath, then a social worker, later editor of the *Irish Socialist* and now a consultant, said the Rape Crisis Centre was a very effective lobby group. 'They influenced the government into spending money on, for example, setting up services for abused children in the hospitals,' he said. 'And this was at a time of stringent cuts in health spending.'

After Fianna Fáil passed the 1981 act, Fine Gael committed itself to reform it. The DRCC met Michael Noonan when he was Fine Gael's Minister for Justice and expressed disappointment at the party's failure to honour this commitment. Monica Barnes, a member of the Oireachtas Committee on Women's Rights, said the committee supported the DRCC's proposals for reform. She said attitudes had changed since 1981. People accepted that a broader definition of rape was required, and there was no longer any 'principled objection to marital rape being criminalised'. She said in 1981 the CSW had been told 'male TDs would not support it'.[14] However, her colleague, Minister of State for Women's Affairs, Nuala Fennell expressed doubt on marital rape. 'I think it would be difficult to get that through,' she said.[15]

Breda Allen was chairwoman of Fine Gael's women's group at this time. She told the group about the case of a young woman who had bled to death after being raped by a man using a broken bottle. He could only be charged with indecent assault, she said. Allen said the trauma for a woman raped by her husband was 'worse than if she was raped by a stranger' and that marital rape was a 'regular occurrence' for some women. The women's group gave its unanimous support to the DRCC's proposals. The Minister for Justice, Alan Dukes, came in for flak from the DRCC when he said at the Fine Gael ard fheis that rape victims should consult with prosecuting counsel before court hearings, under an already existing arrangement with the Director of Public Prosecutions. He was talking, O'Donnell said, 'absolute rubbish'. The DRCC's experience was the prosecution lawyers were 'petrified of being accused by the defence of trying to coach witnesses' and did little more than telling the victim to 'stand up in court and speak out'.[16]

The Progressive Democrats were forced to distance themselves from one of their representatives in Galway after Bridie O'Flaherty spoke up at a meeting in the city organised by the

Galway Rape Crisis Centre to promote the campaign. 'I wouldn't like if one of my sons brought home a woman of loose morals from a disco one night and she cried rape when he was innocent,' said the PD, formerly a Fianna Fáil mayor. Judges should always be told about the sexual history of 'a woman like this', she declared. The DRCC said it was 'amazed and appalled' and that all women deserved legal protection from rape. It called on the PDs to dissociate themselves from O'Flaherty's 'offensive' remarks. The PDs said O'Flaherty had been expressing her personal views and not those of the party.[17]

The Oireachtas Committee on Women's Rights unanimously recommended changes to the law along the lines recommended by the DRCC. Charles Haughey, leader of Fianna Fáil, was a member of the committee. He, too, addressed the DRCC's demands. Speaking at a Fianna Fáil women's conference in Galway at the end of 1986, he described the fear of rape as a 'barrier to equality'. It brought horror to individual women, he said, and it also 'tends to limit the freedom of all women'. He pledged that the next Fianna Fáil government would make reform of the rape laws and a review of services to rape victims a priority. 'A broader definition of rape is needed. It is necessary that women should be entitled to the protection of the law against domestic violence of any kind,' he said. Afterwards, he had his photograph taken sitting on Santa's knee.

In the middle of an early December night in 1986, a man broke into a woman's home in Cavan town. While the woman's three children slept, the man raped, buggered and, using a knife, indecently assaulted the woman. Her ordeal lasted for two hours. A 21-year-old man confessed to the crime, and there was supporting forensic evidence. However, he later retracted his statement and pleaded 'not guilty'. When the case came to court, in May 1987, it lasted three days. The jury took just ten minutes to conclude that the man was not guilty, and he was acquitted.

Judge Frank Roe told the jury the man's initial confession

had been made a day after he had consumed a lot of alcohol. He also told them: 'the raped woman is a deserted wife … we must face the facts. It appears that it is not unusual for her boyfriend and perhaps other men to come to her home quite late at night, sometimes after the public houses have closed.' He added that this didn't mean she was 'keeping a house of ill fame'.

Afterwards, the woman spoke about the trial. 'They really hounded me on the fact that I was a deserted wife and they as much as said that I went out all the time, bringing home men every night and that I was a "scarlet woman" and that I was running some sort of open house. I just felt I didn't have a chance.'[18]

Paddy McEntee was described afterwards in an *Irish Times* editorial as 'one of the most formidable defence lawyers in the state – arguably in these islands'.[19] Senior counsel for the prosecution was the equally able Paul Carney, now a High Court judge. Controversy centred on the fact that Carney opened the case for the state but was then unable to attend the trial for more than an hour a day. This was because he was simultaneously appearing in a High Court case about the constitutionality of the Fisheries Act. It was left to a respected but less experienced junior counsel to conduct the cross-examination of the accused and to sum up for the jury. (This was accepted practice at the time.)

Haughey, by this stage Taoiseach, and his Minister for Justice, Gerry Collins, faced a barrage of questions in the Dáil. Mary Harney called for separate legal representation for rape complainants. The Bar Council set up an inquiry which found that Carney's absence didn't constitute any breach of the Council's code of practice. Collins said the report did little to allay public concern.

The case did, however, raise public awareness about the obstacles facing raped women who wanted justice. *The Irish Times* commented that some of the issues in the Cavan case 'were but symptoms of the inadequacy of the rape laws and the way in which they make the taking of legal action on rape extremely difficult for women'. The editorial backed several of the DRCC's key recommendations. Commenting on the fact that Máire Geoghegan Quinn, who had become Minister of State at the Department of the Taoiseach, had said the government would like to enact new legislation but had to wait for the deliberations of the Law Reform Commission, the editorial concluded: 'In the meantime, the crime of rape continues. Women victims live in fear of taking court proceedings or of being humiliated if they do.'[20]

The DRCC's legal campaign made it one of the country's most prominent voluntary organisations. The *Irish Press* praised it in 1987 and demanded: 'How many more gruesome assaults must provoke public outrage before a fundamental attack is made on the crime of rape?' In an editorial, the paper said the increase in reporting of rape must be 'due in large part to the helping hand put out to rape victims by the DRCC'. It commented on the paucity of state assistance for the DRCC's work and called on the 166 TDs of the 25th Dáil to act to change the law. 'The crime of rape and other crimes of sexual abuse are no longer part of the hidden Ireland. The facts show an unacceptable level of these crimes together with an inadequate response to them ... Without action, how many more victims, young and old, are they consigning to savage assault?'[21]

A particularly shocking answer came with the case of a mutiple sex offender who was freed by the Dublin District Court and went on to rape and murder a young Canadian woman in London. Sentencing inconsistencies continued. A man who raped his three daughters, all under the age of six, got two years in jail. His brother raped one of the girls and got four years. A man who escaped from his social worker's custody and raped a woman got 20 years. Commenting on these and other cases, the DRCC called once again for 'consistency of sentencing and treatment for rapists in prison so that when they are released they don't come out and do exactly the same thing again'.[22] When a judge postponed a two-year prison sentence and freed a man on £100 bail after he pleaded guilty to raping his 14-year-old cousin, O'Donnell said it was a verdict which proved what the DRCC had been saying for a long time: 'The law is a complete ass in the area of sexual violence and sexual abuse ... it just does not protect the victims.'[23]

The Law Reform Commission, chaired by Mr Justice Ronan Keane, later the chief justice, published a consultation document in December 1987. The DRCC was pleased to find that it recommended the recognition of marital rape, that it recommended removing the assumption that boys aged under 14 couldn't rape and that it called for consistency of sentencing. 'We're pleased they considered it worth dealing with rape. A decade ago there was not much talk about it,' said O'Donnell. However, she added that the DRCC was 'very unhappy' that the LRC had come down against broadening the definition of rape, instead proposing the creation of two new offences called 'sexual assault' and 'aggravated sexual assault'. The DRCC also regretted that the Commission hadn't reached any conclusion on the issue of separate legal representation and said it was 'angry' that its document made very few references to the DRCC's own legal document. Máire Geoghegan Quinn also criticised the LRC's conclusions, commenting that whether she was attacked in her anus, mouth or vagina, the experience for a woman was that this was rape and should be recognised as such. She reiterated her support for separate legal representation and for juries to be half male, half female. She said the government had begun work on new rape legislation.

Asked by an RTÉ reporter whether the implementation of the LRC's recommendations would make more women report rape, O'Donnell replied, 'No, not particularly.'[24] The DRCC was also angry about the fact that four of the five members of the Commission were men, and all four were members of the legal profession. 'The law is not the prerogative of lawyers but is supposed to serve the ordinary people of the country,' O'Donnell wrote in a letter from the DRCC to the newspapers. 'We believe the broader the range of people examining and evaluating the relevance, value and justice behind our laws, the better the probability that our laws will serve the needs and concerns of the people of this country.'[25]

9

Aggravating Circumstances

The DRCC had been calling for it for years, but, in the end, it was a convicted rapist who brought about a review of sentencing in rape cases. Edward Tiernan, then 29, pleaded guilty to raping a 23-year-old woman in north Dublin in October 1985. The presiding judge, and then president of the Circuit Court, Mr Justice Thomas Neylon, described the case as 'abominable and bestial' and 'by far the worst rape case I've ever heard over 45 years in the legal profession'. He sentenced Tiernan, along with another 20-year-old man who also pleaded guilty, to 21 years in prison. A third man failed to turn up in court. It was the lengthiest sentence for rape that had ever been given in an Irish court.

The young woman and her boyfriend had been in his car in Cabra when the three attackers arrived. One of them sat on her boyfriend, and one drove the car. They stopped at Ashtown and one of them dragged the woman over a ditch and into a field. They locked her boyfriend in the boot of the car. They told the woman to undress. She tried to run away but was captured and beaten. They raped her repeatedly and performed other obscene acts. Later, they released the couple and 'legged it' back to their homes in Finglas. The judge said the woman would be affected by the ordeal for the rest of her life.

The DRCC said it was very pleased that the judge had 'treated this abominable crime with the seriousness it deserved'. Anne O'Donnell added that jail alone wouldn't rid society of rape. Prisoners should be treated so that their attitude to women changed, she said. The two men were refused leave to appeal their sentences. Subsequently, the Court of Criminal Appeal reaffirmed them. Then the Attorney General ruled that the decision involved a point of law of exceptional public importance and should be appealed to the Supreme Court, which should set guidelines for sentencing in future rape cases.

Representing Tiernan, senior counsel Hugh O'Flaherty said that the sentence was so severe as to be out of proportion to the crime. There had been worse cases, he said. Any rape was 'an attack on the humanity and dignity of the woman, an interference with her bodily integrity and an attack on her essential freedom and a violation of her nature as a woman'. O'Flaherty said there were three degrees of rape. In the first, the woman didn't consent but there were no other aggravating circumstances. In the second, there might be aggravating circumstances such as the age of the woman, violence above and beyond the rape, breaking into a house or vehicle, premeditation, group rape or rape accompanied by unnatural acts. In the third, the rapist might have previous convictions, would be defined as a psychopath, a danger to womanhood in general and would have inflicted lasting physical or mental injury on his victim. O'Flaherty argued that while there might be no mitigating factors in the third category, there should be some distinction between it and the other two.

In defence of Tiernan, he said there was no premeditation – the rape was 'an instantaneous act of lust'. The defendant had made a full admission of his guilt to gardaí. Referring to research in New Zealand, O'Flaherty commented that long sentences didn't seem to act as a deterrent to rapists. 'By a merciful dispensation of providence,' he added, 'the woman is not alleged to have suffered any long-term serious physical or mental trauma.' Michael McDowell, then a senior counsel, latterly a PD Minister for Justice, represented the DPP. He said all the aggravating elements were present in the rape, and if there had been any error by the trial judge, it was that he didn't take Tiernan's guilty plea into consideration or the possibility of rehabilitation.

The DRCC challenged the assumptions behind O'Flaherty's reasoning. How, it demanded, could this rape not be called premeditated? How was the woman's age relevant? If a woman was raped by someone she knew, who was to say that this was better or worse than if she was raped by someone who broke into her house? 'This clearly displays the utter lack of control and position the victim has in the criminal justice system,' said Anne O'Donnell. As columnist Joan Brady remarked, the comments defied all available research on rape. Shouldn't victims be asked about the effect rape had on their lives? she asked. 'Then we might get guidelines which don't simply reflect a narrow and essentially male view of what makes one rape worse than another.'[1] O'Donnell also pointed out that 'very often a rape victim can be so terrified by threats that the offender does not need to use physical violence'.[2]

The Supreme Court declined to provide guidelines, on the basis that its role was to deal with individual cases on appeal. In Tiernan's case, it ruled that his sentence should be reduced to 17 years because of his guilty plea. The Supreme Court said each case had to be decided by the presiding judge. However, the chief justice, Mr Justice Finlay, did make remarks which he said he hoped would assist judges. Rape was a serious crime, for which the appropriate sentence was 'a substantial immediate period of detention or imprisonment'. It was not easy to imagine circumstances in which anything else could be justified. Rape was a gross attack on the human dignity and bodily integrity of a woman and a violation of her human and constitutional rights. It not only caused bodily harm but was inevitably followed by emotional, psychological and psychiatric damage to the victim, which could often be of long-term and sometimes of lifelong duration. It could distort the victim's approach to her own sexuality and impose a distressing fear of sexually transmitted diseases and the possibility of a pregnancy and birth. Particularly welcome, as far as the DRCC was concerned, was the comment that the rape victim's previous sexual experience or the fact that she was 'imprudent' in associating with the perpetrator should not be regarded as a mitigating factor to justify a shorter sentence.[3]

There was further good news for the DRCC when the Law Reform Commission published its final report in June 1988. Anne O'Donnell said the DRCC was 'delighted' by the recommendations, which were broadly in line with its demands. The proposals, if implemented, would allow male rape victims legal redress and this, too, was welcomed by the DRCC. 'An increasing number of men and teenage boys are coming to us who've been sexually assaulted in childhood or raped as teenagers,' said O'Donnell. 'The Oireachtas Women's Rights Committee did recommend very strongly changing the law one and a half years ago. Four of that commission are now in the government. It is time they did something about it.'[4]

In November 1988, the Rape Crisis Centre saw the publication of the Criminal Law (Rape Amendment) Bill. Fianna Fáil's Justice Minister, Gerry Collins, announced that rape in marriage was to be made a crime. The definition of rape was not extended, but indecent assault was replaced with two newly defined crimes: sexual assault, carrying a new maximum sentence of five years, and aggravated sexual assault, with a maximum penalty of life imprisonment. The bill abolished the presumption that boys under 14 couldn't rape. The bill stated that lack of physical resistance didn't constitute consent and that warning the jury about relying on uncorroborated evidence from the complainant was to be left to the discretion of the judge. All cases were to be tried in the Central Criminal Court, and the public was to be excluded. An editorial in the *Irish Independent* praised the DRCC for the pressure it had brought on the government: 'The rapist of the future is in for severe penalties,' it said. 'And no one will have any sympathy for him.'

It should have been a moment of triumph for the DRCC. But it couldn't be savoured. The Centre was in deep trouble. The

Revenue Commissioners had issued a legal writ for £95,000 for unpaid PRSI (social insurance) and PAYE. There was no money to pay it. There were 12 full-time staff and no money to pay their wages. With around 130 new calls (and rising) coming in every month, there was by this stage a waiting list of 300 clients who couldn't be seen because of staff shortages. At least five more staff were needed. O'Donnell was frank about how the situation had arisen. 'We are grossly under-funded by the state and we have been unable to keep up our expenses,' she said. The PRSI-PAYE money was the easiest to withhold – non-payment of rent, electricity or other bills would have had immediate consequences. 'All the deductions were made from staff. We simply used the money to keep ourselves going.'

Bernie Purcell said, looking back, that the collective had known, but not understood, that financial disaster was pending. 'We were not unaware of it,' she said, 'but we felt we had urgent work to do and we just got on with it.' The Centre had an annual grant of £21,000 from the EHB. It received a once-off payment of £10,000 from Máire Geoghegan Quinn, Minister for Women's Affairs, and £5,000 for computers from the Department of Social Welfare. Health Minister Rory O'Hanlon authorised a further once-off payment of £20,000 from the National Lottery. However, spending for the year 1987 was £230,000. The DRCC just couldn't bridge the gap, nor could it raise the same amount for the next year. It issued a statement announcing that, unless help was forthcoming, the DRCC would have to shut down on 23 December.

Back in December 1986, the DRCC had written an open letter to the government, then comprising Fine Gael and Labour: 'We wish all members of the government a happy Christmas, and hope [they] will have time to reflect upon the way in which they have utterly failed to provide adequate financial support for our work,' it said. This had led, for the first time in its history, to it having to turn away clients. 'Perhaps some member of the Government has personal experience of being sexually abused, has a child who has been sexually abused or has a friend or relative who has been raped.

If so, they will know the pain and distress ... and how important advice and counselling could be ... We ourselves, and our clients whom we cannot help, feel totally let down and unsupported by the Government.'[5] In May 1988, when the news of the debt to the Revenue Commissioners had broken, DRCC fundraiser Helen Shortall had said: 'There's no way we can manage to pay our debts and keep going.'[6]

Workers' party deputy Pat McCartan raised the crisis at the DRCC in the Dáil. 'We are faced with the prospect that a unique and comprehensive service is at the end of its financial tether and existence,' he said. No other agency in the state provided the help offered by the DRCC. 'Since the Centre was established in 1979 with the help of a few volunteers and one telephone, it has developed into a professional service second to none and is a credit to all concerned.' He outlined the range of services. Crucially, the DRCC 'remained always at the side of a victim helping them to cope with what is often the complete destruction of life around them'. He said that 70 per cent of callers in the previous year were victims of abuse in the past and that 'because of lack of resources' some 300 of them were in a queue.

'It is important to underline the fact that this is not a handout organisation, one that does not work for itself as well,' he said. 'For example, the financial report for the year to the end of October 1988 showed that their income from fund-raising was estimated at £150,000, £90,000 of which they raised themselves. By way of seminars, lectures, collections, donations and counselling fees, they managed to raise the remainder of that amount, minus the £41,000 [provided by the EHB and Lottery funds].' The vast majority of their resources went on paying the wages of their workers.

McCartan paid tribute to the DRCC's effectiveness in lobbying parliament. Within two years of being set up, it had convinced the government to update the law. It had gone on to provide research and make submissions on the failings of the 1981 act, with proposals as to how these could be corrected. They had won praise for their efforts from all sides of the House, he said, and they had won a commitment from the government to bring in a new law, which was imminent. The impact of the DRCC on society had to be appreciated. In the past year it had counselled 1,234 people. Victims of rape and child abuse were referred to it by social workers, doctors, teachers and gardaí, among others. Professional and voluntary agencies in Dublin and beyond it relied on the Centre.

It was a glowing accolade, but it met with a cold response from the government. The Minister of State at the Department of Health, Terry Leyden, said the DRCC's demand for money was 'unreasonable and unfair'. He said no agency could 'assume an open-ended commitment by the state to their undertakings'. The root of the trouble at the DRCC was that they had expanded their activities 'beyond their own capacity to finance them and beyond the prior agreement and commitment of the public authorities'. They had taken on extra staff and work when they knew they couldn't pay for it, but in spite of this, he had given them an extra £20,000, Leyden said. This amounted to a 100 per cent increase – yet they wanted more. He went on to say that the Department had already made 'very substantial and structured provision for dealing with child abuse' through new services at the children's hospitals at Crumlin and Temple Street, and through local health boards. The new Child Care Bill said agencies like the DRCC had to 'consult with and co-ordinate their work with' statutory agencies to ensure that 'confusion and expensive duplication' didn't occur. It was out of the question, Leyden concluded, 'to present them with a blank cheque'.[7]

An *Irish Times* editorial of the time expressed a better understanding of the role of the DRCC. Rape was a 'social epidemic', it said. The health services were beginning to provide: there was the SATU for rape victims immediately after an attack and the children's hospitals for child victims of abuse. 'But the DRCC must cope with people who suffered abuse in the years when there seemed nowhere to go for help … [it] should not be allowed to close.'[8]

Nor, according to Monica Barnes, should it have to go around with a 'begging bowl'. Barnes was speaking as chairwoman of the joint Oireachtas Committee on Women's

Rights. She said the DRCC performed a vital role and should be state-funded. Máire Geoghegan Quinn agreed to a degree. 'They perform an exceptionally important purpose and function, with the utmost care and attention, giving the anonymity that is so important,' said the then Minister of State at the Department of the Taoiseach. 'We will have to be prepared, as a government, to provide funding on a secure basis.' She said the Minister for Health, Rory O'Hanlon, had undertaken to review funding for the DRCC and for the other RCCs around the country.

However, she added that there were 'question marks' over some of the DRCC's figures. She pointed out that the DRCC had spent £45,000 and a disproportionate amount of time and energy on a fundraising exercise that brought in just £89,000. She said the government intended to appoint a financial advisor to the Centre. Senator David Norris sounded a warning note. The role of the advisor would have to be clearly defined, he said. There had been 'disastrous intervention of this kind before'.[9]

Fianna Fáil MEP Eileen Lemass made an appeal to the Catholic Church to intervene. She requested Archbishop Desmond Connell to donate the proceeds of a mass in every church in the Dublin diocese for one Sunday in December 1988. The Catholic press office informed Lemass that it was Church policy to confine such special collections to projects it sponsored itself. The DRCC retorted that it hadn't been its idea to ask the Church in the first place, nor would it have approved Lemass's move had she asked it first. It was the government's responsibility to sort out the situation.

'We were quite wild in those days and in some ways defiant,' said Bernie Purcell. 'We hadn't been cowed yet.'[10] Indignant feminists wrote to the newspapers deploring the suggestion that the DRCC should rely on church charity – they said rape was not seen as politically important because its victims were mainly women. Geoghegan Quinn had criticised the Centre for its fundraising costs – she should have criticised the inadequacy of state funding, the women added. Lemass hastened to reply that she had only meant the Church money as an emergency measure to keep the DRCC open over Christmas. She agreed that the government should provide and also support a European Parliament resolution on violence against women, calling for information on RCCs to be given out by the police.

A thousand balloons were released in St Stephen's Green. Soccer internationals Johnny Giles and Tony Currie joined members of Def Leppard and Spandau Ballet for a fundraiser at UCD. There was a dance marathon. A northside priest sent money raised by a sponsored 'beard and hair cut' in his parish. Office workers did whip-arounds and sent cheques for £100. Individuals sent £20 notes. A 'rubber band workout' was planned for spring 1989. 'There was enormous public support for the Rape Crisis Centre,' said Breda Allen. 'All the politicians knew that, too, and we were relying on it.' However, goodwill didn't deal with the court summons. 'I had to go down to the Revenue Commissioners and beg and scrape and grovel,' said Allen. 'It was a horrific time for us.' At the last minute, the government allocated £100,000 to the DRCC in the budget of January 1989.

It was a huge relief – though it sparked an angry response from an unexpected quarter. By 1989 there were RCCs in Limerick, Galway, Cork, Clonmel and Waterford. 'On behalf of the Rape Crisis Centres outside the Pale, I would like to strongly express our total disgust and frustration at the government's singling out of the Dublin RCC for the allocation of £100,000 from the budget,' wrote Sandra Barden of the Galway Rape Crisis Centre, which was struggling to survive on 'paltry once-off grants'. Clonmel and Cork RCCs got nothing from the government in 1988. Limerick RCC received £500, and Galway got £3,000. Relations between the Dublin RCC and the other centres had ups and downs. The Dublin centre had provided support and training for most of the other centres, but there was no doubt that the Dublin centre overshadowed the others at a national level, and there was resentment about this.

The promised grant saved the DRCC from closure. However, once the Revenue Commissioners were paid, there would be just £5,000 left. The promised lottery money was not to be paid until after the EHB carried out an evaluation of the work of the DRCC. The calls from distressed victims kept coming, and waiting lists got longer.

The end of 1988 was a low point for the DRCC in more ways than one. In the midst of the financial chaos, the Centre's formidable director, Anne O'Donnell, had to resign for personal reasons. She had become one of the most prominent women in the country and was known as a champion of the victims of rape and child abuse. She'd been given a Millennium Award by Dublin's mayor, Carmencita Hederman, as a tribute to her work. O'Donnell had suffered the loss of her baby twins at birth and had spent much of a subsequent pregnancy, also with twins, in hospital. She lost one of these twins during the pregnancy, and her newborn daughter was premature. The Centre needed a director to sort out the financial trouble it was in, but it couldn't be O'Donnell. 'My priority had to be my family,' she said. 'I had no option but to resign.'[11]

Her view of the financial mess at the DRCC was that it was inevitable given the ever-growing volume of work and the failure of the government to provide. 'I'd be the first to admit, though, that I was not the world's best administrator,' she said. 'We weren't fundraisers – we were campaigners.' Olive Braiden's recollection was that O'Donnell was an excellent administrator. 'She just was not good at delegating authority,' she recalled.

A 1986 profile of O'Donnell in the *Sunday Tribune* by Pat Brennan had described the 'characteristic flair' with which O'Donnell had orchestrated a professional publicity campaign to coincide with the campaign to change the law. Brennan described the good relationship the DRCC had built up with the gardaí and its role in setting up the SATU – 'the envy of RCCs in Britain'. Much of it was down to O'Donnell, Brennan argued. She quoted a Fianna Fáil politician who said she was 'very organised, very ruthless about her cause', that she had made 'talking about rape respectable' and that she never let it 'out of the headlines'. Brennan commented that: 'Her political sense of what can be accomplished, and how, is particularly well developed. It was the DRCC again that made child abuse a national issue.' O'Donnell had listed for Brennan the politicians she knew, as well as the civil servants, judges, barristers and gardaí. 'Personal contact is where it is at,' she told the journalist. 'I feel very strongly about meeting people … then they stop being afraid of me.'

Brennan's view was that O'Donnell had 'mellowed over the years'. She claimed O'Donnell described the DRCC's original militant feminism as 'a bit of nonsense' which the women running the Centre had dropped. Brennan also said that while the DRCC was run as a collective 'there is little doubt whose voice carries the most weight'.[12] O'Donnell wrote to the *Sunday Tribune* to protest about these remarks. She had not dismissed the early workings of the DRCC as nonsense, she wrote. 'Indeed, I remember the early days of the Centre as the most difficult and contentious ones, fighting against massive prejudice and suspicion, laying the base and groundwork on which today's Centre is constructed. The beliefs of the DRCC on rape and sexual abuse are every bit as feminist and radical today as they were eight years ago. It is not the DRCC, or I, who have become less feminist and more radical, but a large segment of social thinking which has, over the years, come to agree with many of our views about sexual violence.' O'Donnell also took issue with the claim that hers was the dominant voice.[13] Several collective members who otherwise held O'Donnell in high regard did, however, recall her as having been 'incredibly controlling' and 'a bit manipulative'. One said, 'she was full of wiry, passionate energy, but sometimes she needed to let other people take charge, and she couldn't do that'.

O'Donnell was the last of the founders of the DRCC to leave the collective. Bernie Purcell took over as director. 'The transformation after Ann was always going to be difficult,' she said. 'I read something recently about excellence and it said that the sign of a successful team is that individual players can leave but the excellence remains.'[14] This was the longer-term challenge for the DRCC. In the short term, staying open was the goal. Emer Neligan joined as a volunteer at this time. 'I found it an amazing place,' she recalled. 'I was in awe of the work the therapists were doing behind their closed doors. You'd hear wailing and at first that used to make me wince. Later, I learned that this was the sound of someone releasing terrible pain, and I'd welcome it. I remember a client telling me how she really appreciated the new building in Leeson Street. She said that the old premises was as grotty as she felt. She'd felt it was all she deserved.' Neligan went on to become a phone counsellor and was later qualified and employed as a therapist.

Funding problems continued relentlessly. 'We had been promised funds, but very much on the government's terms, and nothing like as much as we needed,' said Purcell. 'My year was a "reclaim the land" scenario. We knew the increased government funding would come at a price. We were still seen as a radical group and we knew the deal was that we'd be expected to tone down our criticisms of the health establishment. We were given to understand this. It was a real dilemma because we did want to professionalise, and that was what was expected of us, but we didn't like the compromises we had to make. It sat very ill with us.' The grants were swallowed up by debts. 'We had to crawl for pittances. People were literally writing to everyone they knew who might have anything to give us,' said Purcell. 'It is a wonder that the Centre survived at all.'

'The women in the Rape Crisis Centre changed my life. They gave me so much and I am eternally grateful to them,' said Maura. While the DRCC as an organisation was going through trauma, its work continued. There were hundreds of people, mostly women, receiving counselling, including 10 therapy groups with 20 people in each. Maura was one of the women. 'I was raped in 1988,' she said. 'I was 18 and I'd gone to London from Dublin to join my dad for a week's holiday. I was staying with a friend in Brixton the first night. I got talking to this black guy and he invited me for a drink. I thought he meant in a pub and I agreed, but then he brought me to an off-licence. I was just really naïve. I didn't know what to do in the situation. I ended up in this house with him, in a flat.

'He raped me. Afterwards, I kept saying I needed to go to the toilet and eventually I escaped from the flat. I was naked and I ran down the stairs screaming for help. There were people in the other flats. I could hear televisions, and people talking, but no one would come to the door. He ran after me and caught me. He said no one would help me because they were all his friends. He dragged me back. But someone must have rung the police because they came and rang the doorbell. He escaped. I crawled out onto a window ledge, still naked. I thought it was all a big conspiracy and that the police were on his side, too. They coaxed me in again eventually.

'The police experience was just as bad as being raped. They strip you and put you in a big thing like a plastic bag, with a label on it. They took all sorts of samples and questioned me for five or six hours. I had to come back later to make another statement, too. I didn't tell my dad right away that I'd been raped, and I didn't tell my mum because she was on holiday and I didn't want her to cut it short. I told friends and they all clubbed together and one of them came to London to bring me home.

'I was in a horrific state. My friends moved in to the house and they weren't able to help me. I was going crazy, running round the house smashing things up. I was all hunched up into myself and I wouldn't look at anyone. When my mum came back I told her and she persuaded me to go to the Rape Crisis Centre. She was a very strong believer in what they were doing there and her positive feelings were what got me to go. This was in the Ireland of women's centres being totally frowned upon. She came with me for my first appointment. It was terrifying. I didn't want to go. I didn't want to think about what had happened to me.

'I was in a big group and the work was all *gestalt*. It was body work. We stood in groups in a circle and one woman would be in the middle and she would go through a stream of thought and body movement. It was all about it being trapped in your body. Watching the other people brought it out in me.

I met women who had been really badly affected. There was a woman who hadn't left her house for 20 years. I remember there was this one woman who had big soft brown eyes who looked like she'd understand.

'I had an appointment once a week. It was really hard and sometimes I couldn't face it. Mostly, though, I made myself. I think it is probably the hardest thing I have done in my life, and the more I got better, the harder it got, because then I didn't want to put myself through it. I just wanted to get on with my life. Sometimes I did wish I could have one to one counselling, just to talk. I disturbed my friends by talking about it, and sometimes now I wish I hadn't been so public about it. People don't forget.

'I went for about a year, during which time I was in bits. At the time it seemed unimaginably long. One day I had a real pinnacle moment in the therapy. I got really angry and started beating pillows – I was really furious for myself and for everyone else who had been raped. I empowered myself. I hadn't been able to be angry until then. Other people, my family and friends, had been really angry for me. They were very supportive and I think I was very lucky in that. But I had blamed myself for the rape. Therapy made me realise I'd turned all my anger in on myself. I had been punishing myself. I'd been going round feeling like there was a great gaping hole in me but no one seemed to notice.

'After that breakthrough, I left soon afterwards. I didn't need to go any more. I don't think you ever really get over it completely, but it really helped. I reclaimed my body. I was able to walk strong. It made me more powerful in my life, and since then I've been able to help other friends who've been going through bad experiences. I hardly ever think about the rape now. They never caught the rapist. I don't know why. I think the Rape Crisis Centre does wonderful work. I don't know what would have happened to me if I hadn't been able to go there.'[15]

10

'Not One Iota of Power'

'She's a dead woman.' This was the threat issued by a 26-year-old Dundalk man during his trial in 1989 for the rape of a 27-year-old woman. He and another man had smashed their way into her flat in the middle of the night, tied up her fiancé and raped her vaginally, anally and orally. Two other young Louth men broke into another woman's home, threatened to shoot her, forced whiskey on her, raped her and beat and stamped on her. After they were convicted, a drunken mob descended on the woman's home armed with bottles, stones, a chimney rod and an axe.

In the North, a Fermanagh woman's back and 11 of her ribs were broken as she was raped by a 28-year-old neighbour on her daughter's wedding day. Mr Justice Liam McCollum said there were mitigating circumstances and that the rape was unpremeditated. 'It was not a case of a grossly aggravated rape such as when a house is broken into or a weapon used,' he said, sentencing the rapist to seven years in jail. The victim was left confined to a wheelchair. 'My life has been ruined,' she said.[1]

A 47-year-old man dragged a screaming 93-year-old woman up the stairs of her house by her hair. He attempted to rape her and she thought she was going to die. The man had been jailed for four years in 1984 for raping and assaulting another elderly woman in what was called 'an appalling and perturbing case'. A young woman with a mental age of three who was sexually abused and became pregnant in a care home in Ballina, Co. Mayo, in 1984, was awarded £27,500 in the High Court. A 23-year-old from Co. Kerry murdered 31-year-old Breda Hanrahan and told gardaí he was 'sick of women leading me on'. He told gardaí he felt great after the killing. 'She was just a teaser,' he said.[2]

A 23-year-old man from north Co. Dublin raped his 27-year-old neighbour after she got off a late night bus. A 40-year-old Co. Meath man wrote his neighbour's name and phone number, along with offers of sex, in phoneboxes and public places, resulting in her receiving hundreds of obscene calls. Her husband drove thousands of miles finding and erasing the graffiti. A former soldier from Drogheda indecently assaulted a 20-year-old woman at her home. A senior probation officer told the court the man had shown no remorse and had indicated that the £1,000 he handed over by way of compensation was his way of buying his innocence.[3]

A 59-year-old south Tipperary man pleaded guilty to multiple charges of incest committed against his five daughters over a period of 25 years. All the girls were under 15 at the time of the offences. Two of them had babies as a result of the abuse. One baby was severely retarded and the other was deaf. The court heard that social workers and clergy had tried to intervene but couldn't handle the situation and so the abuse continued. When arrested, the man claimed a priest had absolved him. A psychiatrist said the man exerted complete authority in the home and believed the girls were his possessions. He got three years' penal servitude.

A 51-year-old Dublin man indecently assaulted four of his nieces over a six-year period when they were aged between four and twelve. Mr Justice Frank Roe ordered him to pay his victims £2,000 each and undergo treatment. He said that if he offended again, he'd get a long sentence. Psychiatrist Art O'Connor told the court the man had told him he had a poor recollection of what had happened. One of the victims shouted from the back of the court: 'But we haven't got poor memories.'[4]

The DRCC expressed serious concern about the growing practice of combining suspended sentences with demands for compensation to be paid to victims. 'It sometimes looks as if it is based on the belief that financial compensation can do away with the harm of the offence,' said Bernie Purcell. The DRCC's view was that compensation should be paid – by the state. 'We don't feel at all happy with any deviation from custodial sentences for sexual offences.' She also questioned the requirement that the man seek therapy. The DRCC had campaigned for and supported the therapy programme for incest offenders that had been set up by Dr Art O'Connor in the Central Mental Hospital earlier in 1989, but not as an alternative to prison. 'How does the court assess the success of the therapy?' said Purcell. 'And unless he does get therapy you can be sure that a sexual offender will offend again.'

Less than two months later, a case came to court which proved her right. A 47-year-old man had sexually abused his daughter from when she was 11 until she was 15. He was caught, took part in a pilot programme of counselling for incest offenders and then started the abuse again. A prosecution lawyer told the court there had been 'a degree of bureaucratic bungling' in the case. The man was jailed for five years. Mr Justice Frank Roe commented that the case was 'most unusual' in that the family, including the victim, had 'forgiven' the man. In fact, as the DRCC was discovering, this was a common feature in families that had been completely dominated by an abuser.

The DRCC had also warned that men charged with rape shouldn't receive bail. Again, a court case proved the point. A 49-year-old Dublin man raped and beat his daughters over a period of 18 years between 1971 and 1989, from when each of the girls was about eight years old. During one court appearance he threatened to shove a crutch down one of his victim's throats. While on bail, he had defied a High Court order that he was not to return to his home.[5]

A young traveller admitted making his younger sister, then

15, pregnant. The court was told that the girl was physically handicapped and mentally retarded. She had given birth to a stillborn baby. The court heard they lived in primitive conditions, isolated from other travellers. A Galway man admitted sexually abusing his ten-year-old daughter during weekend access visits. The judge said a custodial sentence would do no one any good and adjourned the case for six months to see how the man would behave in the meantime.

Gardaí warned women in the northside Dublin suburb of Coolock to beware after a woman was dragged off the road by three youths and raped as she walked home from a local pub. They warned women in the western Dublin suburb of Tallaght to beware after a similar attack on a woman there. A survey of women students at University College Dublin revealed that they were afraid of walking on the campus alone following several sexual attacks.

Department of Health statistics showed a 66 per cent increase in confirmed cases of child sex abuse in the year 1986/7. The SATU at the Rotunda hospital was hugely over-subscribed, as were the units set up to work with abused children in Temple Street and Crumlin hospitals. The ISPCC's Childline had 750 calls in one year from children revealing sexual abuse. A new foundation, Children at Risk Ireland (CARI), was set up to provide treatment for abused children. Social workers were overwhelmed. One social worker in the audience of a *Late Late Show* discussion of incest said there was no point in encouraging more people to come forward since existing services couldn't cope with any new influx. The programme, inevitably, led to just such an influx.

A young woman wrote to an agony aunt: 'I am an 18-year-old girl and my father is 45. For the past three years he has been sexually abusing me. Until now I've been too scared to seek help as my father has threatened to beat me. My mother knows what's going on but won't interfere as my father hits her regularly. I am very worried now because I missed my last period and I have noticed sores on my private parts. I am desperate.' Anna, in the *Evening Press*, urged her to contact SATU and the Rape Crisis Centre.[6]

The Rape Crisis Centre revealed in August 1989 that it had already had 357 new clients that year, as compared with 388 during 1988. The rate of contacts was accelerating all the time. 'What is of major concern to us is that this number of people continue to be raped, ten years after we were established,' said Bernie Purcell. 'While the facilities for helping victims have improved, the public attitude to the crime has remained the same.' She admitted that the DRCC was unable to cope with the demand. 'Even without the extra numbers we were stretched to the limit. For every one person we take off the waiting list and place in a therapy group, we replace them with two more.'[7]

There were 250 people on waiting lists at the time. One of them, using the name Nicky, wrote to the *Evening Herald* in response to an article headlined 'Are sexual abusers treated severely enough?' No, she said, they were not. 'I would like to ask also,' she went on, 'Are the victims treated seriously enough?' She said she had already been waiting six months and 'would be lucky' if she was counselled within the next six. 'I would really like to know why the government repeatedly ignores the needs of the victims by ignoring the cash needs of the Rape Crisis Centre and the wonderful, unparalleled work they do,' she wrote.[8]

'We have not had a penny since the financial crisis we had in November last. We are pleased our debt to the Revenue Commissioners has been paid but it is vital that a decision is made soon about the future of the Centre,' a spokeswoman for the DRCC said in March 1989. In the Dáil, Monica Barnes criticised the delay in paying the DRCC promised funds. She noted that the EHB had said the DRCC had no urgent need for funding on a day-to-day basis. This was untrue. 'Ordinary people in the street believe they've got large sums of money,' she said. A meeting was to be arranged with the Taoiseach, Charles Haughey, to discuss the crisis. She later accused Haughey of ignoring repeated requests from the joint committee on women's affairs for urgent funds to be provided for the country's Rape Crisis Centres and other women's groups. The illusion that the DRCC was now rich was fuelled by the fact that it had become a very fashionable charity with glamorous fundraising events such as champagne receptions at the Trinity Ball, a public interview with Richard Harris and the Smirnoff Fashion Awards.

The government fell, and the Rape Bill was not yet passed. Commenting on this, Olive Braiden said, 'Our big concern now is the distinct possibility that by the time the new Dáil sits, we won't be here … sexual abuse is not just a woman's issue but sadly, although we have got a lot of verbal support from some TDs, notably Monica Barnes and Máire Geoghegan Quinn, there is not one single woman in the Dáil with one iota of power.'[9]

Senator Nuala Fennell had made valiant efforts to have the bill amended at committee stage. Women were living in 'petrifying fear' she told the senate. They locked themselves in their cars and homes and they didn't go out at night. Why should half the population be subject to such a curfew? She accused the Minister for Justice, Gerry Collins, of bringing in 'all the old patriarchal attitudes'. Collins replied that it would be wrong to reduce the debate to men versus women.[10]

The DRCC's annual report for 1989 is a subdued affair. The services offered by the Centre are listed. Two thousand people contacted the Centre, and 441 went on to get counselling. Nine out of ten of them were women. Half the calls were referrals by social workers and other professionals, family members or friends. The other half were made by the victim herself. Over 50 per cent of callers had been sexually abused for the first time when they were aged 11 or under. Just 12 per cent of clients had reported to the gardaí. During the year, the Centre ran a mother's group, a male group, several incest groups, rape groups and sexuality groups. The report described the new education department, run by Maeve Lewis and Dolores Heffernan. This was to co-ordinate talks and training courses and provide educational material. The role of volunteers had changed. By 1989 they were mainly involved in staffing the 24-hour crisis phone line and giving talks, while face to face and longer term counselling were carried out by the paid workers.

The section on funding has a weary tone. The financial evaluation was carried out early in the year and 'staff spent a good deal of time' with health board officials.[11] Then came the services evaluation which 'continued for many months throughout 1989, absorbing time and energy on the part of staff'. Then, towards the end of the year, 'when the Centre was desperately in need of the long-promised funding', the officers returned, claiming that the financial information they had received was now out of date. The money was not, in fact, delivered that year.

'The evaluation process was awful,' recalled Bernie Purcell. The evaluation team, led by Brian Glanville, director of psychology at the EHB, decided at an early stage that the information provided by the DRCC was not adequate, so they devised a detailed statistical questionnaire with more than 30 questions. This was provided to the DRCC on 20 December 1988. The team was evidently displeased when, on 13 January 1989, 'it became apparent that work had not yet started ...' The tone of the EHB report, completed in October 1989, indicates considerable friction between the evaluators and the DRCC. The words 'inadequate' and 'unsatisfactory' feature frequently. A great deal of time and energy had been wasted, the report claimed, because of degrees of non-co-operation.

The team wished to meet staff and was clearly annoyed when the director advised that staff would meet with them as a group only and not individually. A compromise was reached, and staff met the team in pairs. Purcell recalled that she urged staff to dress conservatively for these sessions. 'One day a pair of them appeared for their meetings with the Board in the most outrageous clothes – multi-coloured tights and mini-skirts. I was appalled. I didn't know what to say,' she said. 'But it turned out they were having a joke. They had their hair shirts in a bag.' The volunteers were also disinclined to meet the EHB as individuals.

The evaluators asked to sit in on group therapy sessions and were impatient with the DRCC's refusal to allow them. Grace O'Malley, then a volunteer at the Centre, remembered the evaluators as 'incredibly arrogant'. Some of the files the evaluators asked to see were confidential, she said. The report described the workers as being 'extremely confident about the value of the work they are doing ... they believed the service they are providing is one that is not provided anywhere else in Dublin'.[12] Staff morale was found to be 'high, with considerable enthusiasm and commitment expressed'.

Counsellors were said to be 'openly critical of the management style which had operated prior to December 1988'. The 'feminist collective' was still the 'organisational philosophy', the report found, with decisions being made at a monthly meeting attended by staff and a representative of the volunteers. The report is dismissive: 'While this structure may have served the Centre well in its early years we do not consider that it is any longer appropriate, particularly given the degree of isolation under which the Centre operates. Both management and the organisation need the kind of guidance and leadership which would be provided by a strong, experienced and largely independent board of directors under a companies structure.' The team recorded drily that the DRCC seemed to have no plans other than to obtain 'a major increase in the annual grant from public funds'. The report criticised the system the Centre had introduced in 1988 of asking clients who could afford it to pay a counselling fee, on a sliding scale. It noted that EHB social workers had told them this was a 'major disincentive'.

The report said social workers who referred clients to the DRCC criticised the long waiting lists and the difficulty of getting to the Centre from the suburbs, as well as the costs. It said some clients were disappointed that they could have only group therapy and would have preferred individual counselling. However, it conceded, clients' reports had been 'generally positive'. It said the Centre's title was 'misleading'. A crisis service, it claimed, would allow callers to get through directly to a counsellor instead of having to make a second call. The service also needed to be mobile, it stated, and there should be no waiting lists. 'In our view the DRCC is not currently providing the kind of service which is needed by a victim in crisis,' the report stated baldly. It should be asked, 'as a matter of urgency', whether or not it was prepared to provide such a service. If not, the EHB should 'immediately act to ensure that such a service is provided'.

On the counselling of victims of past sexual abuse, the evaluators commented that other services existed which provided 'similar help'. 'In contrast to the DRCC, however, these services have not had a high media profile.'[13] There followed complaints about the lack of information allegedly provided by the DRCC, and the apparently grudging conclusion that the service is 'probably of a good standard'.[14]

In January 1990 Bernie Purcell resigned. Soon afterwards, two of the Centre's other most experienced staff also left. 'It was all just too much,' said Purcell. 'I was overburdened. The Centre needed so much commitment. I had three young children; I was not spending enough time with them. My family was complaining. I was torn. I just couldn't hack it.' Purcell set up a private therapy practice. Grace O'Malley recalled that, 'there was a great storm of anger when they left'. However, looking back, she said she could understand why they did. 'They were very good at what they did, and very much in demand,' she said. 'The DRCC was so fraught and so under-funded.' Olive Braiden, then the deputy director, said people felt they had no option. 'They felt it was a sinking ship,' she said. Personally, she said, she always felt the Centre would survive. 'I saw no reason why we wouldn't eventually get the money.'

Braiden is, by now, known to be made of stern stuff. Her mettle was to be severely tested when she took over as director of the DRCC on 1 February 1990. The DRCC was meant to have a meeting with the EHB on 13 February 1990 to discuss the report. The minutes of the staff meeting from 5 February note tersely: 'The EHB will finally make the report available to the Centre.' The report was meant to be confidential. Someone, and the DRCC has always been convinced it knows that person's identity, leaked it to the press. On 9 February the *Irish Independent* reported that the EHB report contained 'major criticisms' of the DRCC and listed several of them. On

the night of the 12th, Braiden took a call from *The Irish Times*'
then health correspondent, Kathryn Holmquist. What was her
reaction to the 'highly critical' report, Holmquist asked.
Braiden replied that she would not comment on a report the
DRCC had not seen, though she did reject the claim that a
crisis service was not provided. She described the leaking of
the report as unethical and told Holmquist the DRCC would
cancel the meeting scheduled for the next day. That day, the
headline on Holmquist's article was: 'Leaked health board
report castigates rape centre.' Kieran Hickey was quoted as
saying that the leak was 'unfortunate and unhelpful'.[15] When
asked to comment for this book, a senior member of the EHB
team declined, saying that it would be inappropriate.

Looking back on those troubled times, Braiden said she
had always believed the report would be hostile. 'The EHB
behaved appallingly, from the start,' she said. 'They treated us
so badly. The nerve of them, thinking they could just get rid
of the Rape Crisis Centre! I refused to accept the report.'

11

A Rebirth of Optimism

Braiden had joined the DRCC in 1983. She helped out on its annual flag-day, then became a volunteer. 'I was an outsider in a way,' she recalled. 'I hadn't been involved in the women's movement. I'd lived abroad and I had five children, including a baby.' She had taught English in Thailand and was shocked one day when she met two of the little girls she was teaching in the company of European men who were obviously using them as prostitutes. Back in Ireland, with a baby daughter who was deaf, Braiden had been particularly appalled to read in a newspaper report that a deaf woman had seen her allegation of rape thrown out of court because her interpreter couldn't be understood.

From the start, she was not impressed by the feminist collective as a structure. 'I couldn't believe that there was Anne O'Donnell, a paid worker, albeit badly paid, running the whole kaboosh, and I walked in, a total greenhorn, and had the same vote as her. Then, as I got more experienced, I objected to other greenhorns walking in and having the same say as me. I never shut up about it. That and smoking in the Centre, which I deplored.'

To Braiden, the Centre was 'a work in progress'. Too much time was spent talking about feminist theory, to the detriment of the clients, she believed. 'We called them clients because we didn't like the word victims,' she recalled. 'We had a long discussion about it, needless to say.' Although she said the training she received as a volunteer was 'excellent', she became concerned about relatively inexperienced volunteers working as counsellors. 'It was not safe,' she said. She was determined to push for professionalised counselling in the Centre.

She felt the Centre was 'just a bit chaotic', though 'there was a terrific sense of camaraderie and we were all terribly involved'. O'Donnell, she said, was 'a very good manager', Purcell was a 'brilliant' counsellor and director of counselling, and Barbara Egan was 'excellent in her many roles – counselling, fundraising and public speaking'. Along with Purcell and Egan, she became part of the management team at the Centre in the late 1980s. They had already decided that they needed a board of directors and a company structure long before the EHB demanded it.

They were also seriously considering changing the name of the Centre, partly because their fundraiser, Kevin Flanagan, felt it was a deterrent to some donors. The new name hadn't been selected, but the minutes of a staff meeting for June 1989 note that the other RCCs had been informed of this possibility 'and that we would not be involved with network meetings any more'.[1] The DRCC's 1989 report lists among the Centre's aims for 1990, 'changing the name of the agency to more accurately reflect the services and activities'.[2] Half of the Centre's work related to child abuse. Braiden was against the move. 'To me, it was important that we kept our feminist ethos. Sexual abuse is rape. It is the abuse of power. Women were beginning to downgrade their own adult experience. They'd say things like, "Oh, of course, what happened to me was not anything like as bad as what those children went through …"' After the EHB's intervention, she was all the more determined to keep it.

The fightback against the report began immediately. Whoever leaked it 'does not support victims of sexual abuse', Braiden told journalists. It would be 'disheartening' for such victims to read the media coverage, she said. She pointed out that recently raped clients were offered immediate telephone counselling 24 hours a day. The caller would also be offered a counselling appointment at the Centre for 9.30 the next morning.

She agreed that adult victims of childhood sexual abuse had to join a waiting list that had 500 names on it. She agreed that it would be 'ideal' if callers could get through at all times directly to a counsellor. However, she pointed out, the Centre simply didn't have the resources to employ enough staff. The DRCC had made no secret of this, she said. It needed £250,000 a year. It had yet to receive the £20,000 it had been allocated for the previous year.

The EHB's chief executive, Kieran Hickey, issued a statement which said that 'any loss of confidence' in the DRCC 'would be unwarranted'.[3] However, damage had been done. In a furious letter to *The Irish Times*, Grace O'Malley wrote that the fact that the DRCC managed to keep going on its own fundraising efforts with minimal state support showed that it was 'obviously a highly competent and able body – unlike the EHB'. She went on to rebut several more of the report's allegations, though she noted tartly that 'I use the term report very loosely, obviously.' The DRCC's aims and objectives were clearly defined. Its statistics were accurate and available. Its staff were 'highly qualified, both academically and experientially'. So admirable and essential were the services provided by the DRCC to recent rape victims and adult victims of child abuse 'that the EHB avail of it daily through their social workers, guidance counsellors, psychologists, doctors, nurses etc.', she concluded. 'The EHB even sends its staff there for training!'[4]

Some reactions to the EHB report were hostile to the DRCC. One correspondent to the *Irish Independent* said the report 'cast an entirely new light on the activities of the DRCC' and that it raised questions about the Centre's use of public funds.[5] However, there was much support for the Centre. 'These women do a wonderful (and evidently thankless) job for victims who are more numerous than our smug society is prepared to admit,' wrote one man.[6] Anthony Cotter of the probation officers' union wrote to the papers with a strong statement. The Centre was 'competent and professional' and had 'developed many creative, innovative and indeed pioneering ways of providing therapeutic help to victims as well as perpetrators of sexual abuse', he wrote. Some of the EHB's criticisms were 'negative and misleading'. Cotter pointed out that there were many other examples in Ireland of the government first of all failing to provide much-needed services, then providing inadequate funding for voluntary groups and finally criticising those groups.

One of Braiden's first tasks as director was to appoint the Centre's first board of directors. 'I made a list of notables and approached each of them individually,' she recalled. 'I stayed with it until I had a good mix. I was determined to cover all the constituencies.' Chaired by Gemma Hussey, the board had a baptism of fire, dealing with the aftermath of the EHB report.

Cathal MacCoille, then political editor of the *Sunday Tribune*, was on it. 'There was no sense back then and there is still no clear sense in this country of what people are entitled to,' he said. 'There is a policy vacuum. Groups like the DRCC were confronted with a dilemma in terms of trying to work the system because of that. You couldn't engage with it because it was not there.' He said the board had huge sympathy for Braiden as director of the Centre. 'It was a demeaning position. She was left trying to run the place not knowing when the cheque would come and how much it would be for. It had a corrosive effect on morale. The Minister would announce that there was to be an allocation of money to the Rape Crisis Centres, but he wouldn't say for months which centre would be getting what. It was a classic tactic of divide and conquer, and I regret, looking back, that we fell for that. The Rape Crisis Centres would have been stronger if they hadn't been seen to be fighting over the money.'[7]

In May 1990, Gemma Hussey wrote to the EHB requesting payment of a grant of £21,000 promised the previous month. She said that having to engage in this 'endless badgering' was a waste of time.[8] The Minister for Social Welfare, Michael Woods, announced in January 1990 that

£150,000 would be paid to the Rape Crisis Centres. No breakdown was given. The centres were still waiting in July. Finally, the Minister announced that Dublin was to get £50,000, with Galway and Cork each getting £35,000 and Limerick, Waterford and Clonmel getting £10,000 each. These were, Woods emphasised, once-off payments.

In August, Hussey wrote to the Finance Minister, Albert Reynolds, asking for a commitment to state funding on a 'fixed, guaranteed annual basis' and suggesting that £125,000, half the DRCC's needs, would be ideal. The help given by the public was 'magnificent'. State funds, though welcome, had been 'sporadic and uneven'. The Centre urgently needed to employ three more counsellors. Calls from women who had been raped had risen from 255 in the first six months of 1989 to 325 for the same period in 1990. Calls from victims of past child sex abuse had also risen from 478 in the first half of 1989 to 588 in 1990. It was 'deeply disturbing', she wrote, that while the list grew, it was 'clear that the state had no services to which the centre could refer these distressed callers'. It was 'intolerable in a caring society'.[9]

MacCoille said the board's role was to advise and also, crucially, to give the beleagured Centre 'an establishment image'. He felt he was useful not least because 'it did no harm for the politicians to know there was a journalist involved'. He said he was surprised at his first meeting to note that the board was far from being dominated by people obviously associated with the women's movement.

As well as Hussey and himself, the board included Dr Joe Robins, who had retired from his position as assistant secretary at the Department of Health. He had been a long time supporter of the Centre. There was psychiatrist Professor Ivor Browne, who brought gravitas and experience, former DRCC worker Barbara Egan, former advertising manager Neil McIvor, the DRCC's solicitor Breda Allen and Ossie Kilkenny, accountant to U2 and other celebrities. 'I met him on a flight,' said Braiden. Fifteen years later, he is still an active board member.

Much of the board's energies, inevitably, were taken up

with 'hassle about money'. Gemma Hussey, who had retired from politics, was, MacCoille said, a 'great and really gifted' chairwoman. 'She'd learned a lot from meetings chaired by Garret FitzGerald, which went on and on. She didn't let people ramble.'

Braiden's tactic in terms of the Centre's relationship with the state and statutory bodies was, she said, 'to aim for the top and get as high as you could.' She and her board met Kieran Hickey and other senior EHB officials, and, she said, 'I found them not bad. They knew they had to co-operate with the DRCC because we had such public support. We worked together and eventually we got it right. Joe Robins from our board was a great help because he knew how the civil service thought and worked.' Grace O'Malley, author of the withering letter to the press, said she still respects the anger she felt then. 'I saw them as these EHB bureaucrats – but ultimately we knew we had to work with them. It made sense to mainstream the Centre.'

O'Malley had joined the DRCC in 1988 and became a member of staff in 1990. 'I'd done a degree in psychology at Trinity and I was doing a masters in psychotherapy. I'd been involved in the women's group, and especially in the anti-strip -searching campaign.' This campaign highlighted the strip-searching of women prisoners and their visitors at Armagh prison in the North. 'I saw strip-searching as very much part of the sexual violence domain,' continued O'Malley. 'I continued to be a feminist throughout my time with the DRCC, but by the early 90s things were very different. The "all men are rapists" mad stuff was gone, and the collective. We were seen at the time by the other Rape Crisis Centres as bowing to the system. I think we took a reasonable line and got a lot achieved. Olive was very strategic. She moved the Centre forward as a business. If she hadn't, the funding would have stopped and the Centre wouldn't have survived.'

Lean times continued. There was a discussion at a staff meeting about whether or not tea and coffee should still be provided. Staff were instructed to switch off lights, use stationery sparingly and account for every penny of petty cash.

There were bigger issues to face internally as well. One of Braiden's first acts as director was to instruct therapists at the Centre that they were to work a five-day week instead of four, as formerly. 'Originally, workers had done four days plus night work and fundraising,' she said. 'But it had evolved into a situation where people worked four days and then had the fifth day off. My whole thinking was that if we were getting public money, we had to be accountable. I was at war with some of the staff over it, but good work was done throughout it all.'

Rosaleen McIlvanny, then training as a clinical psychologist at UCD, came to the DRCC on placement just as Braiden took over as director. 'There'd been a lot of conflict, and then there was a re-birth of optimism and excitement,' she recalled. 'There was a great atmosphere and a very good service was being provided. You felt a real sense of welcome in the place. You felt privileged to be part of the Rape Crisis Centre. Under Olive's direction, you felt very well minded as a worker, too. It was lovely.'[10]

Therapists Deirdre Walsh and Rosemary Liddy had, in 1989, published a handbook on *Surviving Sexual Abuse*, based on the counselling models developed at the DRCC. The book was designed to encourage women who had been abused to seek counselling as a way of dealing with pain which they had kept secret, but which had overshadowed their lives. Walsh and Liddy acknowledged that women could be abusers, too. Using fictitious life histories, they defined abuse and outlined its effects, short- and long-term, physical and mental. They described the courage and determination required to go for counselling and what counselling entails. 'Remembering and disclosing are only the first stage of the whole healing process. The hardest part of counselling is to allow yourself to feel all the emotions that got buried with the abuse,' they stated. They described the anger, sorrow and pain, fear and shame that many victims experienced as part of counselling. 'Total happiness' could not be promised, but many women spoke 'of being free and feeling free for the first time in their lives'.[11]

'They were very good at trying out new methods and learning from clients' experiences,' said McIlvanny. 'What they did was very good. I learned a lot during my three months there.' She had reservations about the 'professionalising' of the DRCC. 'The feminist movement and the Rape Crisis Centre in particular did so much to raise awareness, and as an autonomous organisation they were able to campaign in a way that people inside the system can't. I wonder did they lose something when they went professional.' However, she felt, in retrospect, that while in the early days the DRCC provided a voice for rape victims, the need for this had diminished as survivors such as Sophia McColgan and Colm O'Gorman, founder of One in Four, came forward themselves. In 1994, McIlvanny was appointed head of Laragh, the Eastern Health Board's new counselling service for adult survivors of sexual abuse. 'We used the Rape Crisis Centre for our training,' she said. 'They were extremely helpful.'

A 31-year-old Kilkenny man and soldier in the Irish army raped an 11-year-old girl at her home in Wicklow in 1988. He was a friend of the family. In court, in 1990, Judge MP Smith was told by one of the soldier's superior officers that he had an excellent record but a jail sentence would mean he would lose his job. The soldier had been on remand in prison for three months before the trial in January 1990, and the judge said he had paid his penalty. 'I don't think it will happen again,' he said and gave him a three-year suspended sentence.[12]

The Rape Crisis Centre, and Women's Aid, protested. The child's father, interviewed by Gerry Ryan on RTÉ, said the child had tried to commit suicide shortly after the rape. It was then that she told her father what had been done to her. The father said she told him she felt 'dirty' and that it was her fault. Before telling him, she said, 'You're going to be very annoyed at me.'[13]

Two months later, a farm labourer from Co. Cavan admitted the rape of an eight-year-old girl he was babysitting. The child didn't tell anyone until eight years later when she went missing and was found shaking and wet on the road a few miles away. She then confided in a friend. A local priest told the court the incident had caused a rift between the rapist's family and the girl's but he was trying to bring them together again. He said the man had made a mistake and learned his lesson. Paul Carney, defence barrister, pleaded for leniency. Mr Justice Frank Roe gave the rapist an eight-year suspended sentence and told him to keep away from the girl.

Afterwards, the girl's family expressed anger at the outcome and publicly rejected the priest's efforts. They wanted nothing to do with the rapist, they said. Olive Braiden said she feared the outcome of the case would act as a deterrent to other victims. There was further outrage when, in September 1990, District Justice Maura Roche released on probation a 17-year-old youth who admitted that he had indecently assaulted the six-year-old and four-year-old daughters of his neighbours. She said he should get psychiatric help. He returned to his home in a Dublin housing estate, but some local residents took the law into their own hands and petrol-bombed his house. Fianna Fáil Justice Minister Ray Burke said the Law Reform Commission was to look at sentencing issues and the government would ask it to include the possibility of appeals against over-lenient sentences. Michael McDowell warned of the risk of 'vengeful demands' for greater severity.[14]

Olive Braiden had earlier in 1990 denied that rape victims were motivated by a desire for vengeance. They went through the trauma of the court case 'because they are afraid the rapist will strike again and they want to save some other woman', she said.[15] In 1991 she found herself defending the Irish court system, commenting on the 'Palm Beach Circus', the trial of William Kennedy Smith for the alleged rape of a woman. The victim was named in 'ludicrous' media reports. Braiden urged Irish women not to be put off reporting rapes. 'The Irish courts are much more protective of the victim,' she said.[16] (Kennedy Smith was acquitted.)

In another case, a 14-year-old girl broke down and had to be helped out of the courtroom when Judge Gerard Buchanan gave the 17-year-old boy who had indecently assaulted her a two-year suspended sentence. His father had told the court the boy was insecure because he was overweight and had spots. A 10-year-old mildly handicapped Dublin girl was said to be 'living in terror' after another 17-year-old youth who had sexually abused her while babysitting was given early release from jail. The youth, who lived near the girl, was released after just eight months. The family of the child was not warned. The girl's mother said her daughter had spent eight months in a psychiatric unit. Accusing the judge of 'copping out' by releasing the boy, she demanded: 'Can you imagine us suddenly meeting him in the street?'[17]

A 34-year-old man who admitted abusing his nephews for five years was given bail and told by Judge Gerard Buchanan to stay away from his victims. The man was taking part in a treatment programme run by psychiatrist Dr Art O'Connor, a pioneer of Irish treatment programmes for sex offenders. [18]

Meanwhile, Dr O'Connor said that less than 5 per cent of Irish incest cases ever came to court. Journalist Padraig O'Morain analysed court decisions over a one-year period and found that only a minority of those convicted of sex offences against children went to jail.[19] An international study found that Irish courts handed down lighter sentences than most other countries for offences such as rape. Commenting on this, Olive Braiden said the DRCC often felt sentencing did not reflect the seriousness of the crime. However, she added that long sentences without 'proper therapy' for the rapist would have little effect.[20]

The dangers posed by sex offenders released back into the community were well illustrated by the case of one Cork family. The father had sexually abused his eldest son and had been convicted and jailed. On his release, there were consultations with the health board, and he returned to the family home. He was later found to have started abusing his 12-year-old daughter, and at that point deserted his family. The health board stated that the son who had been abused was potentially a danger to his siblings and recommended that he be placed in a foster family. One could not be found, so he too returned to his family and sexually abused one of his sisters. His mother had pleaded with the courts to send him to a reformatory. 'I would like him to get help now before it is too late and he ends up being a wife or child batterer,' she said.[21]

In December 1990, the Law Reform Commission recommended that doctors, psychologists, health workers, probation officers and teachers should be obliged to report cases of suspected child abuse for investigation. The DRCC supported mandatory reporting, though its experience showed that it had to be part of a bigger response to child abuse. 'We had our own policy of mandatory reporting for cases in which we had reason to believe that the offender still had access to children,' said Grace O'Malley. 'I reported numerous offenders to social services but no action was taken. They couldn't cope.'[22]

The DRCC also stepped up its campaign for treatment programmes in prison. By 1991 there were limited schemes in the Central Mental Hospital, Arbour Hill prison and Mountjoy. But, Olive Braiden said in 1991, they weren't adequate, while offenders who were given suspended sentences received no treatment at all. The DRCC called for services in prisons as well as for those on suspended sentences, with a follow up of offenders after release. 'We are trying to break the cycle of abuse,' said Braiden.[23]

Lack of treatment was one issue – an even more immediate one was starkly highlighted when a judge had to release a 15-year-old rapist because there was no place available for him to be detained. Judge Dominic Lynch refused to remand the boy on bail because he feared he would abscond. He said he was 'not prepared to make up for the inability of the executive to provide a place of detention for him'.[24]

The DRCC said it was 'appalled' and that this would act as a disincentive for other rape victims contemplating reporting rape to the gardaí. As the boy walked free, the girl's father spoke on RTÉ's lunchtime news programme. 'I was happy the law was going to deal with it,' he said. 'What future is there for justice for anybody? It has kind of destroyed the young one, my daughter,' he said. 'She is trying to find herself. She hasn't been the same since.' He said his daughter had been forced to leave school because of intimidation after the rape. His wife had died before the case came to court. 'How can they expect anyone to have any confidence in the law?'[25]

This was far from being the first young offender who

couldn't be accommodated. 'There is a long waiting list to get juveniles into suitable places of detention,' said an editorial in the journal of the Irish Association of Social Workers in July 1991. It said this sent a message to young offenders that they were 'untouchable and uncontainable'.[26] The previous year, a 15-year-old boy who was found guilty of indecently assaulting two girls aged eight and ten, was sentenced to two years' detention – and released because there was no place available.

Within days of the controversial release in 1991, the boy was in court again because in a separate incident he had indecently assaulted the girl two days after the rape. This time, the judge sentenced him to three years' detention at Trinity House. This time, the DRCC angrily described the sentence as 'derisory'. Again, Olive Braiden warned that this would act as a disincentive. 'We are not advocating long sentences, but the punishment should fit the crime,' she said. 'Two very serious crimes were committed in this instance.' She also said the controversy surrounding the case had further traumatised the victim. She said that in the first six months of 1991, 130 women had reported rapes to the DRCC. Just 30 of them had reported them to the gardaí. Many said they were terrified that the court appearance would be an unbearable ordeal, she said.[27]

Prostitutes had rarely complained of rape to the gardaí, not least because they could leave themselves open to prosecution. In 1991, a 35-year-old father of three approached a 22-year-old prostitute on Dublin's Fitzwilliam Square. The woman got into his car and agreed to have sex with him for £20. She told him to drive to a nearby car-park, but he drove past it. She tried to get out, but he grabbed her hair and held onto it as he drove her to the Phoenix Park. There, under threat of death, he forced her to take off her clothes and orally and anally raped her. Then he made her get out of the van, still naked, and stand with her hands on the roof. The woman, a mother of three, pleaded with him to let her go. She told him she had a three-week-old baby. He sexually assaulted her with a branch.

She told the Circuit Criminal Court in Dublin that while

he did so he said, 'I'm the devil and you're the prostitute. Wouldn't it be funny if the guards found you murdered with this branch up you?' She said she tried to run away but again he grabbed her by the hair. 'I kept screaming. I reefed his glasses off his face. I hoped he was blind without them but he gave me a few digs,' she said. He demanded she give his glasses back as he told her they'd be evidence against him if he killed her. He had already killed two other women, he told her, and buried them in the Dublin mountains.

After all this, he dropped the woman off on a back road. A milkman, out on his early morning rounds, found her and took her to Blanchardstown Garda Station. She was brought from there to the SATU in the Rotunda where Dr Moira Woods examined her. She told the court the woman was covered in excrement, was very distressed and had cuts and bruises consistent with her account of what had been done to her. The man claimed the woman had consented to sex and had been paid for it. He described her allegations as 'absolute fantasy'. He said he had hit her, just once, because she was roaring and screaming at him. 'It is the only time in my life I hit a woman,' he told the court.[28] He was supported in court by members of Alcoholics Anonymous who gave evidence of his 'kindness and consideration'.[29]

The jury found him guilty of indecent assault and buggery. The Rape Crisis Centre welcomed the verdict. Olive Braiden said it was important that the rape of a prostitute had been 'taken seriously'.[30] Anne O'Donnell, who had left the Centre by this stage, said it showed society had become capable of looking beyond what a woman does to what actually had happened to her. She congratulated the gardaí for vigorously pursuing the case.[31] Judge Kieran O'Connor sentenced the rapist to 14 years in jail. 'You acted in a depraved manner and degraded your victim, depriving her of any semblance of human dignity,' he said.[32]

This case was also significant in that it marked the first attempt by the Irish authorities to use DNA evidence to genetically fingerprint a rapist. Gardaí had sent material to England for tests, but the results were rejected in court on a technicality. However, the director of the state laboratory, Dr James Donovan, said Irish forensic scientists were in training to carry out the tests. The use of DNA evidence from blood, semen and saliva would become hugely important in rape trials in the years that followed.

12

UNTHINKABLE PROSPECT

'Her presence ... radicalised the symbolic definition of women in Ireland,' said poet Eavan Boland on the election of Mary Robinson as President of Ireland in 1990.[1] 'The election of Mary Robinson was a great boost for us,' said Olive Braiden. As President-elect, Robinson was the guest of the Rape Crisis Centre at a performance of Handel's *Messiah* at St Patrick's Cathedral. 'We are overjoyed and honoured,' Braiden wrote.[2]

Robinson had always supported the Rape Crisis Centre and had praised its long campaign to change the law on rape. She had written about how, at the turn of the 20th century, 'women had virtually no rights at all ... their husbands could rape and beat them without any interference from the law.'[3] That things had changed, she argued, was down to the work of women like those who set up and ran the Rape Crisis Centre.

Robinson was well known as a feminist and had spoken with compassion about pregnancy resulting from rape: 'Let's look at the hard cases,' she told journalist Kate Shanahan. 'Where a woman finds her 13-year-old daughter is pregnant by her father, or where a woman has been gang raped. Are we saying that under no circumstances can these women have access to a safe and reliable method of termination? I think that is quite wrong.'[4]

Political commentator Dick Walsh wrote of the symbolic importance of Robinson's campaign. He said that post-colonial Ireland had looked for 'an internal focus for its vengeance or an excuse for its own failure to live up to expectations' and had fastened on 'a version of morality that saw sex as the only sin and women as the most provocative temptation'. The result was punitive for women. Robinson's impact on this was as important as the fall of the Berlin Wall, Walsh said.[5]

Robinson focused on the work women were doing in their communities, filling in for a lack of state services, she said. She expressed her solidarity with victims of domestic and sexual violence. 'We must remind them that they are not the cause, but the victims of these outrages and we must do all in our power to encourage them to break their silence and report offences committed against them,' she told a conference organised by the Irish Association for Victim Support. On the crimes she said, 'Let us not flinch from calling them what they are: criminal assaults from vicious spouses or associates.'[6]

Finally, vicious spouses were to lose the protection of the state: the act of rape within marriage was criminalised in Irish law on 18 January 1991. Husbands who raped would, according to Fianna Fáil Justice Minister, Ray Burke, be 'subject to the full rigours of the law'. Men, or women, who forced their victims into oral sex, anal sex or used objects to violate them could also be found guilty of 'rape under section four'. The DRCC had drawn attention to a recent case in which an arthritic woman in her eighties was penetrated by a bottle, tied up and forced to have oral sex during a burglary at her home. Braiden commented that under the 1981 law, her attacker faced 'relatively minor' charges.

Boys under 14 lost their legal immunity from prosecution for rape, and the new offences of sexual assault and aggravated sexual assault replaced the pre-existing charge of indecent assault. The previously mandatory warning given by judges about the danger of convicting a rapist on the uncorroborated evidence of his alleged victim became discretionary.

Defence lawyers were no longer entitled to question a woman about her previous sexual experience with anyone, including the accused, without getting the permission of the trial judge. 'We're very pleased to have achieved so much. We didn't expect it from this government,' said Braiden, in an RTÉ interview.[7] Leading defence lawyer Paul Carney said the exclusion of evidence about sexual history would lead to incidents being tried 'in blinkers'.[8] He also warned that the decision to try all rape cases in the Central Criminal Court, effectively a branch of the High Court, would lead to 'enormous delays' and that at least two more judges would be needed. He was soon proved right on this point. The DRCC's solicitor, Breda Allen, said the new law was 'an extremely important piece of legislation'.

There was still some disappointment, in particular over the refusal of the government to yield on the issue of separate legal representation. The woman would have the right to consult with a legal-aid lawyer, but the lawyer had no right to take a full part in the trial. Ray Burke claimed this measure would 'go a long way in reducing the sense of isolation, bewilderment and helplessness' that many victims felt in court. It was too limited, said Braiden. It might give the rape victim comfort – it wouldn't give her a voice.

When asked if the new law on marital rape would lead to 'an increase in malicious cases brought by disgruntled wives against their husbands', Braiden said: 'No. I don't believe anyone brings a spurious rape charge to court. And I don't believe that some women, as is so often alleged, cry "rape" as an after-thought or for fear of pregnancy.' The real problem was under-reporting: 'We hope that this new legislation will encourage more victims to notify the police and this will help give a more realistic reflection of the level of sexual violence being committed in our society.'[9]

The law, however, was presided over by judges, and the attitudes of judges continued to concern the DRCC. It soon became apparent that judges were, for the most part, continuing to issue the corroboration warning and were allowing evidence of the woman's sexual history to be used. In May

1991, Olive Braiden wrote to the papers regarding comments during recent cases. In one, an ex-soldier was sentenced to eight years for raping a young woman who had accepted a lift from him. The judge said: 'This case should act as a warning to persons not to accept lifts from strangers at any time.' In another, two men were convicted of the multiple rape of a young woman. The judge said: 'the girl involved had been very foolish in consuming a very large amount of alcohol and walking through the town at midnight with six men, only one of whom she knew previously'.

Braiden posed a series of questions: 'A) Is the victim of a mugging or a robbery blamed for the actions of the criminal? B) Is it implied that the bank clerk is to blame when a bank is robbed? C) Is the victim of a road accident blamed for the actions of a dangerous driver?' She concluded: 'The victim is not, and cannot be, responsible for the actions of the offender.'[10] She also described as 'outrageous' the comment by a British judge presiding over a rape trial that women who said 'no' didn't always mean it.

'This is an early warning from the Dublin Rape Crisis Centre … our funds have almost run out … after three months … the doors of 70 Lower Leeson Street will shut.' This statement was issued by the board and director of the DRCC on 4 July 1991. 'We have explored, and continue to explore, all possible avenues of getting more funds. This has become a nightmare as pressure on all sides mounts … We cannot, despite continual efforts, get regular assured funding from the State … in three months we will have to terminate all counselling and therapy,' the statement said.

It was not, Olive Braiden said at the time, a case of crying wolf. The Fianna Fáil/PD government had allocated just £10,000 in the 1991 budget, a fifth of its inadequate contribution of the previous year. The Centre was busier than ever – from January to June there had been 1,362 calls, 800 of them first-time callers. This compared with 2,002 for 1989. There were 13 staff to pay and more needed. There were rent and running costs on the large building. 'We need £130,000 just to get us to the end of 1991,' said Braiden. 'We would need £300,000 to run the Centre for a year. We've had meetings with the Department before but they haven't yielded any money.'

Several women who had used the Centre spoke out at the time. 'What I would have done without them doesn't bear thinking about. I was suicidal before I went there. I don't know if I'd even be alive now … without the place. Anything could have happened. I was on the verge of a nervous breakdown ….'[11] Caroline was speaking to journalist Jacqui Corcoran. Sally, who was still in therapy at the Centre, told Vivienne Clarke that before she had gone there, she felt 'so cut off and abandoned'. She felt she was getting better and said she didn't know what she would do if it closed: 'It will be like being abandoned all over again.'[12] Sarah had been raped by a soldier she met at a party when she was 18. 'If the Centre weren't here, I'd be an alcoholic,' she told journalist Liz Ryan. 'I was cracking up to such an extent I almost lost my job.'[13]

Caroline's story, and Sally's, and Sarah's, illustrates well the emotional complexities with which the Rape Crisis Centre was working. Caroline was raped as a young woman by a male colleague whom she'd regarded as a friend. Afterwards, she told Corcoran, 'I completely flipped. I started to scream. I went back to my flat and sat there for what felt like three or four days, without eating, without being able to do anything.' She went into a blind, confused rage, cut herself and had to go to hospital. A nurse gave her sedatives and referred her to the DRCC, where she got an immediate appointment. 'I was shaking … I was completely out of control. I didn't have a clue what was going on, I just couldn't take it,' she said. The counsellor at the DRCC talked her through a period of extreme anxiety. 'Just being able to talk to someone who had some idea of what it must be like was a help,' she said.

After several sessions, the counsellor recognised that there was some deeper trauma behind Caroline's anguish over the rape. 'My reactions were strange, very magnified,' Caroline told Corcoran. She said that one day, during the counselling, she stood up and said, 'Yes, I have.' Afterwards, she didn't know where this statement had come from. Soon after this, she told her parents about the rape. Her father told her it must have been her fault and screamed at her. Her mother was also unsupportive.

Caroline spent several months getting one to one counselling, then moved into one of the Centre's groups. After her first group session, she had a sudden revelation. 'I had left the Rape Crisis Centre and was walking along by Stephen's Green, when suddenly – bang! The whole thing became completely clear to me. I just had memory after memory coming up like a flood.' Caroline had blocked out these memories and was shocked and horrified by what they told her. 'It was my mother who had abused me,' she told Corcoran. 'As far as I had been concerned, I came from a relatively normal, happy family, but suddenly, this just was not true.' She said she couldn't have survived without the support of the Rape Crisis Centre. She told Corcoran that she was 'actually quite happy and I don't ever remember feeling this way'. While she sometimes got depressed, she never felt desperate, and she knew she would 'eventually be okay'.[14]

Sally spoke about her ongoing therapy by describing a blindfold which was about to be lifted. She'd been sexually abused as a ten-year-old by a friend of her family. She felt that some of her sisters might have been abused in their own family but weren't facing up to the fact. She had been in a good job and was 'supposedly doing well', she said. But she was also drinking heavily, smoking hash and shoplifting. 'I didn't know what was wrong with me.' When she read about the Rape Crisis Centre, she realised that her self-hatred might be linked to what happened to her when she was ten. She'd been on a waiting list for six months before seeing a counsellor. 'But immediately I felt better, especially at the group therapy sessions where I met others who had a similar experience. It was a great relief,' she said.

Things were getting better. She was not drinking and smoking hash, and she was not afraid to be alone. There was less and less 'self abusive behaviour' in her life. 'The effect has been so all-encompassing,' she told Vivienne Clarke. She was able to help children she worked with in a voluntary group because she now understood what had happened to her. Her need for support, however, continued. Her family had 'closed off' when she told them she was going to the Rape Crisis Centre. She still had six months' therapy to complete. 'I don't understand why the politicians don't grasp what is so important here and what great work goes on,' she said. 'Abuse and rape affect so many people ... and this is the only place they can go for help.'[15]

Sarah had refused to 'go the whole way' with the man who was seeing her home. He beat her up and raped her. She passed out and woke up in hospital. Then she faced a court case which was, she told Liz Ryan, 'as bad as the rape'. Everything was disclosed, she said, and her underwear was held up for the jury to view. The rapist was in the army's boxing team, 'a big plus in court when it came to character testimony', she said. She couldn't believe that consent was still the central issue 'even when the victim is black and blue'. She said it was suggested to her in court that she was a sadist who had asked the man to hit her. 'It was to hell and back,' she said, but added that it was worth it to get the rapist jailed for nine years.

Sarah, however, didn't recover after the case. Her experience in court became part of the trauma. She took to drinking a lot and lost weight and confidence. She distrusted men. 'I believe all men have the capacity to rape,' she said. She saw the whole attitude to rape as unbelievable: that it happened. That it took two years to get to court. That the court case was horrific. That the DRCC was under threat of closure.

Nuala Fennell raised the issue in the Dáil. 'The government are not taking the crime of rape seriously,' she said. 'One questions the Minister for Health's perception of this organisation. Does he regard it merely as some worthy benevolent women's organisation?' The Centre was unique and vital, Fennell said, and rape victims and their families 'have nowhere else to go'. There was no duplication of services, she said. The SATU existed to carry out medical examinations and validations for legal action.

She described meeting a victim of rape, an Irish-American woman who had returned from New York to live in the South

East. 'After two weeks she woke up one night to find a man's hand over her face. He assaulted her, he raped her twice, he tied her to the bed, he stuck a knife in her and he choked her. She was almost left for dead,' she said. 'That is the reality of what is happening when we speak of rape.' She said the woman had not found out during the legal process about her rights to damages for loss of earnings and medical expenses. The specialised service offered by the DRCC was needed, Fennell said. The Minister should pay up.

The Minister of State at the Department of Health, Chris Flood, listed the grants given to the DRCC, stated that the role of voluntary organisations in the health service was an important one but said they had to avoid 'duplication of services'. Recent victims of rape were 'dealt with' at the SATU, he said. Most of the DRCC's work was with victims of past sexual abuse and there were 'several other services' providing 'similar help'. He reiterated Health Minister Rory O'Hanlon's advice to the DRCC – that it should 'contact the Eastern Health Board'.[16]

In her diaries from this period, the chairwoman of the DRCC's board, Gemma Hussey, records a series of crisis meetings between the Centre's representatives, the EHB and the Health Minister. 'This week DRCC holding all the lime-light after a lot of coming and going,' she wrote on 24 July 1991. 'Seeing the Minister with Olive today, AGM and board meeting tomorrow, EHB Friday. Will it ever end?' She added, 'Who has come up trumps? The sisters.' The sisters included her old friend Dr Mary Henry, who was the chair of the new Friends of the Rape Crisis Centre group, set up by the board in the summer of 1991 to raise funds. In advance of the meeting with O'Hanlon, Hussey wrote that the Centre was 'demanding £156,000 for '92, the same plus inflation for '93 and £57,000 for this year' and commented, 'Was not I very impertinent?'

Hussey described a meeting at the EHB's Park House headquarters: 'Board and myself confidently faced ranks of EHB and Ministers representatives. To their obvious amazement, one and a half hours of implacability and reiteration followed ... We left in a dignified way. Went to Olive's house and had a gin and tonic in her back garden. God, we badly needed it! The heat was intense.'

The heat was intense, too, in the debate about the Centre's survival. 'How can they be so mean?' was the headline on a front page story in one tabloid account of the budget allocation. A letter writer accused the government of forcing the DRCC to concentrate on raising money to survive rather than on educational and preventative work: 'The government's stinginess and "washing of hands" makes it all the more likely another woman will be raped today.'[17]

Anne O'Donnell wrote that she was 'saddened and appalled' at the plight of the Rape Crisis Centre. 'Let it not be forgotten that 12 years ago, when the DRCC was first opened, discussion about rape and sexual abuse was utterly taboo in Ireland,' she wrote. Now the horror had been exposed. 'Is the work put in by all of us who have worked there over the last 12 years to be obliterated?' she demanded.[18]

An *Irish Times* editorial of 27 July 1991 was headlined, 'Unthinkable Prospect'. It praised the DRCC's role in having the laws on rape changed and on making the public aware 'of suffering once thought shameful and crimes once hidden ... To say the State gets an essential service at a bargain price – little more than one tenth of the cost – is a feeble understatement.'[19]

The Centre needed £300,000, said it would undertake to raise half that and demanded that the government pay the remaining £150,000. The Minister offered £40,000, to be paid by the EHB. Gemma Hussey described the Minister's tone when he rang her with the offer as 'somewhat chiding'. The Centre rejected the offer. Nuala Fennell called it 'derisory'. O'Hanlon was under political pressure to fund the Centre properly and on what the Labour Party called a 'multi annual basis'. Fine Gael and Labour backed the DRCC's demands – so did Fianna Fáil's coalition partner, the Progressive Democrats. Gemma Hussey noted in her diary that she and Olive Braiden had gone to see Mary Harney. 'She was totally supportive, openly hostile to Fianna Fáil and behaving like an

opposition party. Mary's tough out.'[20] They also met Fine
Gael leader John Bruton. 'I told him he had a right to know
this could become a big issue,' Hussey noted. She was right.

The newspapers were full of letters of support. *The Irish
Times* ran a series of them, all headlined 'Unthinkable Prospect'. Ronan Conroy said the DRCC had spent years creating
'the warm, human, healing atmosphere of the centre'. It was a
'wanted' service, 'set up by the Irish people themselves and
loudly supported by them'. It was 'highly professional and
financially efficient'. What, Conroy demanded, was the
Minister's problem? He suggested that perhaps, as a medical
doctor, the Minister was disturbed by what the DRCC represented: 'The existence of a major facility outside the orbit of
the medical profession challenges the paternalistic, Victorian
medical model.'[21]

The Campaign to Separate Church and State saw it as a
sectarian issue and demanded the resignation of the Minister.
He was, said spokesman Dick Spicer, putting the Rape Crisis
Centres out of business while 'illegally funding priests' salaries
in hospitals out of public funds'.[22] Women from the Workers'
Party chained themselves to the railings of the Dáil to mark
the 80th anniversary of women getting the vote. They carried
placards in support of the DRCC. 'Women in 1991 are still
demanding the basic right to walk the streets of their towns
and cities free from fear,' said Marian White.[23] Rape victims
suffered alone until the advent of the Rape Crisis Centres.
'Slowly and painfully' they'd changed attitudes and the law.
Several writers saw the issue as being linked to the government's refusal to make condoms freely available despite the
spread of HIV. One referred to the 'shamans of the flat earth
society' having too much control.[24]

The Minister went on an RTÉ *Today Tonight* programme
to defend his position. The programme surveyed Rape Crisis
Centres around the country and found all of them struggling
and underfunded. The Minister said money was scarce and
that comprehensive psychological and psychiatric services
were already available through the health boards for victims of
rape and child abuse.

Besides, he said, far from struggling, one of the Centres, in Galway, had even made a profit the previous year! This provoked an exasperated letter from the Galway Centre, which pointed out that it had no choice but to keep its expenditure within the limits of what it earned. None of its counsellors was paid. As for health board provision, why then did doctors, social workers and psychologists continue to refer women to the Rape Crisis Centres? Indeed, Sandra Barden wrote, some women came for counselling after bad experiences within the psychiatric service. Raped women were not psychiatrically ill and shouldn't be treated as if they were. In Rape Crisis Centres, 'women are in control of their own recovery'.[25] The Clonmel RCC wrote in similar terms. Some 30 per cent of its referrals came from professionals within the health board.

Reviewing the *Today Tonight* programme for the *Sunday Independent*, Colm Tóibín described the women from the centres as 'concerned, sympathetic and caring' and providing an 'essential service in a calm and professional manner'. Tóibín saw it as a power struggle. 'For many people in Ireland the family as a social entity has failed, but this has never been publicly recognized ... how we deal with this as a society is a crucial issue ...' He described the medical profession as having 'its fair share of fundamentalists and members of the Knights of Columbanus'. They enjoyed their control, he said, and didn't intend to cede it.[26]

Fintan O'Toole wrote in *The Irish Times* that the refusal to fund the Rape Crisis Centres was influenced by an ideology which was 'as hermetically sealed, as paranoid, as self-righteous and as intolerant' as Stalinism. The logic was that Ireland was 'a holy Catholic country, which, left to itself, will be moral and happy'. Those who claimed, as Rape Crisis Centres did, that rape and sex abuse were rampant were part of a conspiracy to undermine all this. Groups like Responsible Society, SPUC, PLAC (Pro-Life Amendment Campaign), Family Solidarity and the Anti-Divorce Campaign had wielded huge influence connected to both church and state 'in spite of the fact that their views are not only bizarre but also what can only be called totalitarian'.

O'Toole accused the Minister for Health of pushing the Rape Crisis Centres into the hands of the health boards knowing that it was there, at local level, that hostility to the Centres was most acute. Like Tóibín, he referred to a battle which was not primarily about money. He said that if the RCCs lost the battle 'then the generous, compassionate and humanistic instincts of ordinary Catholicism will finally have been surrendered.'[27]

One letter writer asked the Minister to explain how it was that, if alternative services were available, there was a waiting list at the Dublin Rape Crisis Centre.[28] Another contrasted the 'shameful' refusal to support the RCCs with the spending of £17 million on a facelift for government buildings.[29] Taoiseach Charles Haughey had recently opened Michael Smurfit's new multi-million leisure complex, the K Club, and the government had provided a grant of £608,643. The Church of Ireland's archdeacon, Gordon Linney, preached in Christ Church Cathedral that there was no way the moral law could approve a system which 'allowed a few to practise a vulgar affluence and greed' while at the same time the state said it couldn't afford to help the Rape Crisis Centre, compensate haemophiliacs, run a proper health service or accommodate homeless children. The *Irish Independent* agreed. In an editorial it said that the archdeacon had 'courageously reminded us that there is a moral law, and that it applies'.[30]

The Catholic Dublin Diocesan Social Service Centre, CentreCare, described the DRCC as an 'innovative, creative' voluntary organisation meeting a need which had been neglected. It would be 'disastrous' if it had to close.[31] Owen Keenan, the director of the child protection charity Barnardo's, pointed out the DRCC was working with Barnardo's on a joint proposal for a 'child protection information and training programme aimed at informing and supporting parents, child care staff, playgroups personnel and others'. The cost of such a programme would, he said, be a 'fraction' of what it would otherwise cost the state. 'It seems incredible in view of increasing awareness and concern about the extent of sexual abuse that services should be curtailed rather than expanded,' Keenan stated.

He demanded that the government examine the wider issue of the role of voluntary bodies and the state's responsibility to them. They were not, he said, regarded as 'social partners'. Perhaps the experience of the DRCC might, he suggested, be a good reason for voluntary organisations to join forces and insist they be treated as such.[32] The Irish Association of Social Workers also supported the demand for the Centre to be funded and said the state 'relied extremely heavily' on the voluntary sector to deliver essential social services.[33]

Peter Cassells, general secretary of the Irish Congress of Trade Unions, wrote to the Minister urging him to fund the Centre to 'provide this essential service'.[34] The Council for the Status of Women and the Well Woman Centre met the Minister and impressed on him their support for the DRCC. In Dun Laoghaire court, Judge Hubert Wine took up the cause. 'It is a terrible thing to have to plead from this court for a voluntary organisation,' he said. 'It is incredible that the authorities do not fund it properly.'[35] He ordered a young man caught with cannabis to pay £100 to the Centre.

'Careful, careful, we have them running,' Hussey wrote in her diary that August. But the Centre's old adversaries made a last-ditch attempt to turn the tide. Bernadette Bonar of the Responsible Society wrote an article in *The Irish Times* which began with a warning about the 'ravages of the permissive society' and went on to describe the concern with which she and others had viewed the opening of the Dublin Rape Crisis Centre. Everyone would have welcomed support for rape victims from 'a genuine caring group', she wrote. But these were feminists, campaigners, and there was concern 'lest a momentum for legalised abortion on the grounds of rape should evolve'. It would be better, she stated, if help for rape victims was integrated into the health service, where it could be monitored.

Richard Greene, also a member of the EHB and a Green Party councillor, wrote to the papers complaining about 'incessant propaganda' for the DRCC and said that the EHB had better things to do with its money. 'Many organisations that do more essential work than the DRCC with less fanfare and publicity are not being funded at all,' he claimed. Furthermore, other organisations were providing just as good a service to rape victims and getting no credit in the media for it.[36] The Green Party disassociated itself and said it supported 'the great service the DRCC provides'. Greene and the eponymous party subsequently parted company amid acrimony.

'Is it any wonder the Dublin Rape Crisis Centre finds itself embattled with the EHB over 12 years?' demanded Gemma Hussey in her written response to Bernadette Bonar's article. Anyone reading the article 'can understand the depth of prejudice and innuendo which permeated officialdom's dealings with the Centre'. She noted Bonar's 'almost perceptible curl of the lip' in her reference to the Centre's origins as a 'feminist collective'. Yes, it was, said Hussey, 'and a fearless and dedicated group of people answering a desperate need which had been ignored'. She laid out the eminently respectable professional credentials of the board and said it was 'proud to continue the work started by such admirable people'.

Hussey derided Bonar's claim that the EHB was the 'conduit' through which public money came to the Centre. 'What money?' she demanded. The funds provided had been 'minuscule' and had been 'dragged out of them painfully and humiliatingly'. Bonar had quoted selectively from the EHB report. The Centre had been 'greatly encouraged by the outpouring of support' from the public.[37] Bonar responded by claiming that the DRCC had been unco-operative with the EHB and that its 'emotive publicity campaign' was 'not constructive'.[38]

But the tide had turned. 'The battle is on,' wrote Hussey in her diary, the week before the Centre was due to close. It was otherwise, she wrote, 'all in all a pleasant and friendly week launching the Friends of the Rape Crisis Centre'. It set about organising its first event, an autumnal fundraising climb of the Little Sugar Loaf mountain, followed by a party in the Avoca Handweavers, owned by DRCC board member Hilary Pratt.

The Centre had demanded that the allocation of funds for

1992 be finalised before 26 August. The EHB said it was not possible for it to complete its assessment of the Centre's needs in time. The Minister, Rory O'Hanlon, wrote a conciliatory letter offering to add £20,000 to the £40,000 the Centre had rejected and committing himself to the same level of funding for 1992. He also offered his personal assurance 'of my determination to achieve a solution to the current problems and to develop a positive partnership'.[39] Hussey replied haughtily that the Centre noted his offer and also the lack of specifics about when funding would be made available. She said Bernadette Bonar's *Irish Times* article 'will give you some idea of why the Dublin Rape Crisis Centre has such difficulty with the EHB' and asked, 'May we expect a public refutation of the quotations from the report of 1989 from the officials of the Board?'

Four days before the deadline, there was a tense meeting between the DRCC and the Health Minister. Ossie Kilkenny's record of it notes O'Hanlon's position: 'He will not be blackmailed – if the service is withdrawn on 26 August, so be it. He would be of the opinion that other services will replace it.'[40] O'Hanlon asked the board to give the EHB more time and it agreed to defer a decision on closure until October. Cathal MacCoille recalled that the media were camped on the steps of the DRCC's Leeson Street premises during a long board meeting. He eventually left, carrying his bicycle, by the back window. In a statement, the board welcomed the Health Minister's 'personal assurance ... and his acknowledgement both of the professionalism of our work and its essential nature'. However, it warned that the amount on offer for 1992 would leave the Centre still having to raise two-thirds of its costs and stated: 'This is too much for the Centre to bear.'[41]

The EHB was criticised by the Joint Oireachtas Committee on Women's Rights over its failure to respond to a questionnaire the committee sent to the health boards as part of an assessment of funding for the Rape Crisis Centres. The vice-chair of the committee, Fianna Fáil's Mary Wallace, said the services of the DRCC were 'very specialised and very essential' and that they weren't being supplied by the state.[42]

Braiden and Hussey again met O'Hanlon in September. 'It was not pleasant,' Hussey wrote in her diary. 'He harped on and on [and said that] the state can't be seen to give in to any organization … I told him I didn't appreciate being lectured [to].' He also raised the issue of funds for the other RCCs. Hussey told him her problem was within the EHB area and that bringing in the other centres was 'an attempt to divide and rule'. Afterwards, she noted, 'I reflected that in his position, I might have tried the same.'[43]

On 15 October, O'Hanlon wrote to Bertie Ahern, then Minister for Labour. He told him he had guaranteed public funding of £100,000 for the DRCC for 1992. It was 'the first time the DRCC has been given such a firm commitment' and he would be making arrangements 'to ensure that adequate funding will also be provided from 1993 onwards'. He was 'satisfied that the new working arrangements which are emerging from the discussions between the Centre and the EHB will provide a sound basis for the delivery of a prompt and effective service in future'.[44]

In November 1991, Braiden and Hussey were 'summoned to see Mary O'Rourke in her new persona as Minister for Health'. O'Rourke was to be Health Minister for just 12 weeks but the timing was perfect for the DRCC. 'I loved Health,' recalled O'Rourke. 'They all thought they had a very sweet woman from the country. They didn't know what I was like, and by the time they did, it was too late. The department secretary asked me when Charlie [Haughey] appointed me if I had any priorities. I said, yes, I'd like to do something about the Rape Crisis Centre.

'Gemma Hussey had contacted me within a day of my appointment. You have to remember that at that time the Rape Crisis Centre was still viewed with suspicion. I was advised that the EHB was quite iffy and squiffy about them. I was advised also that the health boards didn't like Ministers interfering. Especially, I would say, interfering women! I said I wanted them to have regular funds. We got it done as a sub-heading, which meant it would be renewed each year.'

O'Rourke was well aware of the existence of domestic

violence. 'Women used to come to me black and blue,' she said. 'And of course plenty would have said there was no such thing as marital rape – you just lay back and thought of God. One woman came and she told me her husband beat her because she wouldn't have sex with him – she said they couldn't afford to have any more children. I gave her an ad from *Hibernia* magazine for condoms. You could send away for them. She passed it on to other women and, the next thing I knew, the parish priest was at my door. He said, I believe you're giving out advice about condoms. I said, yes. He said it was wrong and I should stop. He said it was a woman's duty to submit to her husband.

'When I was growing up, these things weren't talked about. There must have been a lot of unhappiness, and still is, of course. I had always supported the Rape Crisis Centre. I used to think of a vulnerable woman, terrified, and wondering, where can I go? Dublin is anonymous – women from any part of the country could ring them and get help. I have told women to ring them myself. It was a refuge in the old-fashioned, almost biblical, sense.'[45]

O'Rourke's style was utterly different to her predecessor's. 'Across the bridge of sighs,' Hussey wrote in her diary. 'Greeted by whoops and hugs from Mary. Ebullient as ever and knew the area. We felt very encouraged ... EHB had conceded several points.' Indeed, the EHB's follow-up report on the DRCC in 1991 praised the Centre and recommended that it should 'continue to be recognised as the crisis service for the EHB region'. It said the Centre had become 'noticeably less isolated' and complimented its 'greater openness'.[46]

Encouragement turned to euphoria just before Christmas when, as Hussey noted in her diary, 'Mary came up trumps'. O'Rourke announced that, in addition to the EHB allocation of £100,000 for 1992, the Department of Health would be giving the Centre an additional £25,000 for its educational work. The EHB would provide £27,000 worth of computer equipment, stationery and other services. The Centre had got what it asked for – a commitment that the state would meet half its funding needs. The years of struggling for every penny were over. The battle for recognition as an essential service had been won. 'We are absolutely delighted,' said Olive Braiden.[47]

13

A COUNTRY 'DIZZY WITH SHOCK AND ANGER'

'There was a lot of reluctance to face up to what was going on in the Ireland of saints and scholars,' said Olive Braiden. 'It was one thing to say that a "monster" had jumped out and raped someone. It was far more frightening to say that pillars of society were doing it in their own homes. There were plenty of people in authority who just wanted to put a lid on it. I remember one of our volunteers went to a lecture in University College Dublin. I had written a letter to the papers about the high incidence of rape and this was brought out and read, as an example of the decline of right thinking in a Catholic country. The letter, not the rapes!

'But 1991 was when we made our name. It was a nightmare to fight that battle, and hugely time-consuming but we had right on our side and we had a good, solid history. We had our figures showing the extent of the problem. In the end, the health board was shamed into admitting that they had no services and that we were doing their work for them. We had a right to public funding. Getting it was a huge breakthrough.'

Reflecting on the achievements of the DRCC in 1991, Olive Braiden said it had brought about considerable improvements in the treatment of rape victims. Attitudes, however, had not changed, she said. 'You still get people who can't distinguish between sex and rape,' she said, in an interview with Liz Ryan. 'You still get the rigid, religious family whose father goes to church every Sunday morning and rapes his daughters every night. You still get the people who think women "ask for it" by wearing short skirts or whatever – even though rape victims include nuns, children and grandmothers. And you still get the judicial attitude that regards alcohol as an exacerbating factor if the victim had been drinking and an exonerating factor if the perpetrator had been drinking.' Almost all rapists were men, she said. It was possible that 'some men rape when unable to deal with liberated women who confidently turn down unwanted advances'.

Columnist David Hanly provoked an angry response from the DRCC when he wrote in the *Sunday Tribune* that a barrister friend had told him rape had become a more vicious crime in the past 20 years as a reaction to 'strident feminism'. Whereas in the past 'rape was rape', a matter of the rapist overpowering a woman and getting sexual gratification, in recent times the act was often accompanied by 'acts of un-imaginable cruelty and torture' including mutilation. The barrister told him that the emergence of independent, asser-tive women had 'spawned a reactionary generation of rapists for whom rape is not a sex act, not an act of power, nor yet of humiliation: it is an act born out of sheer hatred of women'.[1]

Responding to the article, Grace O'Malley of the Rape Crisis Centre suggested Hanly's barrister friend 'should be asking why it is that victims are so reluctant to report rape and go through the trauma of a rape case'. She said rape was motivated by 'power, anger and violence'. O'Malley agreed that rape had become more horrific but suggested this might be related to the influence of pornography. She noted 'our deplorable video censorshop laws' and 'the insidious portrayal of women as sex objects'. Was Hanly implying, she demanded, 'that rape will stop if women are submissive, inferior and unassertive?' This was 'ludicrous, outrageous and beneath contempt'. She pointed to a study carried out for the DRCC by Dr Rosemary Cullen on the behaviour of rapists. It 'totally exonerates victims from any possible responsibility in rape cases'.[2]

Cullen's study came about when a benefactor gave the Centre a large donation for research. She conducted a study of convicted sex offenders in prison. The levels of violence the men had used were 'generally beyond levels necessary to gain sexual compliance', she found. Half of the men said they were 'specifically interested in a non-consenting sexual encounter'. They said they had experienced a 'complete absence of sexual arousal' or 'very low levels of arousal'.

Two out of three of the rapists interviewed gave 'non-sexual motivational factors' for the rape, including 'tension, stress, specific problems in their lives and anger'. They commonly said their feelings during the attack included 'anger, hatred, power and dominance'. Cullen concluded that if the incidence of rape was to be lowered, the offender population had to be tackled. She suggested that a helpline for offenders should be set up. This, however, was far from the government's priorities. In fact, in 1991, the sex offenders' treatment programme at Arbour Hill prison was dropped after just 12 prisoners had completed the course.

Braiden said this was 'short-sighted'. The Centre was educated on the potential of treatment by the British pioneer of such programmes, Ray Wyre. The Department of Justice insisted that there were 'extensive services'. In 1992, the then Minister for Justice, Padraig Flynn, had to make a humiliating climbdown. A judge found that a man he had jailed for incest the previous year, with an order that he should receive treatment, was not, in fact, receiving treatment in prison. A senior civil servant had stated in court on behalf of the Minister that the sex offenders, programme at Arbour Hill was 'the best in the world'. However, the principal officer of the prisons section at the department told Judge Michael Moriarty in 1992 that such a claim should never have been made because the programme described didn't exist. Dr Art O'Connor pointed out in court that the programme he ran at the Central Mental Hospital was not available to prisoners. The Rape Crisis Centre described Flynn's claim as 'incredible'. It was 'not only incorrect but irresponsible', said Olive Braiden. 'We must be one of the few countries under common law jurisdiction where no attempt is being made to rehabilitate sexual offenders in prison.'[3]

'Our worst fears have been realised. How bitter it is to say "we told you so".' This was the statement issued by Mary Holland, Anne O'Donnell, Ray Kavanagh and Anne Marie Hourihane of the Anti-Amendment Campaign steering committee after a 14-year-old girl pregnant as a result of rape was prevented from travelling to England for an abortion.[4]

However, Fr Michael Cleary took a different view. 'If a case was made, was planned deliberately, to test this amendment, this is it … I honestly suspect a lot of organisation behind it,' he said on *The Late Late Show*.[5]

In January 1992 the parents of a 14-year-old Dublin school-girl found out she had been raped and was pregnant. The rapist was the father of her schoolfriend. The couple brought their child to the SATU in the Rotunda, reported the rape to the gardaí and arranged for her to have an abortion in England.

It was when the girl's father inquired of the gardaí as to whether they should have DNA tests done on the aborted foetus to provide evidence for a rape trial that the family found themselves plunged into a new nightmare that would agonise the nation and provoke a constitutional crisis which has still, more than a decade later, not been fully resolved. The gardaí passed the question on to the DPP, and the DPP informed the then Attorney General, Harry Whelehan, who invoked the 1983 Amendment to obtain a High Court injunction to stop the 14-year-old leaving the country. The pregnant girl and her family had already travelled to England for the abortion, but returned to Ireland to sort out the legal issues arising from the injunction. This became known as the X case.

The girl was suicidal. The High Court heard she had been just 12 when her friend's father had begun to sexually molest her. He had done so continuously and eventually forced sexual intercourse on her, as a result of which she became pregnant. However, Mr Justice Declan Costello ruled in favour of the unborn. The girl was not permitted to leave the country for nine months. If she tried to, she could be jailed. A child was to be forced to bear and give birth to the child of a rapist.

The people had voted two to one for the 1983 amendment, but there was huge sympathy for this child, and anger. President Robinson said the Irish people were experiencing 'a very deep crisis in ourselves' and said we should become a more compassionate society.[6] Ten thousand people took to the streets of Dublin in emotional protest. Some placards read, 'Jail the rapist, not the victim'. There were similar protests around the country. Rock star Sinead O'Connor stood outside Leinster House with a placard that read, 'Stop this legalised child abuse now!' Martyn Turner brilliantly illustrated the situation with a cartoon which appeared on the front page of *The Irish Times*: '17 February 1992 … the introduction of internment in Ireland … for 14-year-old girls,' read the caption. The cartoon showed a map of Ireland, with the Republic surrounded by a high fence with barbed wire on top. Inside stands a girl in school uniform, clutching a teddy bear.

A young woman phoned the Marian Finucane radio show and talked about how she had been raped at the age of 12, became pregnant and had an abortion in London. Her mother had supported her. She disputed the Catholic Church's claim that abortion was another act of violence: 'To force someone to bring a baby to full term which has been conceived during rape is an act of violence,' she said.[7]

An *Irish Times* editorial demanded: 'With what are we now to compare ourselves? Ceausescu's Romania? The ayatollah's Iran?' The case was reported in similar terms in newspapers across Europe and the US. However, the Catholic Church was undaunted. Rape was an 'unspeakable crime' but an 'innocent human being cannot rightly be made to pay the penalty of death for the crime of another'.[8] Fr Michael Cleary claimed on *The Late Late Show* that the X case had been 'planned deliberately' to test the 1983 amendment. 'Why did the police have a telephone contact for her over there? And why did they come meekly back when the police said, "please come home"?' he asked. He said if he was the father, he 'would have lied' and claimed it was too late. There was applause from a section of the audience.

'I was absolutely shocked at his remarks,' Olive Braiden said at the time. 'He also said there was a very low incidence of pregnancy from rape, yet in 1990, 52 women who came to us were pregnant from rape, and that was only in Dublin and only the people who came to us.'[9] Braiden revealed that eight rape victims in 1990 had already terminated pregnancies before coming to the Centre, while seventeen opted to continue the pregnancy and keep the child, and nine put the baby up for adoption. Braiden also highlighted the fact that 1,000 girls had reported being sexually abused in 1990.

Monica Barnes was incensed at Cleary's remarks. She wrote to Archbishop Connell questioning Cleary's fitness as the Catholic emissary for youth. She told him the people were 'in pain and crisis' about this 'heartbreaking case'. She asked him to dissociate the Church from Cleary's offensive remarks. She received from the archbishop's secretary a one-line acknowledgement that her letter had been received, but she got no further reply.

Barnes commented on the 'steady and sinister erosion of women's rights' resulting from the amendment, including the closure of non-directive pregnancy counselling services and restrictions on freedom of information. 'A police state could emerge,' she warned.[10] Two weeks later, Archbishop Connell compared the spread of abortion with the corruption of power seen under Nazi and communist rule.

'When somebody is raped, all their control is taken away from them,' Olive Braiden told *Newsweek* magazine. 'To be banned from travelling for an abortion is a second victimisation.'[11] She told the *European*, 'Until now we have encouraged women to go to the police. But we will not be involved in forcing anyone to have a baby against her will.'[12] Looking back, Braiden said the Centre had to be careful what it said on abortion.

There were still endless requests for abortion information. It was illegal to give it, following a series of court cases during the 1980s in which the Society for the Protection of the

Unborn Child (SPUC) had successfully invoked the 1983 Amendment to prevent the Well Woman Centre, students' unions and others from providing women with contact details for clinics in England. 'It was very frustrating getting those calls,' recalled Grace O'Malley. 'Each one had to be treated as if it was genuine, just in case.'

Braiden said the Centre's position had always been that a rape victim should have the right to choose her own options. 'We referred women who were, or thought they were, pregnant to the Well Woman Centre, Cherish or the Irish Family Planning Association,' recalled Braiden, who was on the board of the Well Woman Centre at the time.

Acutely embarrassed by the situation, the Fianna Fáil–Progressive Democrats government funded an appeal to the Supreme Court. The panel of male judges ruled by a majority of four to one that the girl had the right to have an abortion – and in Ireland. One judge said the failure to enact laws to give effect to Article 40.3.3 was 'inexcusable'. The 'anti-abortion' amendment was found to allow the right to abortion if there was a 'real and substantial risk to the life' of the mother, which could be avoided only by termination of her pregnancy. Anne O'Donnell said it was 'utterly hypocritical' of Irish people to declare themselves delighted that the raped girl could go to England for an abortion and said she should be able to have the operation in Ireland.[13] An opinion poll carried out soon after the X case became public found that four out of five Irish people believed abortion should be available in some circumstances. Almost half thought it should be available in cases of rape, incest or when the mother's life was threatened.

The rapist subsequently tried to stop his trial going ahead because of the adverse publicity around the case. He was convicted in May 1994 and given two seven-year sentences to be served consecutively, meaning he should spend 14 years in jail. However, this was not the end of the X-case rapist's story.

On a May evening in 1992, a man grabbed an 11-year-old girl from a street corner in Dublin and dragged her to a nearby canal bank, where he stripped her. She managed to escape, running naked along the street until a motorist stopped and rescued her. It was a year full of evidence of shocking levels of sexual violence against children.

Dr Mary Henry, chairwoman of the Friends of the Rape Crisis Centre, launched an appeal for funds to help the X-case girl and her family. Any surplus was to be donated to the Rape Crisis Centre and the SATU. 'This is not an unusual case at all,' she said, adding that the SATU had been 'flooded' by teachers and social workers bringing in raped children.[14]

Joe O'Toole, then general secretary of the Irish National Teachers' Organisation (INTO), said child abuse was 'endemic'. The DRCC welcomed calls by the teachers' unions for training in relation to abuse, and education officer Maeve Lewis called on the Department of Education to fund it to carry out the work.

A survey carried out in Cork found that more than two-thirds of child sex abuse victims attempted suicide in later life. The survey received little attention in the aftermath of the X case, but its findings heralded another looming scandal: one in ten male victims had been preyed upon by a priest or religious brother.[15] Meanwhile, CARI announced the opening of Ireland's first long-term therapy programme for child sex abuse victims.

Childline claimed that one in ten Irish children had been sexually abused. Gardaí revealed that while 230 babies were born to minors (and therefore after statutory rape) in 1990, just 35 cases had been reported to the police and 4 convictions secured. Sixty-two births were to girls aged under 15. The youngest was 11.

The DRCC was aware of one case in which a mother found blood in her baby daughter's nappy, evidence, it emerged, that the child's older brother had been raping her. He got a suspended sentence and was counselled by a nun. The DRCC believed the young man should have gone to prison and questioned the nun's qualification to provide such therapy. Dr Noël Browne had challenged the government to say whether or not it would force a pregnant rape victim to go through with the pregnancy in 1980. He did so when Oliver J. Flanagan was attempting to block the funding of the DRCC. During the X case, Browne wrote that the world would now know how 'with constitutional authority, the religious fanatic obscurantist mad Irish "cherish" their children'.[16]

A Co. Dublin fisherman armed with a screwdriver chased a 14-year-old girl, caught her and sexually assaulted her. He was jailed for three years. A man indecently assaulted his 13-year-old niece, who described a litany of abuse by him, her father, who had since died, and another man. The man got a suspended sentence. A young Waterford girl told the Circuit Court that her father had been raping her for five years, since she was 15. The case collapsed after the state failed to produce crucial evidence. A Co. Westmeath man admitted raping a 14-year-old girl in a field near Ballinasloe. He was jailed for three years.

A Donegal girl became pregnant as a result of rape at the age of 13. She had a baby shortly after her 14th birthday. She gave evidence in the trial of six men on charges of multiple sexual assaults. Three men pleaded guilty and were released with suspended sentences. Three were acquitted because there was no corroboration of the girl's evidence and the judge ruled that it was necessary. The girl told journalist Eamonn McCann that when some of the men returned to Donegal they drove round the village green blowing their horns and cheering. A garda told McCann it was like a football team returning from some triumph. Some of the men also held a celebration in a local hotel. The girl was asked to leave a local disco on the grounds that her presence was 'disturbing people'.[17]

'I was in court for another case and I saw Lavinia being escorted out screaming,' recalled Olive Braiden. Lavinia Kerwick, who was 18, had just witnessed the release of the young man, also 18, who admitted raping her. 'He got away with it! He got away with it!' she sobbed as relatives helped her from the Four Courts. Kate Shanahan, who interviewed Lavinia for her book *Crimes Worse than Death*, said that, outside the court, Lavinia kept asking her mother what had gone wrong. 'Did I look like a whore to the judge?' she begged.[18] Mr Justice Fergus Flood adjourned sentencing the young man and said he was giving him 'a chance as a human being'. If he transgressed, the judge said, he'd go to jail for ten years. Counsel for the accused, Michael McDowell, said his client knew he had done wrong, but that there were 'strong mitigating factors' and he had 'given in to his strong sexual impulse without any forethought'.[19]

Lavinia Kerwick was not represented in court. Her injuries were not described. There was no one to say that she had been starving herself since the rape and had attempted suicide. The first inkling Lavinia had that her rapist was not going to jail came when one of the gardaí urged her mother to get her out of the courtroom fast: 'Get her out. It's going bad. Get her outside.'[20] Supported by her family, the distraught young woman decided that her side of the story needed to be told. She felt, she later said, that she was representing the women of Ireland. On 16 July, the day after the court case, Lavinia Kerwick abandoned the anonymity to which she was entitled by law. It was one of the most important interviews ever to be broadcast in this country.

'I can't believe it. He might as well have raped me yesterday again,' she told Gerry Ryan on his morning programme on 2FM. The rapist had been her boyfriend, and she described going to a New Year's Eve disco with him. Walking home, he had become 'forceful, angry and excited', she said. 'He raped me not just once but several times.' She said the attack lasted more than an hour and left her with bruises on her face, legs, back, private parts: 'Everywhere.' He had warned her not to tell anyone. He told her that even if she did, and it came to court, he'd walk free. Afterwards, she felt 'guilty and dirty'. She felt she was to blame and that she shouldn't have worn the clothes she was wearing. She started taking tranquillisers and sleeping pills and she stopped eating. 'I couldn't go on with my life any more.' He lived near her, and she was 'terrified' to go out. The gardaí had been '100 per cent', but she regretted reporting it, she said. She had been 'let down by the whole justice system'.

She appealed to the Minister for Justice, Padraig Flynn, to meet her.[21] Lavinia was interviewed again on RTÉ television that night. She appealed to the Minister: 'I'm begging him from the bottom of my heart, if he has any consideration for girls, and for me, and for people who have gone through it, and for people who will probably go through it tonight, even, please, I'm begging him to bring it back up.'[22] In press interviews she revealed that she had been a virgin before the rape. She had been terrified she might be pregnant and had taken the morning-after pill. Every town should have a special unit for rape victims, she said. A rape crisis counsellor should be available in court.

'Rape girl fury,' was the front page headline on the *Star*. The story was on every talk show, every front page. Olive Braiden said the Rape Crisis Centre was 'shocked and disillusioned' by the outcome of the case. She said she feared it might deter other women from reporting rape. She wrote in *The Irish Times* that 'recent sentences lead us to believe that there is no justice for rape victims in court' and that society colluded with this situation.[23] In a powerful analysis of the week that followed, Justine McCarthy wrote that 'the country has been dizzy with shock and anger'. She put the case in the context of other recent ones: a rapist who had got off on a technicality; a rapist who couldn't be jailed because there was no place for him; the High Court injunction in the X case.

'Every time some controversy like this erupts, women all over the country raise their hopes like distress flags on drifting ships. We have endless days of screaming headlines, sanctimonious politicians and talking head experts on the airwaves. Then they all go back to whatever they were doing before and women and children continue to be raped by husbands, boyfriends and strangers in the dark.' She pointed out that although just a small minority of rape and sex assault cases ever reach court, there were 27 such cases listed for hearing in Dublin for the following week.[24] The *Star* called for mandatory sentencing in rape cases.[25] 'Something must be done to stem the huge flow of sexual violence,' said Olive Braiden.[26]

The sense of outrage was fuelled by the intervention of a barrister, the late Greg Murphy. 'It is a very emotive issue. These things happen. There must be a distinction between the cold rapist and something which is, at the end of the day, just a matter of consent,' he said on RTÉ's *Morning Ireland*. 'It is not a case of someone jumping into someone's house and raping an old woman. These people were only 18 years of age. They'd known each other for up to five months. It's a case of things having gone too far.' He accused the Rape Crisis Centre and other women's groups of being 'vengeful' and attempting to deny the rights of men accused of rape.[27] A few days later he claimed he had defended many 'ordinary common or garden rapists'. The situation usually involved a young couple who had a lot to drink: 'A girl who knew nothing about sex was late home, her knickers in flitters and she was worried whether she was pregnant or not. The easiest thing was to scream rape.'[28]

Olive Braiden denounced Murphy's comments as 'absolutely outrageous'. The Centre had never called for mandatory sentencing for rapists and had always strongly advocated the need for therapy for rapists and child abusers. She said victims of what he had dismissively called 'date rape' were likely to feel more disillusioned and betrayed than those raped by strangers. They might also face sceptical and less helpful attitudes from the police and the public and were likely to blame themselves.[29] She said the phonelines at the Rape Crisis Centre were jammed with callers who were 'jumping up and down with rage' at Murphy's views.

Women with their mouths gagged with black ribbons protested outside the Four Courts. They included Carmel Foley, then chief executive of the Coucil for the Status of Women (CSW). 'The law silences women,' said their placards. Lavinia Kerwick was admitted to hospital suffering from anorexia. She said she hated her body. If she died, she wanted her body to be burned.

Lavinia spoke in interviews about the fact that she was receiving counselling from the Rape Crisis Centres both in Dublin and Clonmel. Concerned about her health, Olive

Braiden publicly advised Lavinia 'to rest and not to give any more interviews'.[30] Braiden, along with Roisin Mac Dermott, chairwoman of Women's Aid, and representatives of the Irish Countrywomen's Association and the CSW met the Minister for Justice. He promised that new legislation would be introduced within months, allowing appeals against lenient sentences. 'We have all come to realise that there is a high level of violence against women,' Flynn said.

Carmel Foley said afterwards that the Minister had accepted that rape was a crime of violence and not of passion. Braiden said the DRCC had also pushed the Minister to bring in separate legal representation for women. A fair trial allowed women to feel psychologically vindicated and gave them a sense of being protected by the state, she said. Having someone in court to represent their interests was 'the only thing which will encourage women to come forward and bring cases', she said.[31]

Flynn also agreed to see Lavinia Kerwick, who discharged herself from hospital to travel to Dublin for the meeting. 'He was a very nice man and spoke to me like a daughter,' she said afterwards. 'He gave me a lot of good advice and hope for the future.'[32] She said he had become very angry as she told her story and had banged the table. 'He said he would change the law so that what happened to me will never happen to any other woman in court,' she said. She told reporters she had made him a promise which she was keeping a secret. Then she went back to hospital.

That night, about 1,000 women took part in a Reclaim the Night march in Dublin. Speakers called on Judge Flood to resign. They said the protest was inspired 'by the courage of one woman who spoke out', and was dedicated to 'the hundreds of women who have been raped but have never spoken out because of fear'.[33] Women's Aid revealed that it had only £25 in the bank, that there was an acute shortage of refuge places and that women needing barring orders against violent partners were having to wait up to a year to see a legal aid solicitor.

Social worker and commentator Kieran McGrath, who

had long taken a close interest in issues associated with rape and sexual abuse, called for reports on the effects of rape on its victim to be presented in court. Rape Crisis Centre chairwoman Gemma Hussey agreed. 'As the debate goes on, more things are coming out,' she said. 'It must amaze ordinary people who would have thought as a matter of course that the judge would know the state of the victim.'[34] Mary Harney, then a PD Minister of State, called for the restoration of criminal injury compensation for pain and suffering. The Fine Gael–Labour Party government had removed entitlement for such compensation in 1986. Harney said it was particularly important for rape victims. The Rape Crisis Centre said it had received a surge of calls after Kerwick had courageously spoken out and pointed out that it needed to raise £200,000 towards the next year's work.

In the aftermath of the Kerwick case, the Minister for Justice made further sweeping promises about ending violence against women. He would ensure for women that 'the very first time their partner's hand is raised against them they can make sure it's the last'. He said he would end the 'cycle of violence' whereby boys learned to treat women violently from their fathers.[35] He also announced details of the new legislation he had promised Kerwick. The Criminal Justice Act of 1993 allowed the DPP to appeal lenient sentences, judges to order an attacker to pay compensation to a victim and victim impact reports to be presented in court so that a judge knew how the rape had affected the victim.

The Department of Justice and the gardaí organised a Women and Safety conference at Dublin Castle. 'It was,' the *Star* reported, 'a unique gathering of those who fight for, represent and help the rapists and batterers and those who fight for, represent and help their victims – women.' Reporter Anne Sweeney said, 'the heavyweight women's organisations were powerfully represented – this lobby of mostly cash-starved voluntary organisations helping to pick up the pieces of women's shattered lives as they fight for change'. Susan Denham, later to become the first woman on the Supreme Court, spoke at the conference and a large number of judges attended.

In her speech, Olive Braiden commented on the euphemistic title chosen for a conference about violence against women. She welcomed the changes proposed by the Minister, but repeated the Rape Crisis Centre's demand for separate legal representation. The government said it couldn't be done, she said, but that was what they had said about changing the law to criminalise rape in marriage, too.

Lavinia, in the audience, heard speaker after speaker praise her for her courage. Just weeks later, another brave family spoke out. Joyce, Paula and June Kavanagh, along with their mother, also Joyce, took part in a superb documentary shown in the RTÉ *Tuesday File* series in October 1992. The Kavanagh daughters had been raped and abused by their father throughout their childhoods. In 1988, they had watched *The Late Late Show* which featured Constance Nightingale talking about having been abused by her father.

The Kavanaghs went on to report their father to the gardaí. In 1990, he was convicted of rape, indecent assault and incest. His victims also included a niece and grandniece. He was sent to jail for seven years. His wife, Joyce, later obtained a judicial separation.

The rapist tried, but failed, to prevent RTÉ showing *The Silent Scream*, which was produced by Moya McColgan and presented by Miriam Fitzsimons. The Kavanagh sisters gave a moving account of their lives. They remembered and described what they had felt when they were small children experiencing the abuse. Their father was religious, and they believed God was punishing them. Among the comments they made were: 'God knew I was bad, that's why he let Daddy do it.' 'Everything was a bribe – if he had sex with you, you got money. We'd the best of toys.' 'He told us my mother would leave us.' 'I just wanted to please him so that he'd love me.' 'It was not sex – he liked to hurt you. He liked to see you cry.'

The women revealed that one of them had told a priest – who told her to come back to him with her father. One had told a doctor, who said he would 'sort him out', but that was the last she'd heard. The programme revealed much about the complexity of the relationship between abused children and their abuser. 'Bad and all as he was, he was all we had,' one of the women recalled. Their mother hadn't known, they said. The father had a way of separating the child he was about to abuse so that no one else in the family knew.

A special freephone number for the Rape Crisis Centre was given out at the end of the programme, and hundreds of callers phoned it. There were ten lines staffed by counsellors, but still there were those who couldn't get through. Callers included women and men of all ages, including elderly people, many of whom had never spoken before about the abuse they had been subjected to. Three out of four of these callers were women. Callers also included men who admitted that they were abusers. Olive Braiden commented on the dearth of services to which to refer these men. Braiden said the Kavanaghs' experiences of trying to get help proved the need for training for professionals who came into contact with children.

The Kavanaghs said that at one stage during their therapy they were paying out so much in counselling fees that they were working just to pay for it. 'Why is there no fund available for victims?' they demanded. Braiden agreed there should be state support for victims. Crisis counselling sessions at the DRCC were free, and six free sessions were allocated. Those who could afford to pay were asked for donations on a sliding scale – those who could not pay were not asked to do so. At the time the programme was shown, there was a waiting list of 100.

Braiden said the programme was a milestone. It recognised a problem which had been a dark secret of Irish society for too long. Joyce Kavanagh said the family was delighted that so many people came forward for help after it. 'Child sexual abuse is a huge problem,' she said. 'Something had to be done and I'm glad we did it.'[36]

14

Rape As a War Crime

'There are some crimes so horrendous that they either hush us into silence or else hurl us into screams,' said South African Judge Albie Sachs in relation to war rapes in Bosnia.'Women are held in brothel camps in hotels and barracks. Here they are not just raped, they are also tortured and killed, often in front of their children,' said Indijana Hidovic Harper. 'The world is actually sitting and watching this happen as if it is not quite real.' Harper, from Bosnia, was speaking before addressing a meeting about women and war in the former Yugoslavia in Dublin's Mansion House in 1993. She said rape was being used to create ethnic hatred.

Another speaker, Maja Kovac, from a Serbian background, said rape was being used as a weapon of war. 'While women are the victims, men are the target,' she told journalist Anthea MacTeirnan. 'In a patriarchal society where women are regarded as property, there is no more effective way of humiliating a man than to rape his mother, wife or daughter.' Serbian nationalism, she said, 'has a strong male face ... the main ingredients of this war are national chauvinism and extreme violence'. The future for women would be 'very, very dark', she warned. 'Our gender has been attacked and we may be a long time healing.'[1]

Olive Braiden was in the audience at the Mansion House and was moved by what she heard. 'I'd been following the war in former Yugoslavia and there had been talk about rape camps for some time,' she recalled. 'Then two women from Foreign Affairs were included in a delegation headed by Dame Anne Warburton to investigate the extent of the problem. After I read their report, I was incensed, and incensed that there were still people who didn't believe it.'

The EU report found that Serbian forces had taken part in the organised rape of at least 20,000 Muslim women and girls and that rape was being used as a 'weapon of war'. Many victims of gang rapes, including children aged as young as seven, had died from their injuries, women had become pregnant and, the report found, the psychological trauma suffered by survivors 'has yet to be addressed'.

'I realised we could do a training programme for those working with these survivors,' said Braiden. She drew up a proposal and sent it to the then Tánaiste and Minister for Foreign Affairs, Dick Spring. The Fianna Fáil-Labour government had also been briefed on the situation by Amnesty International. Spring called Braiden immediately, and they met at Iveagh House. 'By the time I got back to Leeson Street the press corps was on the steps asking, "How do you feel about getting £50,000?" My heart was in my mouth, because I hadn't even told the board.' Although it supported the project, there would be, over the years, a degree of tension between Braiden and the board over such 'solo runs', as Hussey privately called them.

In March 1993, Braiden and the DRCC's head of training, Maeve Lewis, set off for Croatia, armed with a letter from Spring to ease their way diplomatically. They were assisted by Irish police and army personnel based in the area. The plan was to select participants for a course to be held in Dublin. 'We met as many women's groups as we could and we went around transit camps and met people working there,' recalled Braiden. 'It was very surreal – we were staying in this exclusive hotel in Zagreb and then we'd be out in these bleak camps. We selected ten women, some of them social workers, doctors and teachers. Some had lost their homes and family members. The Burlington gave us rooms at a cheap rate. When they came over, all the taxi drivers in Dublin were asking us who these gorgeous women were.'

Lewis, along with Angela McCarthy, devised a two-week training course. They were helped by the SATU and other women's groups. 'There was already a good network of women's groups, some of which had worked on domestic violence, and people were receptive. Our initial idea was to set up rape crisis counselling,' said Lewis, 'but we soon realised this wouldn't work. In the Muslim tradition, to lose your virginity was seen as a shame to the family no matter how it was lost. It was hard for the women to talk, though on one of my visits to former Yugoslavia we met a group of women from a village and they told us that all of them had been publicly raped, and all the village men had been taken away and probably killed.'

The DRCC knew that those they were training to provide counselling had themselves been traumatised by the war. They knew many of the women who had been raped had also been tortured and mutilated, and many had endured forced pregnancy. They knew rape was one trauma among many for thousands of Bosnian and Croatian refugees. One of the women, Nives Novina, said Serbs were putting women and children in 'concentration camps'.

The DRCC went on, in 1994, with further government funding, to provide courses based in Zagreb for the original participants and new groups. Training was provided in crisis counselling, play therapy with children, long-term therapy, dealing with post-traumatic stress disorder and group facilitation. Geraldine Connolly made a major contribution to these courses. 'It was very intense work,' recalled Angela McCarthy. 'There was a lot of fear in the air and people were exhausted. People were so traumatised and so alone. We ran several courses in a lovely family guesthouse near the sea in the Croatian town of Split. The war was ever present. You couldn't protect the women. One day we did a little visualisation exercise. You picture yourself as a rose and you describe it and then you draw it. Group members then broke into pairs and quietly talked to one another. In the closing minutes, one of us said, "Does anyone want to say anything in the large group?" There was this damburst of emotion, all the loss they'd suffered. We had to spend ages helping them to process what had happened. It was things that went beyond our known levels.'

The training continued through the late 1990s. Courses were held in Split and, after the Dayton agreement, in Bosnia, in the towns of Tuzla, Gorazde and Travnik. Trainers included Deirdre Ní Chinneide, Geraldine Connolly, Joan White, Ann O'Duffy, Maeve Lewis and Angela McCarthy. 'In Bosnia, women had to use a secret tunnel near the airport in Sarajevo and climb Mount Igman at night to get to the training,' recalled McCarthy. 'People went to incredible lengths to get there.' The DRCC also urged the Irish government to push for the prosecution of war criminals after the conflict. In 1999, training was provided in Kosovo (see chapter 16). Lewis, after leaving the DRCC in 1995, went on to do similar work in Rwanda and Sierra Leone.

While the appalling news of the Bosnian rape camps was reaching Ireland, the story of another sort of rape camp emerged, this one an Irish family home. In March 1993, a 27-year-old woman was interviewed on RTÉ television. She described 16 years of rapes and beatings at the hands of her father, a Co. Kilkenny farmer who had just been sent to prison for seven years. Prosecution counsel in the case had said in court, 'This case concerns nightmare events of almost Kafkaesque proportions, a human tragedy on an enormous scale ...' The rapes had begun in 1976, when the girl was 11. 'I thought I was naughty in some way and it was his way of punishing me,' the unnamed woman told then legal affairs correspondent Kieron Wood.

At the age of 14, her father had made her pregnant, and she had given birth to a son in 1982. She was forbidden to name the father. 'My father put it about that I was a real prostitute,' she said. 'That was what they called me ... I used to get calls at three o'clock in the morning when the pubs kicked them out – "How much do you charge? What positions do you do?"' She described how on different occasions her father smashed her fingers with a hammer, in front of her son, broke her ribs and blinded her in one eye with a kick. He had also cut her with knives and would subject her to 'ranting and raving'. He had made her work slavishly on his farm, while he spent long periods drinking.

The family – her father, mother, sister and herself, and, latterly, her son – lived in a small terraced house in a village. Asked if local people ever offered to help her, she replied, 'People were afraid to talk to me. They would say "hello" in passing and go on.' Her mother, she said, 'was as afraid as I was'. She, too, had been routinely beaten and abused. The young woman had been seen by doctors, social workers, hospital staff, public health nurses, gardaí and teachers at various stages. She had spent some time in a women's refuge.

She told Wood that she didn't feel the seven-year sentence her father had got was long enough. 'I had to go through hell,' she said. She believed her father's rage would be such that she and her mother would have to go on the run when he was released. In a later interview, she said that for years she had felt that 'my spirit was broken'. However, in the end, it was a surge of her own anger, and the perseverance of Garda Agnes Reddy, which brought about her father's arrest and prosecution.

The scandal received huge media coverage. In her diary, DRCC chairwoman Gemma Hussey noted her feelings as she read the details of 'Yet another horrific rape/incest case', adding: 'it doesn't bear thinking about but it must be thought about'. The Minister for Health, Labour's Brendan Howlin, launched an inquiry, headed by Catherine McGuinness, then a barrister. Olive Braiden warned that this was 'not an isolated case'. She said that over the years the DRCC had seen 'many clients who have been brutally beaten and impregnated by fathers, brothers and uncles'.[2] She said that for years the DRCC had been calling for 'comprehensive training' for professionals so that they knew 'what to look for and what questions to ask' and that they should then have 'clear guide-lines' on what to do. 'The reality is that an abused person, especially if the abuse is occurring within the family, is seldom going to tell anyone what is going on. Therefore, it will often have to be someone from outside the family who has to intervene. To do that, they must know how.'

She said that it was the DRCC's experience that abused children were often desperately looking out for an adult to confide in, but were terrified of the abuser, who would have warned them not to tell. It took a skilled person to 'make them feel they can tell the truth and they will be protected'. She described the Stay Safe programme in primary schools as an important first step, but added that programmes were also needed in secondary schools and were not available in most of them. 'The crucial question is,' she said, 'Are we willing to intercede for a child in a family situation?' [3]

Reviewing Kieron Woods' book, *The Kilkenny Incest Case*, the then head of clinical services at the DRCC, Rosemary Liddy, said the book dwelt too much on the physical details of the sexual violence.[4] This was 'a minor part of the trauma most survivors experience. The real trauma lies in the deepest part of a survivor's psyche, burnt into mind, heart and soul ... the real horror ... [lies] in the battle for survival and sanity ... Trust shattered, love betrayed, humiliation, treated as of no value, powerless, terrified and helpless to do anything. The techniques used to get through another day, the feelings of isolation, alienation and hopelessness that are the lot of every abused child.' She praised the courage of the young woman and wished 'for healing for her and for her son and for love to come into her life'.[5]

The DRCC made a submission to the Kilkenny Incest Investigation, calling for training for professionals, better funding for Rape Crisis Centres and mandatory reporting of child abuse. The report, published in May 1993, included all these in its recommendations and paid tribute to the 'excellent work' done by RCCs and Women's Aid. It suggested that it was 'the women's movement and the work of Rape Crisis Centres which forced societies to recognise that sexual abuse of children does occur in families'. The lower socio-economic status of women and children was part of the complex picture and 'ambivalence towards family violence goes right across the community', it said. Reviewing the literature, it stated that the vast majority of perpetrators of sexual violence were men. While the Constitution stressed the 'inalienable' rights of the family, the report said children had traditionally been regarded as property 'without valid opinions and virtually without rights'. It called for a constitutional amendment to introduce an 'overt declaration of the rights of born children', a pointed reference to the fact that the 'unborn' had such protection.[6]

The report to a huge extent agreed with the DRCC's analysis of sexual violence, and board member Joe Robins described its recommendations as 'enlightened and comprehensive'. However, he argued that the investigating group had been 'far too reticent' in its comments on the role of the South Eastern Health Board. For 'at least a decade' it had been public policy for the health boards to develop measures against sexual abuse, he said. There were guidelines. The girl had grown up and was outside childcare legislation for some of the period of the abuse, but her child, also at risk, should have been protected by it. 'It is clear that the misery suffered by this young woman for so long arises less from the lack of legal provisions and health board resources than from what appears to be gross indifference by far too many people in authority to the brutalisation of women and children,' he concluded.[7]

Catherine McGuinness, now a Supreme Court judge, recalled the investigation. 'The Rape Crisis Centre had opened the public mind on child abuse, and this case bore out all the things they had been saying all along. Plenty of people knew these things had been going on. But there was a huge reluctance to interfere in what was seen as the private affairs of a family, and that is still the case. It was striking too, the way the community tried to say the family was not really part of it. They said they were outsiders, protestants. The report helped the Health Minister, Brendan Howlin, to get the funds to implement parts of the Childcare Act. The Rape Crisis

Centres and Women's Aid are better resourced now, and hopefully it did something towards that, too. I think there is more sympathy now, less of a tendency to say of a rape victim, "Oh well, she was wearing a short skirt, after all." But it takes a long time to change people's minds.'[8]

The government allocated £23 million towards implementation of the 1991 Childcare Act and £248,000 from lottery funds to the country's Rape Crisis Centres, a 90 per cent increase on the previous year. There was also £52,000 for the DRCC for education and training. This brought state funding for the Centre to £227,500. The Minister said the work of the Centres was 'vital'. The DRCC welcomed his 'swift response'.

The Kilkenny incest rapist was sentenced to seven years in jail, the maximum penalty available under the existing law. Part of the sentence was suspended. He would be released in just four years. The Justice Minister, Fianna Fáil's Máire Geoghegan Quinn, said there had been an unprecedented public response to the sentence and that she would convey the 'immense anger' expressed to the judiciary, though she favoured 'self regulation' rather than state-imposed reform on sentencing policy.

She also met with the young woman at the centre of the Kilkenny case and heard a plea from her for a longer sentence. The Minister told her that, while she favoured the availability of longer sentences, it was impossible to alter those already given. She said that when the new Criminal Justice Bill (1993) became law, the DPP would be able to go to the court of criminal appeal to have a sentence reviewed if it seemed unduly lenient.

In July 1993, following the earlier adjournment of sentence, Lavinia Kerwick heard Mr Justice Fergus Flood announce that he was not sending the young man who raped her to jail. He imposed a nine-year suspended sentence. A shocked Lavinia said she regretted ever reporting the rape. The DRCC joined in criticism of the sentence. However, columnist Sam Smyth claimed that 'those who encourage the young rape victim to become an emblem of wronged Irish women, a martyr for emancipation, want to offer up another sacrifice'.[9] The DRCC had, in fact, encouraged Kerwick to retreat from the public eye and concentrate on her own recovery. The chairwoman of the Council for the Status of Women, the late Anne Taylor, had also said, 'We want Lavinia to become a survivor instead of a victim, a model, not a martyr for women.'[10]

Nuala Fennell suggested that seminars on violence against women should be directed at men, to bring about a change of attitudes to women. The Irish Family League responded to her assertion that women had less freedom in 1993. 'Young people ... have been deprived of the moral guidance they received in the past,' wrote its honorary secretary, Mary Kennedy. The 'natural order' had beeen rejected. 'Boys and girls were warned not to go to lonely places together. If they were foolish enough to do so, they were ashamed to talk about it. This folly has been raised to heroine status by the feminists.'[11]

'Lavinia Kerwick cannot change history but she has changed the future,' Geoghegan Quinn told a seminar on Women and Safety at the garda training centre in Templemore in July 1993. She said Lavinia had been responsible for bringing about the fastest legal change the country had ever seen. Geoghegan Quinn also praised the 'very courageous woman' in the Kilkenny incest case, whose criticism of her father's sentence had led to the new law being amended to increase the maximum penalty for incest with a female aged between 15 and 17 to 20 years. In 1995 this was increased again to life imprisonment, under the Criminal Law (Incest Proceedings) Act.

Senior gardaí had already credited the two young Kilkenny women with prompting them to announce the setting up of a special unit in Dublin to investigate sex offences. The Domestic Violence and Sexual Assault Investigation Unit was established as part of the serious crimes squad and had a policy of referring victims to the DRCC and other agencies. In its first year, it dealt with almost 5,000 cases. The unit provided a protocol for gardaí outside Dublin and ran training courses.

The Minister praised Garda Agnes Reddy, who had played a crucial role in both the Lavina Kerwick case and the

Kilkenny incest case. She announced a new measure to prevent sex offenders harassing their victims from prison. This followed the revelation by the Kilkenny incest survivor that her father had been sending her abusive letters from Arbour Hill.[12] The Minister also described the new treatment programme for sex offenders which was to be introduced on a pilot basis at Arbour Hill prison. This was welcomed by the DRCC, which took part in the conference and would later make an input into the treatment programme. The Centre also once again called for 'community-based facilities for both the treatment of sex offenders and the monitoring of them following release from custody'.

The DRCC believed that it had made a further major breakthrough when the Minister for Justice declared that she supported its call for separate legal representation for the victim in a rape trial. In a statement, it said legal representation would give such women 'courage and confidence to go through with this harrowing procedure'. [13] However, separate legal representation has not, to date, been achieved.

'By the early 1990s we were in a lot of demand for training,' recalled Maeve Lewis. 'We were seen to have experience and expertise. We'd become part of the mainstream mental health services and we got huge recognition.' The Centre was training care workers, social workers, pastoral workers, psychiatric nurses, trainee counsellors, probation officers, teachers and parents – not just in Dublin, but all over the country. It provided training for other Rape Crisis Centres, too. Fees were charged – the education department was self-financing. After the outcry over the Kerwick and Kilkenny incest sentences, the DRCC revealed plans to train judges. 'Every professional needs to keep up to date with developments in their field,' said Olive Braiden. 'Judges are no different. Police, doctors and welfare workers all attend courses to get new information on rape and its effects. Judges are the only ones who don't, yet they have the final say in what happens to an offender, and, indirectly, to the victim.'[14] The DRCC was supported by the Bar Council, and by the Council for the Status of Women, which met the Minister for Justice to push for the training. In the senate, Mary Henry said that many judges lived 'fairly rarefied lives'. However, the judiciary has yet to take up the offer.

When Carmel Foley took over as head of the Employment Equality Agency in 1993, she revealed that the biggest cause of complaint from workers was sexual harassment. One woman, Maura, said of her experience: 'We went through the usual formalities, then, suddenly, the door was closed behind me and this repulsive old man with a Pioneer pin was kissing me all over my mouth ... I don't remember how I got him off, but I do remember that I then proceeded to interview him politely ... while at the same time measuring the distance between my chair and the door, wondering, how am I going to get out of here?

'When I got to the door, I shook his hand and he started feeling my breasts. I should have kneed him in the balls but instead I walked out, said "Cheerio" to the girls in reception and went back to work.' Maura found herself wiping her mouth with her hand as she spoke of these events. 'His lips were all wet and soggy – disgusting. I felt so unclean afterwards,' she said. There were further incidents, one of which scared Maura. She told a union representative and her boss. Both said she should make a complaint of sexual harassment. But she didn't. 'I feel I handled it all wrong,' she said. 'I did nothing. I was a young woman in a new job ... trying to prove her ability ... I was an outsider – he was a pillar of society. I was afraid people wouldn't believe me or that they would have said I must have encouraged him ... I was afraid my family would be ashamed ...'[15]

The DRCC was soon to provide powerful evidence of the need for legislation to outlaw such harassment. A study conducted by Fiona Tiernan for the Centre found that, despite a 1985 Labour Court ruling that sexual harassment was discrimination punishable by law, it was prevalent, and many businesses didn't know what to do about it. While 40 per cent of companies surveyed had received complaints from staff about sexual harassment, almost 90 per cent of companies had no training on how to deal with it, 50 per cent of companies had no policy to deal with it and 25 per cent didn't even know the law on it.

'In the main, women have suffered most from sexual harassment,' wrote Tiernan. 'It has many guises ... [and] if it is allowed to prevail it can often escalate ... to very serious sexual assaults.' International studies showed, she said, that most cases went unreported, most victims ended up resigning and many lost faith in their own abilities. The DRCC report, undertaken because the Centre had received a large number of calls from victims of sexual harassment, recommended that, while the government should introduce legislation to punish harassers, 'prevention is the best tool for eliminating' it, and employers had a responsibility to introduce policies to this end.[16]

Commenting on the survey, Olive Braiden said, 'It is clear Irish companies have little or no understanding of the seriousness of the problem.'[17] In a lecture to delegates at SIPTU's national women's forum, the DRCC's Grace O'Malley distinguished between sexual harassment and office flirtation – the former was sexual behaviour which was 'abrasive ... unwanted and unreciprocated', the latter 'freely and mutually entered into'. She said women were often too afraid to complain. Over 90 per cent of victims were female, she said, quoting British figures. O'Malley pointed out that in the US two out of three women soldiers said they had been subjected to sexual harassment, but in Ireland equality legislation didn't apply to the army, so women could not complain. 'Either we accept the unacceptable or we start educating and changing attitudes fast,' O'Malley said.[18]

The Centre ran training programmes for a range of companies, including the ESB, and in 1994 produced a training video presented by journalist Olivia O'Leary. This won an award from the Institute of Personnel and Development, presented by Richard Bruton in 1996. Accepting the award, Braiden described sexual harassment as a 'complex, soul-destroying problem' that was 'completely preventable'.[19]

The dynamic of sexual harassment was like that of rape, as were its effects. 'Harassment isn't about someone being carried away. It is about bullying and intimidation. It is about power,' said Carmel Foley.[20] And power was overwhelmingly in the hands of men. In 1993 there were just 20 women TDs out of 166, one of the worst rankings in the EC. No women were county or city managers, or county secretaries. Out of 77 government bodies, only 11 had reached the 40 per cent quota of minimal representation by women recommended by the Second Commission on the Status of Women.[21] The Equality and Law Reform Minister, Labour's Mervyn Taylor, appointed just one woman, his secretary, to his office, which had a staff of ten. A study of the gap between male and female salaries could not find enough women managing directors to provide an effective sample. However, it found that women managers were paid 19 per cent less than men.

The DRCC had always emphasised that the fear of rape inhibited women's freedom and was pervasive. In 1993 a man who became known as 'the Northside rapist' terrorised a whole community. Over a period of several months, the 'skeleton' rapist, reportedly a tall, thin young man with crop-ped blond hair, attacked and raped several women. The attacks happened in or around DART stations at Kilbarrack, Sutton and Howth. 'This is a crisis situation for a community – they must, and are, taking precautions. We are getting several calls a day from women who are worried and traumatised by this man,' said Olive Braiden. Some were women fearful for themselves and their daughters. Others were women whose memories of past rape experiences had been triggered. Women felt helpless, she said. One woman told a reporter that she was afraid but had to walk home alone from the station. 'I can't have a bodyguard with me all the time,' she said. A local man said his brother's life had been made a misery because he looked like the garda photofit of the rapist.

Local women did courses in self-defence, and some took to carrying aerosol cans and screwdrivers, though Braiden warned that weapons could be taken from the woman and used against them. 'Generally a rapist is stronger and he has planned what he is going to do,' she said. 'The woman is taken by surprise.' She urged women to report attacks to the gardaí. Once again, she challenged those urging women to stay at home. 'Women have had enough restrictions,' she said. 'Most victims are known to their attacker, and of course women are raped in their homes. At times like this, men would like to have a curfew for women. It would be much more realistic to have a curfew for men because the effect of that is that women would be safe.'

Gardaí warned women not to walk alone at night, but while one woman was attacked at 11.15 p.m., others were attacked in the morning on their way to work and another at three in the afternoon. Braiden said there was a risk that women would blame themselves for being attacked, because they had been warned.

In December 1993, Olive Braiden accompanied a 31-year-old Kildare woman to the Four Courts. The woman had alleged that a man had raped and beaten her. The man was her husband. It was the first marital rape case to come to court in Ireland, and there was considerable media interest. 'I was there to support the woman,' recalled Braiden. 'But it ended up causing a major hassle between me and Paul Carney.' After the case began, gardaí approached Braiden and asked her to leave. She refused. Michael McDowell, SC, representing the husband, objected to her presence, and Mr Justice Carney called her into the witness box to account for herself. 'I felt very strongly about it,' Braiden recalled. 'I said I was there to support the woman and I pointed out that her father and brother had both died in tragic circumstances and she was alone and without support. I said the legislation allows the woman to have someone there with her. Carney sent out for the Act. I was allowed to stay.'

However, the Centre's troubles were far from over in the case. 'I have noted that the Rape Crisis Centre has shown in the past an indifference to truth,' Mr Justice Paul Carney told the Central Criminal Court. His comment was widely reported. It was a reference to a previous case in which three young girls had been raped and abused more than 400 times.

The Centre had criticised Mr Justice Carney, alleging that he had claimed in his summing up that the girls were 'mentally unscathed'. The comment had in fact been made by the prosecution barrister and was quoted by Carney.

During the marital rape trial, the fact that the woman had been unfaithful to her husband with several men was established. Counsel for the DPP said her morals were not the issue. 'The wide spectrum, from the harlot to the celibate nun, are entitled to protection under the law,' he said. A husband had no right to use his wife as a 'chattel', he said. After a three-day hearing, the jury unanimously acquitted the accused. Mr Justice Carney warned at the conclusion of the case that while 'temperate criticism' was acceptable, he would 'deal severely' with anyone who misrepresented him or the proceedings.

Afterwards, Braiden said the Centre accepted the verdict. She appealed for the woman in the case to be left alone. 'The trial shows the particular difficulties for women in marital rape cases. Where a consensual sexual relationship has existed there are major problems in establishing the withdrawal of that consent.'[22] 'We sincerely hope that this will not discourage women from reporting rape within marriage.' The man who had been cleared of the rapes said he had been through 'hell' and asked to be left alone. Some members of his family called on the government to stop funding the Rape Crisis Centre.[23]

The *Sunday Independent* ran a two-page spread heavily criticising the DRCC. In what Gemma Hussey described as a 'savage attack', Senator Shane Ross said the Centre was tainted. It had departed from its 'fine original aims' and its role of 'comforting victims' and was 'indulging in an anti-male crusade', 'spreading … politically correct disease' and 'putting pressure on a courageous judiciary'. Agony aunt Patricia Redlich said 'feminism in the form of Olive Braiden of the Rape Crisis Centre was involved in the whole sordid proceedings' and that 'a charge of rape within marriage … where there is no physical or psychological violence, is not realistic'. Another writer said feminists had 'cynically attempted to appropriate rape as a political weapon'.[24]

Responding in a letter to the *Sunday Independent*, Braiden and Hussey wrote that the DRCC had 'always appreciated that its work is difficult, sensitive and often controversial'. Accompanying women to court was one of the services it offered: 'It is not our role to sit in judgment on the merits of a case.' Far from being 'anti-man', the Centre provided counselling and support for male victims of rape and sexual abuse. The letter even pointed out that the majority of its board of directors were men and spelled out the board's impeccably respectable credentials.[25]

Mary Corcoran wrote that she hoped the DRCC wouldn't be intimidated. Its role 'should indeed stretch far beyond victim support' to include changing attitudes and the law. Certain journalists were 'using strange propaganda' to 'create hostile reaction to anything remotely labeled "feminist"'. It was not the work of the DRCC that should be called into disrepute, she said, 'but the behaviour and attitudes of many men and the mainstream of Irish culture that should be challenged'.[26] The Galway Rape Crisis Centre said it was angry about media coverage of the case and that women might be discouraged from reporting rape or seeking help from Rape Crisis Centres. The board was worried about the hostility expressed towards the Centre, and Braiden recalled it as a 'shaky time'. 'After that, I didn't go to court,' she said. 'I was too obvious with my red hair – and my orange coat. I didn't want my being there to draw attention to the person I was accompanying. Victims were always fearful of being recognised.'[27] The DRCC revealed that it had been contacted by 37 women in 1993 seeking help as a result of marital rape.

15

FROM STAY SAFE TO FR BRENDAN SMYTH

'Say no! Get away! Tell someone!' These were the simple messages taught to children as part of the Stay Safe programme. The programme had its opponents: 'Children are being told to tell teachers if anyone interferes with them, even if it is their father. This is a direct attack on parental responsibility,' said Dr William Coulson, speaking at a meeting to oppose Stay Safe.[1]

When psychiatrist Dr Maria Lawlor and psychologist Deirdre MacIntyre were planning the programme in 1990, they were very clear about what they wanted it to achieve. 'We were seeing so many people ending up into residential psychiatric treatment with huge problems as a result of child sexual abuse,' said Lawlor. 'If kids knew to tell, and to keep telling until someone helps them, the damage can be stopped at an earlier stage. Hopefully, there will also be kids who won't be abused at all, because they will know how to say no.'[2] The programme, which taught 'simple strategies for dealing with potentially dangerous situations', was piloted on over 1,000 national-school children, and 97 per cent of parents declared themselves satisfied with it. One of the recommendations of the Kilkenny incest report was that the programme, introduced in the EHB region in 1991, should be implemented across the nation, a proposal supported by the Rape Crisis Centre.

A former Irish international swimmer who alleged that he was abused by the Irish Olympic swimming coach, George Gibney, called for the introduction of a Stay Safe type scheme. It emerged that sex abuse by coaches was rife amongst young Irish swimmers.[3]

Holy Ghost priest Fr Brian Gogan wrote that it was based on feminist morality and 'was not suitable for use in Catholic schools'. He argued that it could damage childhood innocence and undermine trust between parents and children.[4] His pamphlet opposing Stay Safe was distributed to Catholic schools. After a stormy *Late Late Show* debate on Stay Safe, one woman wrote to the *Irish Independent* asserting that such programmes had already led in many parts of the world to 'a tremendous rise in crime, addictions of every kind, venereal disease, as well as child abuse'.[5] Conservative philosophy lecturer Dr Gerard Casey suggested that it represented 'social engineering".[6] Parents Against Stay Safe (PASS) groups were set up and schools using the programme were threatened with legal action. PASS claimed that reports of child abuse were 'grossly exaggerated'. This, according to columnist Fintan O'Toole, was 'the unacceptable face of fundamentalism'.[7]

O'Toole pointed out that Gogan's arguments relied heavily on the work of an American Lutheran cleric, Dr Ralph Underwager. He quoted an extraordinary interview in which Underwager claimed that 'paedophiles can boldly and courageously affirm what they choose. They can say that what they want is to find the best way to love.' Underwager denounced 'child sexuality hysteria', which was fuelled by female jealousy of 'male bonding and paedophile sex'. O'Toole acknowledged that Gogan had repudiated Underwager's views on paedophilia, but demonstrated that his booklet relied heavily on Underwager's work. Gogan also claimed Stay Safe 'coincides with the intentions of' paedophile groups.[8] Responding to O'Toole, Gogan said Stay Safe could 'weaken children's defences against a skilful abuser' and could 'provide an early introduction to a permissive (pansexual) approach to sexuality'. He said parents should decide how to protect their children.[9] At this time, Bishop Jeremiah Newman of Limerick declared that 'extremist' feminists were leading an 'anti-family revolution'.[10] Kieran McGrath, then editor of *The Irish Social Worker*, joined the debate, quoting a US review of one of Underwager's books which said it appeared to have been written for lawyers defending those accused of child sex abuse.[11]

Eddie Hernon, chairman of the Accused Parents Aid Group (APAG), wrote to defend the book. 'Dr Underwager is recognised as one of the foremost experts on child sexual abuse, and as such he is gravely concerned by the epidemic of false accusations now sweeping the world,' he wrote.[12]

Hernon was incensed when the US state department used Dublin DRCC statistics in its annual report on human rights around the world. The report quoted the DRCC's 1992 annual report, which revealed that 5,009 calls had been received. It concluded that violence against women in Ireland was 'serious'.[13] Hernon said the fact that the 'land of saints and scholars' was now regarded as 'a country of paedophiles, child sexual abusers, perverts and wife batterers' showed that 'the seeds sown by the "experts"… are now bearing fruition'. He said 'grossly inflated figures' had been 'bandied about', including the 5,000 'alleged' cases of rape reported to the DRCC in 1994. Had these been reported to the gardaí? 'If not, perhaps the DRCC will tell us why not.' In 1993, there were 143 allegations of rape made to the gardaí and just seven convictions. There were 14 alleged incest cases and just one conviction. A 'far cry,' he said, from 5,000. He reminded readers that the DRCC had been accused of falsifying figures in the past.[14]

As a spokesman for Victims Of Child Abuse Laws (VOCAL) Ireland, Hernon condemned in its newsletter 'quacks and zealots' who traumatised families 'in order to keep the child sex abuse industry' going.[15] Hernon was not just concerned with cases involving allegations of sexual abuse. In 1993 APAG accused the media of 'crucifying' the parents of 15-year-old Kelly Fitzgerald, who died after a visit to her parents, who were living in Co. Mayo. When she arrived back in London on a flight from Knock, she was emaciated, in a wheelchair and couldn't speak. The case caused outrage. In 1994, her parents were convicted of cruelty and neglect and sentenced to 18 months in prison. It emerged that Kelly had been on an 'at risk' register while in their care in London.

Stay Safe was working. In January 1995, a 56-year-old Dublin man was convicted of sexually assaulting two 11-year-old girls and jailed for 21 months. The girls revealed that the father of one of their classmates had interfered with them while they were at his house visiting their friend. They told their parents what had happened, after participating in the programme at school. By 1995, less than 2 per cent of schools in the Dublin area were refusing to use it, while less than 5 per cent were refusing to use it in the rest of the country.

'Resistance to Stay Safe was concentrated in areas with a very strong Catholic ethos,' recalled Deirdre MacIntyre. 'But the programme demonstrably worked – it made a significant difference in terms of children telling about abuse. When you'd hear it come up in court cases that was very encouraging. It has become part of the school furniture now. It is no longer controversial.' She said the Rape Crisis Centre's role was pivotal. 'Our awareness about the sexual abuse of children came out of our awareness of the sexual abuse of women, and our awareness of that came from the Rape Crisis Centre. They woke the country up.'[16]

In June 1994, Fr Brendan Smyth was convicted in a Belfast court of 17 charges of child sex abuse against five girls and three boys. The offences spanned 20 years and dated back to the 1960s. The 67-year-old Catholic priest was shown on the television news walking into the court. Watching the news while preparing dinner for her partner and children, one Belfast woman saw the man who had abused her 25 years earlier. She had kept silent, and the secret had almost destroyed her life. Now she decided to act. She went to the RUC, and she went to a journalist, Chris Moore. 'It was,' Moore later wrote, 'the first link in a chain which would stretch all around Ireland, to

Scotland, Wales and even across the Atlantic to the United States.'[17]

Moore's investigation into Smyth's career, *Suffer Little Children*, was shown on UTV in the autumn. He revealed that the Norbertine order, which had educated Smyth as a boy and which he had joined in 1945, had known for decades that he 'had a problem with children'. He may have first begun his abuses when he was a student in Rome. Ordained in 1951, he returned to Kilnacrott and the Norbertine abbey. Local parents were impressed by the activities he organised for children. In fact, he was using them as cover for beating and sexually assaulting boys and girls. Parents complained – the abbot sent him off to Scotland. He was sent back, under a cloud, and continued his 'work' in Ireland. He was exposed again, got sent to Wales and later to the US. Local bishops were not told of his sexual proclivities. Ordered out by an American bishop, he was placed by his order in Belfast, where he continued to abuse.

In the 1960s another Norbertine priest had tried to get the order to act to stop Smyth. A decree was issued stating that he was to be confined to the abbey. It was ignored. From time to time, as his activities came to light, the church authorities sent him for treatment. He always resumed his sexual crimes. Then, in 1990, a family, several members of which he had abused, reported Smyth to the RUC.

In 1991, Smyth was charged and released on bail. The Norbertines sent him to work as a chaplain in hospitals in Tralee and Cork, without mentioning the charges. Smyth refused the RUC's repeated requests to return to the North, and, eventually, in 1993, the first of nine extradition warrants was issued. The Republic's office of the Attorney General didn't process these. Finally, in 1994, Smyth returned voluntarily to Belfast and the trial proceeded.

Within weeks of the screening of Moore's explosive documentary, Labour Ministers in the Fianna Fáil–Labour coalition government resigned, and the government collapsed. This followed a protracted row about the failure of the Attorney General's office to extradite the paedophile priest, and the fact that the Taoiseach, Albert Reynolds, had since made the Attorney General president of the High Court.

The DRCC reacted angrily when Whelehan said that the Smyth file hadn't been regarded as urgent. 'A statement such as this, coming from the highest legal office in the country, is disturbing, in that it reflects, unfortunately, the level of consideration which is given to victims of rape and sexual abuse within the judicial system,' Grace O'Malley said. 'Such statements will ensure that the level of reporting remains low – less than 30 per cent – and gives the impression that our judicial system protects the perpetrators of such crimes, rather than their victims, mainly women and children.'[18] She called for the immediate, full implementation of the recommendations in the Kilkenny incest report. 'How many more scandals must be exposed before action is taken?' she demanded. Olive Braiden said it was time for those in public office to 'face up to the reality of child sexual abuse and the recidivist nature of it'. She said the DRCC had worked for years to raise awareness about child abuse. The Smyth case and the 'deplorable' delay in dealing with the warrants showed how serious the problem was, and also 'how hard it is for victims to get justice'. All public offices had to 'put their houses in order', she said.[19]

While the political controversy raged, calls to the Rape Crisis Centre doubled. The monthly average number of new calls at that time was 170 – in November 1994 it rose to 372. Almost four out of five of the calls (77 per cent) were about child sexual abuse, which had previously accounted for 63 per cent. Clergy were responsible for 16 per cent of cases of abuse of males, but just 3 per cent of females. Grace O'Malley revealed that many of the callers had been abused by priests or teachers, including Smyth. Before the Smyth revelations, the Centre was already handling four calls a month on clerical abuse. That month it took 68 such calls. One man was 80. He had never spoken to anyone about what a priest had done to him when he was a ten-year-old child.

'It was tragic really,' one man told journalist Alison O'Connor. 'I survived it but a lot of other kids wouldn't have done.' The man had been repeatedly abused by Smyth in the 1950s, when he was 11. 'As a child that age brought up in a very Catholic environment, I was in awe of him. I was exploited through sheer ignorance and blind faith.' He had repressed his memories. He was living in Australia when he read details of the Smyth controversy. He was angry. He had ceased to be a Catholic.[20]

A woman abused in the 1970s told her story on RTÉ radio. The 'monster', as she called Smyth, had visited her in hospital when she was small. Then he began to come to her home. Her parents were 'delighted that this kind man had come to visit their daughter'. He regularly interfered with her and made her masturbate him. He was always welcomed by the nuns at her boarding school, and once he left semen stains on her uniform. The head nun beat her and humiliated her in front of the class. 'I could hardly tell her the monster had done it, for fear of getting slapped again.' She tried to kill herself with overdoses and by swallowing needles. She felt dirty and that no one could love her. She felt 'utter horror' and guilt when she learned that Smyth had abused others after her. She had gone to the gardaí and encouraged others to do the same. 'It will be hard for us all but if we support each other we can rid ourselves of this monster which [sic] has been lying dormant for so many years and has been the root of our troubles,' she said. 'Death would be too sweet for him.'[21]

The then Catholic cardinal, Cathal Daly, insisted he had been unaware of the disgraced priest's history, and that he had no jurisdiction over him. He admitted meeting his abbot for a talk about Smyth after the RUC had begun investigating him. Dozens of complaints of abuse by priests were pending. It emerged that the Church had established a committee of bishops in 1990 to look into abuse by clerics. After Smyth, it promised an interim report in 1994. The DRCC agreed to advise the committee but Olive Braiden stressed that 'our first responsibility must be to the victim'.[22] A subcommittee was set up within the Centre to look at the issues. The board agreed that caution was required: 'It is vital that we maintain our own independence while dealing with the bishops' committee,' it noted. 'We cannot give them answers to their problems.'[23]

An RTÉ *Tuesday File* documentary broadcast in 1994 revealed that the Church was still in denial. While there were admissions that 'mistakes were made', bishops and other clerics continued to cite canon law to excuse inaction. One man abused by a religious brother told the programme that when he told a priest about it in confession, the priest did the same thing to him. 'That school was a paedophile's hunting ground,' he said.[24] The DRCC ran a special helpline after the programme. After Gay Byrne interviewed some of Smyth's victims on his morning radio show around this time, the Centre took 77 extra calls in one day.

In 1997, when Smyth had served his sentence in the North, he was brought to court in Dublin where he pleaded guilty to a further 74 charges of indecent assault on children, the most recent of them in 1993. He died in jail later that year and was buried, under cover of darkness, at Kilnacrott. 'Why did he die a priest?' asked one of his victims.[25]

'We are absolutely horrified.' This was Olive Braiden's reaction to the decision, in March 1995, by the Court of Criminal Appeal to reduce the sentence of the man convicted of raping the girl in the X case. Originally sentenced to two periods of seven years to run consecutively, the appeal court reduced this to two periods of four years to run concurrently. Judge Hugh O'Flaherty said the case had been a tragedy of 'epic proportions' – for all sides. However, while the court must impose a sentence commensurate with the crime, it must also hold out some possibility of 'hope and redemption' for the man. The girl who was raped and made pregnant by the man was devastated. She and her family heard the news on the radio. In a statement they said they rejected the judgment. If the man had suffered 'grievously', as the judges believed, 'it was him who brought suffering to all concerned', they said.[26]

O'Flaherty said the appeal court, consisting of three men, had reviewed 50 cases of unlawful carnal knowledge which had been before the Irish courts between 1987 and 1993. In only three cases were there sentences at the level of seven years, and one of the longer ones was reduced on appeal. This case was not 'out and out rape'. There were 'no circumstances of force or duress'. This was a 'good family man'. Braiden said the original sentence had not been excessive. The girl had suffered so much and for so long, she said: 'What message is this giving to children and young girls who are raped and become pregnant?'[27]

Braiden also pointed out that the man had only pleaded guilty at a very late stage, after a DNA test on his blood proved that he had made the girl pregnant. 'He left this young victim to believe she would have to give evidence to the court,' she said. 'He also implicated a young man who was questioned and who suffered severely because of this.' His remorse was declared only when he knew he would be found guilty: 'That's not really remorse,' she said.[28] Braiden said that if what happened to the girl was not legally defined as rape, 'then the law will have to be changed because a child cannot consent to intercourse, so it is rape'.[29] Braiden said many young women awaiting trials would be left wondering if it was worth going through the whole procedure. Political columnist Dick Walsh wrote that the Irish justice system was 'still steeped in the shoddiest of Victorian values'.[30] Nuala O'Faolain concluded a passionate rejection of the judgment with the declaration: 'Four years! There is not a woman in the country thinks that just.'[31]

However, Mary Kennedy of the Irish Family League wrote that while there was abuse of trust, and she didn't condone the behaviour of the man, the girl had been 'involved in sexual incidents' with him. Rape was 'not involved', she said. 'Why did she stay there or return after the incidents?' she demanded. 'In the past youth were taught about "occasions of sin" and were warned to avoid lonely places with a member of the opposite sex,' she stated. RTÉ, with its 'preoccupation with sex', along with the 'contraceptive lobby' and sex education, had led young people away from 'moral virtues'.[32] Efforts to introduce sex education into secondary schools were, in fact, at this time, meeting strong resistance. Family Solidarity, meanwhile, said the case showed the return of 'the calm of reason' and that the Supreme Court should now reconsider its original decision in the X case.[33] Patricia Redlich, writing in the *Sunday Independent*, denounced the 'lynch mob' and claimed that the sentence for the man in the X case 'should be influenced by the fact that he was a businessman with a very real stake in this society, for whom any prison sentence for a sexual offence was something akin to a social death blow'.[34]

In the week preceding the X-case appeal judgment, a Donegal newspaper carried a letter from a member of a 'pro-life' group, criticising the funding of a regional Rape Crisis Centre. Several newspapers carried pictures of a 13-year-old model who was described as 'a catwalk kitten' who was 'flaunting her schoolgirl sexuality'. Her photograph appeared on one front page beside a report of a man who had raped his stepdaughters, who were aged between 8 and 13. The judge said of the man, 'He lived in a world of total unreality, with longstanding psycho-sexual difficulties.' In another case, a man who pleaded guilty to raping an 11-year-old Portlaoise girl was given a suspended sentence. An 11-year-old Cork girl who had been raped was revealed to be pregnant.

In the same week a dead baby was found in a bucket in Co. Kildare. The abortion information bill was passed in the Dáil, but the Fine Gael Minister for Health, Michael Noonan, said he had 'no intention' of legislating on the 'substantive issue' of abortion which had emerged in the X case. 'This is a country where leering at "catwalk kittens" is permissible, where rape may go unpunished, where helping women and girls to end crisis pregnancies is forbidden,' this author wrote. 'A land where dead babies in buckets, ditches and grottos will continue to be found. A land of unreality and psycho-sexual difficulties.'[35] This was not to be the end of the violent career of the X-case man.

In the angry aftermath of the X-case sentence, the Rape Crisis Centre and Women's Aid, along with the Council for the Status of Women, met with Justice Minister Nora Owen. They urged her to fund a working group to look into matters arising from the case and threatened to send a report to the UN rapporteur on women's affairs if progress was not made. The CSW agreed to set up the group, and Owen agreed to fund it. After the meeting, Olive Braiden said there was a gulf between the attitude of many judges and that of the public. The under-reporting of rape and child sex abuse was due in part to the fear on the part of the victim that she or he would not get a fair hearing. That fear was understandable, she said.[36]

After her office Christmas party on 22 December 1995, Marilyn Rynn, a 41-year-old civil servant, caught the Nitelink bus from O'Connell Street to Blanchardstown, then took a shortcut through Tolka Valley park. The alternative would have involved walking along a lonely road. She never reached her home. After a lengthy search, her body was found 16 days later, in undergrowth in the park. She had been raped and strangled. She had struggled fiercely for her life. 'This crime has affected Irish women very deeply,' said Olive Braiden. 'We have so many people on to us ... Marilyn Rynn was very mature, sensible, strong, used to living alone and used to being on her own. Women who are like that now feel deeply threatened by what happened to her ... This murder is indicative of the lack of respect towards women. We really need to have some public debate about that, that will force us to look at the inequalities,' she told Pat Kenny on his RTÉ radio show.

She said she accepted there was no way to make Ireland 100 per cent safe for women. 'But that doesn't mean women should stay locked in their houses. We must remember that the majority of women are raped by somebody they know and trust. So a woman is not necessarily safe in her own home. Women are raped at every hour of the day ... We shouldn't put all the responsibility back on women to protect themselves from males. Why should one half of the population be afraid of the other half?'[37]

There was ample recent evidence for her assertions. Joyce Quinn was also raped and murdered in January 1996. She was abducted as she left the shop she ran in Co. Kildare. In the North, an 85-year-old woman died after being raped by an intruder. In the Republic, the late Veronica Guerin reported that Imelda Riney had been raped in her home on the morning of her disappearance. She and her little son, Liam, were abducted and killed along with a local priest, Fr Joe Walsh. Troubled local youth Brendan O'Donnell was convicted of their murders. A Dublin man raped his 68-year-old mother at their home. The Central Criminal Court heard that he, his siblings and his mother had been the victims of his violent father in the past.

Women's Aid released figures in late 1995 revealing that they had received 8,000 calls that year. After the bishops asked priests to address the issue of domestic violence in their homilies, several north Dublin priests invited Women's Aid director Roisin Mac Dermott to speak at mass. She spoke about physical, sexual and mental abuse, of rape, poverty, shame and hopelessness. She said society had created a silence and a stigma. She was applauded. Braiden was critical of the Church's attitudes to violence against women. 'Church teachings have encouraged men to be more violent towards women,' she said. 'Catholics are taught that women are subordinate to men and women are told by the church that they must obey their fathers and husbands ... Violent husbands and boyfriends think they have a right to beat women. Rape victims find they are asked to forgive and forget before they have even begun to cope with what has happened to them.'[38]

In the *Sunday Independent*, however, Patricia Redlich ridiculed the feminist response to violence against women, as epitomised by what Braiden had said about Marilyn Rynn. 'Hidebound by ideology, she missed the whole point,' she said. 'It doesn't help to talk about rights. What we have to do is talk about the kind of society we would like to have.'[39] In 1997 a neighbour of Marilyn Rynn was convicted of her murder. At the time it was the most significant use of DNA in a criminal investigation in Ireland and led to calls for the establishment of a DNA database. This has yet to be established. Also in 1997 a young man in his twenties was convicted of murdering Joyce Quinn. The court heard that he had raped his victim, 'who may have been dead at the time'.[40]

Talking about social change and how to bring it about had

always been central to the DRCC's work. January of 1996 had also seen the suicide of 24-year-old Imelda Hartford from north Dublin. She left a note revealing that she had been raped by a family friend at the age of 13, and for ten years thereafter. She had made several suicide attempts during that period. 'He has taken my life away from me and because of that I will never be as happy as I was before,' she wrote. 'What he did will stay in my mind for the rest of my life. I won't forgive or forget ... I hope he rots in hell.'[41] Commenting on the tragic case, Olive Braiden said, 'The surprise is that more people who have suffered as she did, do not decide to end their deeply painful lives. The country has been made tragically aware, during 1995, of sexual violence, particularly as it affects children, yet ambivalent attitudes still exist at every level of the community. Raising awareness is vital.'[42] By May 1996, ten women had been murdered in Ireland, six of them in their own homes. During one four-day period, three women were killed.

'I was on duty the night of *Dear Daughter*,' recalled Mary de Courcy, now a private psychotherapist. A former teacher, she had joined the DRCC as a volunteer in 1995. On 22 February 1996 RTÉ showed Louis Lentin's powerful documentary about Christine Buckley's childhood in Goldenbridge, an orphanage run by the Sisters of Mercy at Inchicore in Dublin. Christine had been abandoned as a baby and spent her child-hood in a series of orphanages. She was 13 when she arrived at Goldenbridge in the late 1940s. Her name was taken from her on admission – she was to be known as No. 89. In *Dear Daughter* she told of beatings and scaldings, constant humiliation and extreme cruelty from the nuns. Other former residents told similar stories. 'We got to the stage that it was so horrific we couldn't believe it was happening,' Buckley said. 'It was the only way we could survive.'[43]

The Sisters of Mercy apologised, though the nun who had been in charge, Sister Xavieria, later claimed that the pro-gramme had exaggerated things. Although there were no allegations of sexual abuse in the programme, the order, through the Conference of Religious of Ireland (CORI), had asked the Rape Crisis Centre to co-operate with them in setting up a phone counselling service to take calls after it was shown.

'There was an enormous response to the programme, with eight crisis lines open on the night,' according to the minutes of the DRCC's board. The lines were staffed by DRCC volunteers and one staff member for six days. After that, two counsellors, recruited by the DRCC on behalf of the nuns, took over, paid for by the Sisters of Mercy. 'They asked for an ongoing involvement but we cannot afford the staff time,' the minutes noted.[44]

There was also an upsurge in calls from men when the DRCC staffed a helpline after a groundbreaking RTÉ documentary on male rape, in which men gave harrowing accounts of being raped and abused. One man described how many people tried to get him to 'push it back down'. 'If they only knew what it's like to be told to forget about it,' he said.[45]

Finding staff time was all the more difficult, not least because staff were leaving. 'I came in as part of a training group of 24,' said Mary de Courcy. 'Twelve of us were accepted and only five stayed for any length of time. There was a time when it seemed like there was just hardly anyone there. There were so many clients the Centre could only offer six sessions of counselling, and they had to keep closing the waiting lists.' One senior member of staff said when she was leaving that therapists were 'not valued'.

Joan White, now a therapist who does supervision work for the Centre, had joined as a volunteer in 1989 and became a full-time telephone counsellor soon afterwards. 'I think the conflict in the Centre has a huge amount to do with the fact that we were working in the context of destruction and annihilation. You'd see the destruction of a beautiful woman's sexuality, sometimes permanently. You'd get full of rage and disbelief.

'But often people go in there as clients and are transformed. You take a wee 17-year-old girl who's been raped and through the counselling she has to find new levels of understanding of herself. She comes out bigger. It is a crucible. For the counsellors, there is the longing and need to believe that there is good in the world. You require a lot of your leaders and if you feel let down by them, there's dreadful disappointment and anger which gets directed at others around you.'

Mary de Courcy agreed. 'The shadow of the violence was all pervasive. People were working with ugly, dark stuff. If that has nowhere to go it gets channelled into potentially destructive behaviour. It taps into things inside yourself. I remember feeling sicker and sicker and I couldn't find the words to talk about it. The Centre has become more aware of needing to protect people from what they are hearing. There is a price – there is one call in particular that I took that I will never forget. But there are huge benefits, too. I don't regret for a moment working there. The Centre is very alive – it is open to everything.'

'Olive was nice to us volunteers – though we didn't see much of her. She'd waft past, dressed in flowing orange. She let us use the money we earned from talks to run workshops on subjects like dreams and art therapy. It was obvious to us when there were storms going on in the background. You'd see therapists going about glowering.' 'Psychologically,' said Joan, 'Olive was very powerful. She had a steeliness.' Mary agreed. 'She was hated and reviled and loved,' she said. Another long-time worker at the Centre felt that Braiden had kept other workers on too tight a rein. 'You had wonderful, passionate, articulate people there, but they were silenced,' she said. 'Some amazing women got lost along the way and didn't fulfil their potential.'

Grace O'Malley was deputy director at this time and director during Braiden's four-month leave of absence while she stood as Fianna Fáil's candidate in the European elections of 1994. Unsuccessful in the elections, Braiden returned to the Centre, after declaring that she was not a member of Fianna Fáil. 'Olive and I were the management team,' said O'Malley. 'In retrospect, some of our work practices weren't good. We gave short term contracts, we changed people's work practices at short notice …' Mary de Courcy felt that some of the tension arose inevitably because of the old issue of running an organisation which includes volunteers and paid workers. 'Olive was very impressed by the altruism of the volunteers,' she recalled. 'She sort of expected altruism from the therapists as well, but naturally enough, they didn't see it that way. It was their job.'

Braiden said the volunteers were the 'backbone' of the Centre. 'They could stay a year and then sign up for another year, but after that people could get burned out. They could be taking 40 calls a night after a TV programme. We had a ceremony for volunteers who were leaving. We had a dinner and we presented them with a beautiful silver brooch designed by Emma Stuart Liberty, based on the Centre's logo, the unravelling of trauma.' The therapists were equally crucial, Braiden said. 'We were delving into deep, dark waters. It was work for highly skilled professionals.'

Geraldine Connolly joined the Centre in 1995 as an education and training worker, left in 1997 for a year and returned in 1998 as director of clinical services, a position she held until she left in 2003. 'There are particular problems in a voluntary organisation that has become professional,' she said. 'Organisationally, the DRCC hadn't made the transition fully. There were vestiges of thinking that belonged in a voluntary group – working all hours, not having salaries commensurate with experience and qualifications … workers end up feeling exploited.

'I was very determined that anyone working as a therapist in the Centre had to be a fully qualified psychotherapist with at least two years' post-qualification experience, with supervision. Our clients deserved no less. By this stage, a lot of people who could afford it were going to private therapists. Many of our clients were from the lower socio-economic groups.' Over the years, she said, a huge expertise and skill had been built up in the Centre. 'There was also a sense of camaraderie, and a passionate commitment to the work that is very rare in the modern world.' She didn't socialise with other staff and management; she said: 'I didn't feel it was appropriate to have particular friends.'

Connolly set about negotiating large pay increases for the

counsellors and therapists. 'I had come in myself on a short-term contract and low pay. It was a legacy of the days when there was no money – I was determined that salaries were going to be equal to those paid in the health board. It took long negotiations, but by 2001 therapists had got substantial pay increases. Not that we found it easy to get staff – people saw the work as "heavy". People who had worked as volunteers sometimes trained and came back as workers – there's always been great loyalty to the Centre.'

Some women involved or formerly involved in rape crisis work have misgivings about the direction taken by the DRCC. Some RCCs still use the collective model and most train their own counsellors. 'Rape Crisis Centres need to maintain a strong feminist vision,' said one former RCC worker. 'There's pressure to conform to a more conventional model of service provision to get funds, but we must remain radical and challenging.'

The board of the DRCC was, by the mid-1990s, concerned with giving it a fresh image. 'We wanted to raise the profile and to create a sense of openness and caring,' said board member Neil McIvor, who left in 2000.[46] 'We wanted people to see the faces of those involved. We weren't abandoning the campaigning side, but we wanted to stress the soft, client level of what we were about.' A public relations company was hired. From then on, DRCC annual reports were large and glossy and featured photographs of white lilies strewn about and studio photographs of staff, volunteers and board members. The stark feminist symbol that used to be the DRCC's logo became a soft, Celtic-looking swirl – the 'unravelling of trauma', in Braiden's description of the silver brooch.

'But the trouble is, you can change an image but if you haven't the resources to sell it, it isn't much use,' said McIvor. 'Rape is a sensitive issue – and for that very reason the Rape Crisis Centre should be up on walls and in every bus and train. But we had to go cap in hand to the government for our bit of funding. Rape is hugely prevalent in this society and what is worse is the way we ignore it. We have male-dominated politics. There aren't many votes in it. We are still in denial. It is a deep-seated part of our culture.'[47]

16

RAISING PROFOUNDLY SILENCED VOICES

'The most profoundly silenced voices in the justice system are those of ... victims of sexual and other violent crimes,' according to the report of the working group set up after the 'intense public outrage' over the X-case judgment, published in October 1996. This formidable group included Olive Braiden, Anne Marie Gill, chief executive of the National Women's Council (the renamed CSW), Roisin Mac Dermott of Women's Aid, Bridín Twist, president of the Irish Countrywomen's Association, and Mary Ellen Ring of the Irish Council for Civil Liberties. It was chaired by Ailbhe Smyth, director of the Women's Education and Resource Centre at UCD. Group member Grainne Healy of the NWC remembered Braiden's participation: 'She was very shrewd, very sharp, very strategic – very impressive.'

The X case was the last straw, but the group's concerns were 'the cumulative result of almost two decades of decisions and commentaries from the courts reflecting at best mis-understanding of the nature of sexually abusive crimes against women and children'. The report included personal accounts of bad experiences of the justice system. One woman who reported ten years of abuse by her father and brother said of her failed attempts to have them prosecuted, 'Slowly but surely my life shattered in front of my face and became unbearable.' Another said the reason she was not bitter after a similar experience of the system was, 'I've had so much self-development through counselling that it would only hurt me to be bitter.'

The report credited feminist activism and research with naming the issues. 'Men's violence is not simply about individual incidents and individual men,' it said. 'It is central to the maintenance and reinforcement of patriarchal relations of power.' There was profound denial about its prevalence. It would be eradicated only 'through massive transformation' of society. The traditionally dominant position of men, the sanctity of the family and women's economic and social dependency had to be challenged, as did the construction of masculinity as aggressive and femininity as passive.

It cited research describing society's simultaneous 'prohibition and promotion' of men's violence. Public condemnation was accompanied by 'systemic reluctance' to attribute responsibility, dispense sanctions, develop preventative strategies and provide adequate services and supports for the victims of the violence. Braiden was quoted: 'Society colludes with the minimisation of sexual crimes ... Ambivalent attitudes towards women who are sexually assaulted continue to exist at all levels of society.' The report noted that 'justice is dispensed and administered overwhelmingly by men'. Women comprised just over 6 per cent of the gardaí, concentrated in the lower echelons of the force. Just 12.5 per cent of judges were women.

The report commented that sexual violence was increasingly extensively covered in the Irish newspapers. It analysed headlines such as one broadsheet's 'Sinister Crime Monster Stalks the Land' over a report on the rape and murder of Joyce Quinn. 'Violence against women is not extraordinary but everyday,' said the report, 'and those who perpetrate it are "ordinary" men.' Reporting on the trial of Michael Bambrick in 1996, a tabloid referred to one of the women he murdered as 'pretty Patricia McGauley' and the other as 'Sex Monster's lesbian lover'. The report criticised also the 'salacious' detail with which the women's deaths were described. (Bambrick had cut up the women's bodies and buried them.) There was sexist stereotyping, sensationalism and the description of serious crimes as 'domestic disputes'.

RCC figures were analysed. In 1979, it received 76 calls. In 1995, it received over 6,000. Of the 2,864 first-time calls included in this figure, 46 per cent concerned rape and 54 per cent child sexual abuse. Women were 83 per cent of those calling. Less than 30 per cent of the rapes were reported to the gardaí. From 1986 to 1991, 493 rapes were reported to gardaí. There was a 7 per cent conviction rate. There were no national statistics available on child sexual abuse.

The report called for a standing committee to be established to collect and monitor statistics, along with a national study on all forms of male violence against women and children, with particular reference to, among others, traveller women and prostitutes. It called for training for professionals, including judges, with an input from Rape Crisis Centres and Women's Aid.

It recommended that the 1990 Rape Act be amended to include penetration of the anus by an object. Where consent was an issue in rape trials, it called for the onus of proof to be shifted to the defendant, so that he had to prove that he sought and obtained the consent of the complainant. It called for separate legal representation and for guidelines on sentencing. It recommended a range of treatment programmes for perpetrators. It called for the full implementation of the Kilkenny incest report and for a National Commission to review the legal framework.[1]

Bridín Twist remembered with pride the way the diverse women's groups on the committee had worked together as a network. 'The Irish Countrywomen's Association was mainstream and respectable and it was very important for us to stand beside organisations like the Rape Crisis Centre and Women's Aid, which were seen as radical. It was support for them, and it was also acknowledging that we knew the things they were saying were true. I myself have a close relation who was raped so I knew the value of what the Rape Crisis Centre does, and I have a huge regard for it. I also have people belonging to me who are perpetrators. We were all hearing about violence, especially in the home, but it is ingrained in rural Irish women to keep up a front and pretend all is well. Those that tried to get help didn't always get it, either. That was a time when issues were just coming out.' It was also the year in which divorce was finally introduced in Ireland, after a referendum to amend the constitution.

The report didn't have the impact its authors had hoped for, which was, said Ailbhe Smyth, 'very frustrating'.[2] However, it led, indirectly, along with the Task Force report on domestic violence, to the setting up by Labour Minister Eithne Fitzgerald of the Steering Committee on Violence Against Women, which reported in 1999.

In the summer of 1996, the bodies of two little girls who had been sexually abused and starved to death were found buried in the garden of Marc Dutroux near Charleroi in Belgium. Two girls who had also been imprisoned and abused were rescued by the police. Dutroux had already served a sentence for child rape. The DRCC and the ISPCC said the case should act as a warning for Ireland, proving, once again, the need for a complete overhaul of child protection services.

The Rape Crisis Centre had long believed that mandatory reporting of child sexual abuse was, as Olive Braiden said in 1995, one of the two most important steps 'towards confronting and dealing with this dark and disturbing aspect of our society'.[3] (The second step was separate legal representation.) Mandatory reporting would require those with responsibility for children, including counsellors, to report cases of suspected abuse to the gardaí or the health authorities. It had been recommended by the ICCL working group in 1998, though it cautioned that 'this change alone will not bring about an improvement unless it is accompanied by structural changes in the manner in which reported cases are investigated and subsequently processed'.[4] The Irish Association of Social Workers opposed mandatory reporting, not least because these changes hadn't taken place. At this time, child protection services in Dublin were overburdened almost to the point of collapse, with 2,400 children waiting to get a social-work service and an acute shortage of foster parents.

In 1996 the DRCC, Barnardo's and the ISPCC launched a campaign for its introduction. Olive Braiden said it would 'help undermine our culture of secrecy and traditional reluctance as a nation not to inform' and would free the informer from the risk of a lawsuit if the case was not proved.[5] Fianna Fáil called for its introduction but, following consultations, the Fine Gael Minister for Health, Austin Currie, announced that he would not introduce it. Braiden expressed 'bitter disappointment'. She said it was unacceptable that adults 'should leave children to suffer abuse in silence because the current system is failing'.[6]

When Brian Cowen became Health Minister in the Fianna Fáil–PD government that took office in 1997, he declared he would make it a 'key priority'. Joe Robins, who had taken over from Gemma Hussey as chairman of the DRCC's board in October 1994, wrote of 'the human destruction wrought by paedophiles' and said the DRCC had 'time and time again come across victims, sometimes of two generations, who have been abused as children by the same person'.[7] Olive Braiden said mandatory reporting would be 'a hell of a lot better than anything else we've experienced or had proposed'.[8]

The DRCC already informed clients that counsellors could not guarantee complete confidentiality 'for both legal and ethical reasons' in certain circumstances. These included information about abuse of minors by a client, sexual or physical abuse of minors in a situation known to the client, when a client was suicidal, when files or notes were subpoenaed by court.[9] However, the Network of Rape Crisis Centres opposed mandatory reporting, claiming that it breached confidentiality and had been shown not to work in other countries.

Taoiseach Bertie Ahern said in 1998 that it would be introduced, then set up a working party, chaired by Maureen Lynott, with Olive Braiden representing the Rape Crisis

Centre. In 1999 it called for new child abuse guidelines, but stopped short of calling for mandatory reporting. This led to the Children First child protection guidelines of 1999.

'I would kill myself if I had the child, because it is not my child.' This was what the 13-year-old girl in what became known as the C case said, to a psychiatrist, of the pregnancy forced on her when she was raped. The rape raised once again the abandoned issue central to the X case, the right to abortion. Initially, the girl's father said, on RTÉ, that she should have an abortion. Then, apparently after coming under the influence of militant anti-abortion activists from Youth Defence, he changed his mind. The girl was taken into the care of the EHB, which went to court to establish its right to bring her to England. Youth Defence funded the parents to appeal Judge Mary Fahey's ruling that she did have a right to an abortion because her own life was at risk. The girl's father publicly appealed for £100,000 so that the girl could bring the baby back into his own 'happy growing family'. He said the family would wear black and burn black candles if she had the abortion. The High Court upheld the Fahy ruling, and the girl was brought to England.

The C-case girl's family lived in appalling squalor on the periphery of a traveller's halting site in South Dublin. She was one of 12 children. Her mother had in the past received stab wounds and injuries apparently inflicted with an iron bar. The girl's father claimed that the stress of the publicity surrounding his daughter's situation had him drinking two bottles of spirits a day.[10] He has since drowned in the River Shannon.

The man who raped the child was a friend of her father's and a member of a large traveller clan. After she had babysat for him, he offered to leave her home. Instead, he drove her to a quiet place, tore off her clothes, hit her and raped her. His wife came to the van and banged on the door. Still naked, he drove off. When the rapist again stopped, the girl tried to run away. He caught her and punched her. Then he drove her home and told her if she told anyone he would cut her up. She said she took this seriously because he always carried a knife. Her family was also threatened, but another traveller reported it to the police. The rapist initially claimed that the girl had seduced him. In December 1998, however, the 25-year-old pleaded guilty to the rape and was sent to jail for 12 years, with 4 years suspended on condition that he underwent treatment in prison. Mr Justice Quirke said the rapist had 'violated an innocent girl' and his action had also 'led to the death of another child through abortion'.[11]

An opinion poll taken in 1997 during the controversy found that almost 80 per cent of people believed abortion should be permitted in Ireland in certain circumstances. Olive Braiden called on the government to work on the legislation that successive governments had avoided since the X case. It should show 'leadership and courage', she said. 'It is appalling that all the debate is focused on whether the girl should have the baby or not,' she said. 'Nobody has spoken about the fact that she is a victim of rape or the care that she might need as a result.'[12] She also criticised the publication of a photograph of the girl, with her eyes covered, in a newspaper. 'It is a long and harrowing road ahead for this girl, without people knowing her. She needs to recover from this in private.'[13]

While she was on leave of absence from the DRCC as a Fianna Fáil European election candidate in 1994, Braiden had criticised SPUC for being 'vindictive' in pursuit of costs against students following their prosecution for providing information on abortion. She said the students had been found guilty under 'illiberal, repressive laws that could not be defended in any modern pluralistic society'.[14] In 1995 there was a suggestion at a board meeting that, given the evidence that 'most people agree with it after rape', the Centre should consider joining the abortion debate. However, Braiden insisted on caution and it was decided to await legislation.[15]

In 1999, *Irish Catholic* columnist Fr Tom Stack wrote that Braiden was a 'pro-abortion activist'. Braiden vehemently denied it. 'I have never spoken on abortion and it is the policy of the Rape Crisis Centre not to.' The controversy arose after Braiden commented on a British case involving a 12-year-old rape victim who was pregnant. She had said it was appalling that a 12-year-old should become a mother.[16]

'Most prostitution anywhere in the world begins with rape,' Andrea Dworkin wrote in her book *Life and Death*.[17] In July 1998, a 49-year-old Limerick man was sent to jail for seven years for sexually assaulting a 14-year-old girl in a Dublin hotel. He was a former journalist and press officer. She was a child prostitute. He was defended in court by Michael McDowell SC, who pointed out that the girl was a 'willing participant' in the assaults and that her pimp was in the hotel bedroom where they took place. This did not excuse the man's behaviour, he said, but the fact was she had been 'seduced into an evil form of prostitution by another man'. The court heard she had been 'befriended' and 'groomed' by this other man when she was ten. Her services were advertised in several Dublin magazines. The accused booked the hotel room and provided sandwiches, crisps and soft drinks for the girl. The pimp brought her there, under an alias, and took the £50 fee. She was one of a group of girls who spent time at the pimp's house. She had 'allowed herself' to be photographed in lieu of money she borrowed from him, and she and other girls 'engaged in sexual activities with him'. She had also operated in an apartment in Bachelor's Walk on Dublin's quays where she 'went willingly for paid liaisons'. Although the girl refused to co-operate with preparing a victim impact report, her parents said that after disclosure of these matters, 'a huge weight had been lifted off her shoulders'.

Gardaí had arrested the accused at a premises in Limerick where they found 69 child and bestiality pornographic videos. He admitted engaging in sexual activities with schoolgirls. He said he liked young girls with big breasts. He told gardaí his marriage had collapsed after his wife found pornography in their home. Despite 'glowing testimonials' from his friends, Judge Cyril Kelly said he 'posed a continuing threat' to young girls.[18]

The pimp was later sentenced to six years in prison for sexual assault and unlawful carnal knowledge of six girls aged from 11 to 13. It emerged that the former company director had lured children into his house with the promise of money, sweets and cigarettes. He had shown them pornography featuring bestiality, and he also took pornographic photos of them. His victims appealed his sentence to the DPP on the grounds that it was too lenient, and in 2000 it was increased to ten years.[19]

When Joseph McColgan was raping his children, he used to take photographs of them, his own private pornography. So did the father/rapist in the Kilkenny incest case. Serbian soldiers in Bosnia photographed women being raped. Any photograph of a child engaging in sex is a photograph of a rape. And such pornography is then used in further rapes. 'Adult men and women, abused as children, come to us and talk about being made to watch blue movies and forced to copy the behaviour,' Olive Braiden said. 'Women raped by partners and husbands talk about being forced to act out scenes from porn movies.' She said that, in rapes by strangers, the DRCC was hearing about increasing levels of violence and gross indecency. Braiden said pornography was desensitising society and contributing directly to a rise in the number of rapes.[20]

A 1995 study of prostitutes attending the Women's Health Project in Dublin found that a third of them said they had been sexually abused as children. A 1997 Eastern Health Board survey found that paedophiles were able to 'put in an order' for child prostitutes, and that children as young as 13 were involved. Such was the demand that some women were dressing to look like schoolgirls.[21]

The 1996 working group report included a review of research on pornography and concluded that consumption of pornography was associated with an increase in aggressive attitudes to women and greater acceptance of myths, notably that women enjoy being raped. The linking of sex and violence eroticised violence. It cited research by Liz Kelly and others that found that 'dissociation', the process whereby a victim of sexual abuse cuts herself off emotionally from the experience, was frequently found as a coping strategy among prostitutes and those working as 'models' in the pornography industry.

Volunteers at the Rape Crisis Centre met with women working in prostitution as part of their training. 'While constituting an explicit form of violence in itself, sexual and other forms of violence against women working as prostitutes are also endemic,' the report stated. Research by Anne-Marie O'Connor in 1995 found that 55 per cent of clients of prostitutes used violence, but that 83 per cent of prostitutes surveyed said they would go to the gardaí only if they were very badly hurt. The Criminal Law (Sexual Offences) Act of 1993 left them exposed to being prosecuted for loitering or soliciting. One woman said clients knew this, and this made prostitution even more dangerous.[22]

In the month the report was published, a 36-year-old was convicted of raping and sexually assaulting a woman while she was working as a prostitute. A traveller, he had claimed the charge was a conspiracy because he had 'exposed' garda brutality against the travelling community.

The woman told the court she was working to feed a heroin addiction. The accused, accompanied by another man, had approached her and she had agreed to oral sex for £30 with him. He drove out into the Wicklow mountains, where both men raped her for several hours. The man on trial said to his accomplice at one point, 'Look at her – she loves it.' She said she was crying and screaming. They called her a 'tramp' and threatened to kill her. She was eventually thrown out of the car.[23] At Christmas that year, a young Sri Lankan prostitute, Belinda Pereira, was murdered in an apartment in Dublin. In June 1998, another young prostitute, Sinead Kelly, was murdered on the banks of the Grand Canal in Dublin. She had been raped and beaten up two months earlier.

'Rape doesn't happen in isolation,' Olive Braiden told a reporter in 1992. She said women working in the DRCC got 'rather battle-weary' when their challenges of sexist remarks met with demands to 'lighten up'. She said women should challenge everyday sexism more.[24] In 1995, Braiden said of the ending of a 36-year ban on the sale of *Playboy* in Ireland that it was part of the continuum that led to the subjugation of women. 'If we are working towards women's equality and women's right to say "no", why then have dollied up women for men's fantasies?' In 1997, the DRCC successfully complained to the Advertising Standards Authority over an advertisement which it claimed was sexist because of its depiction of a distraught woman with intimations of violence.[25]

Reacting to the fact that hardcore pornography featuring bestiality and children in sexual acts was being openly sold in the Capel Street area of Dublin, Braiden called on the Department of Justice to criminalise such material. It was 'outrageous', she said. Audrey Conlon, a board member at the DRCC since 2004, spent nine years watching pornographic videos – it was her job at the Censor's Office to classify or prohibit sexually explicit material under the 1993 Video Recordings Act. 'Gardaí and customs were seizing thousands of videos,' she said. 'It was pretty grim. Some of the antics were extraordinarily violent. Pornography is very prevalent here. The shelves of the sex shops would be restocked within hours of the gardaí raiding them. Increasingly, sexual violence is also to be found in mainstream film and on the Internet.'[26] Magazines which were banned would simply be renamed. She welcomed the 1998 Child Trafficking and Pornography Act, which made it an offence to possess child pornography, including on the Internet, to encourage children to be used in pornography and to traffic in children.

The DRCC made its own use of advertising when, in 1997, it launched its own cinema and poster campaign. The poster appeared on DART trains and on buses. The cinema ad had a woman's voice saying, 'Maybe you'd been drinking, your skirt was short, you'd thumbed a lift, you led him on, he paid for dinner, you went back to his place, you thought about having sex with him, you didn't get a taxi home, or maybe you were just minding your own business … whatever you were asking for, it was not rape.'[27] In 1998, the Centre advised and helped scriptwriters and actors at RTÉ when the soap opera

Fair City tackled the subject of rape. The plot had a young woman raped by her fiancé, a doctor – consistent with the DRCC's finding that in a majority of cases the rapist was known to his victim (in 20 per cent of cases he was her partner) and that rapists came from all social classes. The Centre's number was advertised at the end of the programme and there was a surge of calls.

Rape was 'the great shame of contemporary society', said Joe Robins as the DRCC revealed that it had received more than 6,000 calls in 1996–7. The number of convictions in cases dealt with by the DRCC was, at 2 per cent, desperately low. Over half of those contacting the Centre did so to talk about past child sexual abuse, and seven out of eight of these cases were not reported to gardaí, and only two of those reported resulted in convictions. Eight out of ten callers to the DRCC were women. Eleven women and girls had become pregnant as a result of rape. Olive Braiden said the fact that people were more aware of sexual crime was 'a social advance', but there was 'disquieting evidence' of an unspoken acceptance of sexual crimes as 'just another distasteful aspect of our society we have to live with'.[28]

There was a rise of 30 per cent in calls to the Centre in 1997–8, and in 1998–9 the Centre received over 7,000 calls, 822 of them regarding recent rape and 67 regarding marital rape. While violent crime reported to the gardaí was declining during this time, the number of rapes reported to them was rising dramatically – by 40 per cent in one year. In 1999, gardaí were dealing with one new rape every day. The DRCC was dealing with 55 recent rapes a month – in Dublin alone. The increase in reports to the police was leading to a serious backlog of cases awaiting trial. The state had only one video-link facility, and since the law had been changed so that under-17-year-olds gave evidence in this way in 1993, this meant huge delays in hearing child abuse cases. By the end of 1999 Mr Justice Paul Carney was warning that the situation was getting 'out of control'. He said he was already setting dates for trials up to two years ahead.[29]

The concern of the Rape Crisis Centre was to make the justice system meet the needs of more of the victims of sexual violence, and in 1998 it published the results of an ambitious piece of research. This was funded by the European Commission under its Grotius Programme, following an application by the DRCC. Olive Braiden recalled that it was thanks to Paul Carney that the Centre learned about the availability of the research funding. 'The Legal Process and the Victims of Rape' was conducted by the School of Law at Trinity College, Dublin, for the DRCC. Ivana Bacik, now the Reid Professor of Law at Trinity, was one of the authors of the study, along with Catherine Maunsell and Susan Gogan. Sally O'Neill, who had worked in the DRCC, became administrator.

'This was a comparative study of legal procedures in fifteen European states, five of them in depth. We had just a year to do it! It was a huge undertaking,' recalled Bacik. 'We had to build links with lawyers, academics, police, Rape Crisis Centres and individual women. There was a psychological element involving interviews with victims, and a legal element. It was fascinating. Belgium was in turmoil at the time – there was a shrine to the victims of Dutroux on the steps of the courts building in Brussels.'

The team found that victims had a much stronger role in proceedings in countries with an inquisitorial system – rather than an adversarial system as in Ireland – and in countries in which they also had some form of separate legal representation. In Denmark, which has what Bacik defined as a 'hybrid, part inquisitorial, part adversarial' system, feminist pressure had resulted in the introduction of separate legal representation. While Irish rape victims surveyed expressed the highest satisfaction with the police, all of them felt that the state prosecutor hadn't adequately represented their interests. Irish victims complained of delays in the process and of not being kept informed as to developments in their case.

Irish victims 'felt less confident, were less articulate and experienced more stress about testifying in court than the interviewees in any other country'. This was attributed to the adversarial mode of trial and to the sort of cross-examination faced. Ten out of fifteen Irish interviewees said the defence lawyer had raised the issue that the victim had provoked the rape. 'Victims felt that they were on trial.' [30]

The study called for a broader definition of rape 'to encompass all forms of penetration'. It said the test on consent should be whether a reasonable person would have considered the woman was consenting, and that it must be stressed that failure to offer resistance was not the same as consent. Victims should be kept informed and should have a lawyer to do this. 'The Civil Legal Aid Act of 1995 allows victims to have pre-trial legal advice, but gardaí weren't advising them of this,' said Bacik. Measures were called for to discourage 'the use of hostile or aggressive cross-examination' and defendants should be prohibited from conducting their own cross-examination of victims. It should be presumed that sexual history was inadmissible, and judges should stop warning juries about convicting on the uncorroborated evidence of the victim.

The report saw a role for the victim's lawyer in these parts of the trial. 'As a result of the study, Liz McManus of Labour brought in a private members bill, the main principle of which was incorporated into the Sex Offenders Bill, 2001. This provides that victims now have the right to have a separate lawyer appointed to represent their interests, in the absence of the jury, when the defence seeks permission from the judge to introduce evidence of the victim's past sexual history,' said Bacik. She recommended that such representation rights should be extended further, as they have been in Denmark. She also argued that 'in particular, victims should be provided with a lawyer from the time when they first report the crime at a garda station, since so many prosecutions depend greatly on what is said in the original statement of complaint.' President McAleese launched the report in Dublin Castle. The DRCC has continued to campaign for separate legal representation.

The National Steering Committee on Violence Against Women, which included the DRCC, was set up after the working group report on violence against women and children. In its first report in 1999, it recommended jail sentences for all convicted rapists and consistency in sentencing policy. It called for treatment programmes for offenders and a national helpline for women, and for the recruitment of more female judges. Launching the report, the junior Justice Minister, Fianna Fáil's Mary Wallace, said the message was that violence against women was a crime and always wrong.

'It was the worst that could happen to me ... I remember he was very forceful. He wanted to hurt me. But he could never hurt me as much as my soul was hurting me.' This was a young woman's account of rape in a Serbian detention camp when she was 15, as related in the war crimes tribunal in the Hague in 2000.[31]

Olive Braiden spoke about the setting up of the tribunal. 'In 1993 women's traumatic accounts of rape during the Bosnian war helped create the International Criminal Tribunal for the former Yugoslavia at the Hague,' she said, addressing an audience at St Patrick's Cathedral in 1998. 'In a historic move, the Tribunal declared for the first time ever that rape was a war crime and I am proud to say that the Dublin Rape Crisis Centre played a role in this major groundbreaking change.'[32] The DRCC kept pressure on the Irish government to highlight the lack of progress on rape trials at the tribunal, and in 1999 it began a campaign to draw attention to the fact that Slobodan Milosevic was conducting a new campaign of ethnic cleansing in Kosovo.

Horrific accounts of mass rape began to emerge, as thousands of people fled their homes. 'Our government must make its voice heard on the Council of Europe,' Braiden wrote. 'Milosevic must be given an ultimatum to halt the oppression and aggression against the 90 per cent Albanian population or face NATO air strikes against Serbian targets.'[33]

Within the DRCC, it was Angela McCarthy who led the move to develop training programmes for Kosovan refugees. 'Having worked on our programmes in Bosnia and Croatia for five years, when I saw Milosevic up to his old tricks, I was very upset,' she recalled. 'We discussed it with the Irish aid agencies, Goal and Concern, and we went to Albania to assess the situation.' The board of the DRCC was 'not particularly supportive' of this project, Olive Braiden recalled, and it was a struggle to persuade the Department of Foreign Affairs to provide funds.

In the event, the DRCC got the necessary funds from the Department and decided to work with Concern, providing a psychosocial programme as part of its rehabilitation work in the Western Kosovan town of Peje. The Department provided funds for eight training trips over two years. 'Deirdre Ní Chinneide and I went out,' said McCarthy. 'It was quite hair-raising at first. The refugees had just returned and things were very raw. Most of the houses had been destroyed. There were bullet holes in the walls, and sometimes gunfire. There were packs of dogs roaming around, rubbish piling up, only erratic supplies of electricity. There were fresh graves everywhere. On the other hand, there was less of a feeling of total despair and depression than there had been in Tuzla. These were people returning, rebuilding broken communities.

'We'd been told that rape was a taboo, a terrible dishonour to a woman's family, and that people would think it was better for a woman who had been raped to have died than to bear such shame. We didn't advertise at first that we were from the Rape Crisis Centre, but the group we worked with, local Kosovan Concern workers, were fantastic. They were so responsive that within two weeks we were able to talk about rape and attitudes to it. We trained them in counselling skills, ways of relaxing and debriefing. We did a lot of work on dealing with bereavement. We used lovely scented things, like candles and incense, and relaxation tapes. There began to be a big demand for those things when shops reopened.'

The programme was extended to include work in outlying villages. 'We trained two women in each village. The idea was to create a core of women to whom other women could come when they needed to.' They found that the Kosovans were dealing with the aftermath of Serbian oppression which went back for years. 'We stayed with Concern and the support was great and the safety – but Kosovo did take its toll on me,' admitted McCarthy. 'I felt it was my project and I went into it with great passion. I was like a sponge soaking up terrible distress. I was fairly shaken by it.' Braiden praised the work McCarthy and Ní Chinneide did in Kosovo. 'It was incredible and counsellors in the Centre learned a lot from their experience,' she said.

The Centre had also expanded its services locally, in Dublin, opening an outreach office in Coolock in 1998. The office was in the Well Woman Centre in the Northside Shopping Centre and was formally launched by Mary Banotti, MEP, in April 1999. She praised the partnership of the Well Woman Centre and the DRCC. 'I well remember the attempts in the early days to demonise the work of the Rape Crisis Centre as it bravely and resolutely exposed the sexual violence experienced by women,' she said. 'Now we know that such acts were widespread against children, too.' Senator Helen Keogh, chairwoman of the Well Woman Centre, said the new service was a 'vital part of the nation's growth' and would serve men as well as women. The DRCC launched its new website on the same day at www.drcc.ie.

Emer Neligan had joined the DRCC in 1987 as a volunteer and became a telephone counsellor. 'I remember taking 36 calls one Friday afternoon,' she said. 'It was great then to see someone you'd talked to coming in to get therapy. I always knew they'd be in safe hands in the Centre.' She then trained as a psychotherapist, working as a receptionist at the DRCC to pay her fees. 'It was three years' training plus two years to get accreditation,' she said. 'A big commitment, but worth it.' Olive Braiden asked Neligan to run the Coolock service.

'It was good to be in the Well Woman Centre in Coolock because it meant local women didn't have to feel any awkwardness about being seen to come in to talk about rape. The staff there were really sensitive and they looked after me. My room was tiny and it had no window. Clients used to say they liked it – they felt safe there. They said it was like a womb. People came by word of mouth, and they came from places like Navan as well as from all of north Dublin.' In time,

Neligan began to look for a bigger premises in order to do art therapy and group work with her clients. 'The Civic Centre in Coolock gave us this beautiful room with carpets and lovely chairs and windows and its own bathroom, for a very low rent, so now the Centre has moved to there and two counsellors job share.'

In 2004, Neligan left to take up other work. 'It broke my heart to leave, but it was time to move on,' she said. She said she had learned a lot from Olive Braiden. 'She believed in empowering the client – she really respected them and never sold them short. She was brave. She'd speak out in a small country, and I felt a sense of pride in her. She was also totally charming. Every Christmas she'd write a card to each of us and there would be a personal message. If something was happening in your family, you'd get beautiful flowers. On Fridays, she'd kick off her shoes and open a bottle of wine after work and sit with whoever was there. She was very entertaining – and she knew how to throw a good party.'

'It was not conceivable to put out the programmes without a helpline – I was terrified of the very real prospect of people committing suicide,' said Mary Raftery, producer of RTÉ's powerful and shocking television series about sexual and physical abuse of children in Irish industrial schools run by the Catholic church during the 20th century. 'The state had no services, and Faoiseamh[34] had been set up by the Church, which was going to put a lot of people off. The Rape Crisis Centre was independent and secular and the most damaged people could go there for help,' said Raftery. There was a huge response to the first programme. 'The minute our number went up, the lines lit and for a solid two hours after that we had five counsellors in the Centre taking calls,' said Olive Braiden. Braiden said the callers had cried and spoken, some for the first time, about 'really terrible childhoods' in institutions. For the later programmes, the Centre opened eight lines, all of which were 'inundated', according to Braiden. 'The people in here have been devastated by the calls,' she said.

States of Fear revealed that thousands of children had been forced into institutions in which they were subjected to extreme violence, starvation, mental torture, neglect, sexual abuse and slave labour. The cruelty was as depraved as it was routine. The final programme was about contemporary institutions and revealed the contents of the report into abuse at Madonna House which had been completed in 1997, but which the government refused to publish. The programme was very explicit about male rape. 'Actually talking about what male rape was had been a taboo,' said Raftery. Most of those raped in the institutions were boys. 'They were regarded as objects and it was well known they were being abused. It was tolerated,' said Raftery.

In 1993, nuns in Drumcondra had sold land to a property developer which contained the graves of the so-called Magdalens who had worked in the High Park convent laundry. Relatives of the women were outraged and the story of the way 'fallen women' had been treated in the Ireland of the 19th and early 20th centuries. It emerged that while the laundries had been set up to provide refuge for single, pregnant women, the women sent there also included prostitutes, women who had killed their babies, unmarried mothers, orphans and women or girls who were considered to be 'soiled goods' or 'at moral risk' by priests or other authority figures. Inevitibly, some of the Magdalens were women and girls who had been raped. Once incarcerated, they lost their names, had their hair cropped and were paraded as 'penitents', a warning to others about the perils of 'getting into trouble'. In 1999, June Goulding published a shocking account of the treatment of unmarried mothers in a convent in Co. Cork, which further demonstrated the punitive attitude of the Catholic Church towards women who had sex outside of marriage – regardless of whether it was chosen or forced on them.[35]

'There was a warped view of sexuality in the institutions,' said Raftery. 'When girls had their periods the nuns saw it as something filthy, a manifestation of sin. There was one reformatory set up by Archbishop John Charles McQuaid for girls "with tendencies towards sexual immorality". This, obviously, must have included girls acting out sexual abuse [some children who have been sexually abused behave in a sexually precocious way as a result] and there would have also been girls put into institutions by their mothers because they were at risk of sexual abuse by their fathers. Children born as a result of incest were among those sent to institutions. About a third of the children were illegitimate. The church, and the state which funded it to run these places, took a eugenic view: that girls were likely to be like their mothers, so if the mother was deemed "promiscuous" the child was seen as "damaged goods" and wouldn't be given up for adoption. They were a sort of underclass. When girls came into the institutions and said they'd been abused, they weren't believed.'

Raftery said the DRCC played a critical role in ensuring that the impact of *States of Fear* was not lost. 'Olive Braiden went on the radio after each of the programmes and talked about the Rape Crisis Centre's awareness of the abuses described. She moved the debate on. Some people had been shocked speechless. The Rape Crisis Centre kept up the momentum and in my view helped bring about the taoiseach's apology on the day of the final programme.' Bertie Ahern apologised to the victims of abuse in state institutions. He also announced the establishment of a commission and a national counselling service. Kieran McGrath pointed out that social workers could not be got 'for love or money' and that there was a serious shortage of skilled professionals within the existing services. Braiden warned that unskilled counsellors could 'do more harm than good'. She said the DRCC could offer training. Meanwhile, those calling the Centre who wanted to see a counsellor had to go on a waiting list. *States of Fear* had opened new floodgates.

17

A Shocking Tolerance of Rape

'Irish society is not as open and liberal as it likes to think it is. While it has moved on in leaps and bounds, the narrowness and conservatism is still there,' said Olive Braiden, in an interview marking the announcement that she was to leave the Rape Crisis Centre after 17 years, 10 of them as its director. 'The services have expanded and improved beyond imagining ... there is great public awareness now, nevertheless there is still a stigma attached to somebody coming out openly and talking about these experiences,' she told journalist Kathryn Holmquist.

'When a woman is raped, people still persist in asking in-criminating questions, such as, "Why were you there at that time of night? Didn't you know it was dangerous?" All these questions that imply a victim was in some way responsible for what happened to them. Attitudinal change doesn't happen quickly. It is the area that disappoints me most ... There is a fundamental lack of understanding.' The Rape Crisis Centre had commented in 1997 on the case of a woman who was raped in Co. Kerry by a local man. Despite intimidation from some people in the area, she reported the rape. After the rapist was convicted, there were death threats against the woman and her family, and they left Ireland. Braiden said people were intolerant towards the victims of sex crimes, while remaining 'shockingly tolerant' of violence and alcohol abuse.[1]

Braiden told delegates at the MacGill summer school in Glenties that there should be sustained public anger about the fact that thousands of Irish women and children were being regularly raped, assaulted and abused in their own homes – but there was not. 'From time to time, when particular horrific cases of systematic abuse of women and children hit the headlines there is an outcry of disbelief and shock, but all too soon it fades away and it is left to the voluntary sector to carry on and work with all the other people whose histories of torture and neglect will never be heard outside of a counselling session,' she said. Most of the violence was from men against women and children, and while physical violence was easier to document, 'living with the constant threat of being raped or beaten' was often more terrifying.

Society must start educating children in how to express anger and frustration in non-violent ways. 'It is only by highlighting these problems, treating them seriously and resourcing the services that deal with them that we can hope to undo the consequences of generations of neglect,' she said. 'The die is cast at an early stage. Our aim must be preventing children from growing up to be rapists and abusers.' It was, she said, a huge task, but not an impossible one.[2]

When a Belfast salesman was convicted in the North in 2000 of raping his wife – the first such conviction in Ireland – Braiden welcomed the verdict. She said 10 per cent of cases reported to the DRCC in 1999 were rapes by husbands or partners, but that most wives were afraid to report marital rape because they felt they wouldn't be believed, unless they had been 'battered and bruised' as well. 'It's very sad to see what a woman has to go through before people will accept she was forced to have sex without her consent,' she said. The rapist had told his wife it was his 'right as a husband' to demand sex. The raped woman told the court that her husband accused her of not respecting him and said she had to be punished and shown that he was 'God'.[3]

A 46-year-old labourer was the first man in the Republic

to be convicted of raping his wife in 2002. However, the Court of Criminal Appeal overturned the conviction as unsafe in 2004 and ordered a retrial.

'He is going to be let out no better than he went in and it is all due to financial reasons in a country that prides itself for its humanity and is in a financial boom but cannot provide this treatment.' This was how Mr Justice Dermot Kinlen expressed his anger about the fact that a man he had jailed in 1996 was to be released in 2000, without having had the treatment the judge had ordered him to undergo. The 32-year-old Galway man was 'one of life's unfortunates who never had a chance', the judge said. He said he was 'horrified' for the prisoner and for society. His father had savagely beaten him as a child, and his mother was an alcoholic. He was taken into state care and placed at St Joseph's in Clonmel, where a religious brother severely abused and raped him. (The brother was jailed for nine years for the offences.) In 1995, the Galway man raped a 14-year-old boy. At his trial, it emerged that he had already served four years for rape in England.[4]

A similarly damaged young man committed suicide in Wheatfield Prison in Dublin in April 2000. Anthony Cawley had been serving the longest sentence for sexual crime ever handed down in Ireland. He had been sentenced to 20 years in 1987 for the rape and attempted murder of a young woman in Dublin city centre. He was on temporary release from prison for other violent offences at the time. In 1989 he attempted to kill another prisoner and in 1998 he became the first person to be prosecuted for 'prison rape' after he raped his cell mate in Arbour Hill.

Cawley was a traveller from a family of 15. His parents were alcoholics and several men in his extended family had also been convicted of violence against women. He had been taken into care as a two-year-old child and had been raped and beaten at Trudder House in Wicklow by the man who ran the home. This man was already on the run from sexual abuse charges in Britain. He was never charged with the crimes he had committed in Ireland. He has since died abroad. Cawley had a history of serious self-harm. He had asked to be taken into a treatment programme in prison, but was not approved for it and was instead receiving counselling. Shortly before he killed himself, a newspaper had advertised a feature about him in which he was referred to as 'the Beast'. This was said to have upset him deeply. RTÉ later expressed regret for broadcasting the advertisment.

At the time Cawley died, there were 357 sex offenders in Irish jails and just 10 places on the Arbour Hill treatment programme. Of 103 prisoners released at the end of their sentences in 1998, just 11 had completed the programme, and out of 80 released in 1999, just 5 had done it. During a Dáil debate, the Minister for Justice, Fianna Fáil's John O'Donoghue, claimed there was a range of treatments available. However, he was criticised for providing the equivalent of two full-time psychiatrists for 2,600 prisoners.

In 2002, a report for the Irish prison service by Dr Francesca Lundstrom called for a multi-disciplinary programme available to all sex offenders in prison. It criticised the failure to act on similar recommendations made in 1993 and pointed out that there was still no Department of Justice, Equality and Law Reform community-based facilities for offenders after their release.[5] In 2003, Joseph McColgan was released from jail amid public outrage having apparently undergone no treatment programme.

The Rape Crisis Centre had been campaigning for years for treatment programmes in prison and in the community, and also for the introduction of a sex offenders register. Such a register had been introduced in the North in 1997 and was eventually introduced in the Republic in 2001 under the Sex Offenders Act. It also made it an offence for sex offenders to apply for work or a voluntary post without informing their employer of their convictions, if the position would given them unsupervised access to children. The DRCC welcomed it. It had highlighted the importance of such a measure when the X- case rapist was released after serving just three years in jail in 1999. However, it also argued that most offenders were never convicted, so they would never feature on the register.

The more important issue was bringing them to justice in the first place.

Clashes with authority figures had been a feature of Olive Braiden's time at the DRCC, and this was the case to the end. In 1999, Mr Justice Paul Carney suggested during a talk in South Africa that rape victims might come under pressure to go to the police and that such pressure might come from, among others, Rape Crisis Centres. He said he didn't know if such pressure existed, but he would be concerned if it did. The *Sunday Independent*'s Patricia Redlich applauded him and claimed the 'victim industry' had created 'an atmosphere of fear and intimidation which makes it hard for those who have been raped to let it go'.[6]

Responding to the judge's remarks, Braiden said, 'We don't force anyone, nor could we. It is the DPP who decides.' Carney had also said that 'a genuine complainant whose rapist is acquitted suffers more on that account than from whatever happened to her on the night of the rape'. Braiden disagreed. 'In fact more pain and suffering ensues from decisions not to prosecute,' she said.[7] Speaking at a summer school in 2003, Carney described his own experience of this suffering. 'I will never forget one particular acquittal where the prosecutrix's screams from the Round Hall permeated every corner of the Four Courts complex and seemed to go on for a couple of hours,' he said. 'What I find personally upsetting about these incidents is that from processing, if not actually hearing, up to 100 of these cases a year, I believe I can profile them to a high degree of accuracy and predict in which cases the acquittals are going to come.'[8]

Rapists knew, Braiden said, that they were committing a 'low-risk' crime and were unlikely to be prosecuted. She said that increasingly long delays, in some cases of more than two years, between reporting rape and getting to court were part of the problem for rape complainants. 'They can't get on with their lives,' she said. The accused – 80 per cent of whom were known to their alleged victim – was frequently given bail. The DRCC called for an increase in staff at the DPP's office, for more judges to be appointed and for more courtrooms to be made available so that the legal process was speeded up.[9]

By late 2000, rape and serious sexual assault cases accounted for almost 80 per cent of new cases listed for the Central Criminal Court, and there was a serious backlog of over 100 cases awaiting trial. The number of rape cases had increased by 265 per cent in seven years. One woman described the effect on her family of a last minute adjournment of the trial of a man accused of raping her son three years previously. The boy had been waiting in the video link room for the trial to begin when the judge decided to give precedence to a murder trial. 'My son was terrified of the trial but he was determined that he was about to get justice and then this happened,' she said. 'We left the court just devastated. It is tearing us apart.'[10] After a lawyer representing a defendant who had been in custody for three years asked for his case to be given priority in 2002, Mr Justice Paul Carney said it would be 'meaningless' for him to make such an order because of the backlog. He spoke of the 'pain and suffering' of victims and relatives in this situation and said it was 'beyond comprehension'.[11] He said the situation could be remedied only by the appointment of more High Court judges.

However, if Carney agreed with the DRCC on this, he clashed with it over the issue of sentencing. The judge criticised the DPP for being 'very trigger-happy' in appealing sentences which were allegedly too lenient. The DRCC responded by defending the DPP's right to appeal and calling for that right to extend to rape victims themselves. Until they had that right, the DPP was 'their only lifeline', said Olive Braiden.[12]

Braiden also challenged the then Attorney General, Michael McDowell, after he claimed that legalising abortion for rape victims could lead to a 'series of false accusations of rape' by women seeking terminations. He did so after calls for the law to be changed in this way. Braiden said she was surprised the Attorney General had spoken out on the 'non-issue' of false claims of rape. She challenged him to say if any study had been done on the numbers of such claims. 'I would say it is extremely low,' she said, adding that McDowell was just diverting attention away from 'other human rights concerns' in relation to rape victims.[13]

Braiden was leaving the Centre in the year of its 21st anniversary. There was much to celebrate. The Centre had grown to have 30 staff and 2 trained volunteer groups, providing a 24-hour crisis line and attending, again on a 24- hour basis, at the SATU. There was a well-respected education and training department which operated in Ireland and in war zones abroad. The Centre's subvention from the government had grown to £320,000 and it had a highly effective fundraising structure. Major research had been done, and more was being undertaken.

The Centre was represented on the Courts Services Board, the Judicial Advisory Board, the Irish Radio and Television Commission and the National Steering Committee on Violence Against Women. To celebrate the 21st anniversary, the DRCC invited President Mary McAleese into the Centre along with TDs and guests. 'She was wonderful,' said Braiden. 'She always did anything we asked her to do for us, and she made astounding speeches at our events.

'The best night of my life was the going away party the staff organised for me,' she recalled. 'I was mesmerised – I thought nothing could happen in that building without me knowing about it. Then the Minister for Health Micheal Martin gave an official party in Dublin Castle to thank me.' Looking back, she said one of the achievements she was most proud of was 'getting the front door to the house on Leeson Street left open for clients to come in to the Centre'.

The early years of the new millennium were marked by a continuing catalogue of horrific sexual crimes all over Ireland. A Dublin man kicked his girlfriend to death and had sex with her body the next morning. A man was convicted of raping and murdering schoolgirl Siobhan Hynes in Connemara. An 18-year-old man was convicted of raping and murdering Rachel Kiely (22) in Co. Cork. A young man sexually assaulted and strangled an elderly nun, Sister Philomena Lyons, in Co. Monaghan. Three men kidnapped a woman and took her to a remote part of Wicklow where they tied her to a tree and raped her. A man forced two girls, one 16, the other 14, to work as prostitutes in Waterford, battered them and then, after they gave evidence against him, said to court reporters, 'Tell them two sluts they are dead.'

It took a detective garda three hours to read out the charges against a Donegal man accused of hundreds of sexual assaults against young boys. A barrister spoke of hearing a conversation in which drug dealer John Gilligan threatened journalist Veronica Guerin that he would rape her child. Gilligan was suspected of murdering Guerin in 1996, but was acquitted at trial in 2001. A man imprisoned his wife and teenage daughter, padlocking and chaining them in a bedroom for weeks on end. He mutilated them with blades, screwdrivers and a spike and threatened to kill them. They were released only to do house-work. He had been raping the girl since she was 14. Eventually the mother escaped. The man was jailed. The girl, who was then 16, became homeless. The Rape Crisis Centre was among the organisations to express outrage at the state's failure to take care of her, and pointed out that report after report had warned that the system needed to be radically overhauled. The then Minister for Health and Children, Micheal Martin, admitted that 'the system has failed and failed badly'.[14]

Judge Peter Kelly dealt with a series of cases of children failed and failed badly by the system. Among those he had to send to remand centres because there was no suitable altern-ative was a 15-year-old girl who had been lured into pros-titution, was taking drink and drugs and was out of control. Another 14-year-old girl who had been in and out of state care had been sold into prostitution by her mother. Hundreds of victims of child sex abuse prepared to sue their attackers after the government announced that it would remove the statute of limitations in such cases – the statute the McColgans had to struggle with when they sued the state in 1997.

Self-styled human rights activist Vincent McKenna was exposed by his brave daughter, Sorcha, when she gave evidence that he had sexually and physically abused her throughout her childhood in Co. Monaghan. After he was convicted and sent to jail for just three years in 2000, Sorcha McKenna protested. There was public fury and the DPP appealed the sentence. It was later doubled. McKenna was released in 2005.

A woman whose father had raped her and her brother and sister over a 12-year period, as well as forcing them to perform sexual acts with their mother, said in court: 'I was just an object to meet his needs. How would my life have been if I had not been abused as a child?' She also said she was concerned at the lack of therapy for sex offenders. 'These people need help. What about our part – the blind eye in allowing these sort of situations to continue. We are also part of the problem.'[15]

'My father's actions imprisoned all my young life,' a young Connemara woman told Mr Justice Phillip O'Sullivan after he had convicted Patrick Naughton (49) of raping and buggering her from when she was 11 until she was 21. He had also threatened to kill her by throwing her in a bog with a stone around her neck. The woman asked that her father be named. He was jailed for 11 years. The case became notorious after it emerged that Bobby Molloy, then a PD Minister of State, had made what the judge called a 'totally improper approach' to him, on behalf of a sister of the rapist. This woman was seeking leniency for her brother. Molloy later resigned.[16]

Mr Justice Paul Carney jailed a 36-year-old Wicklow man for kidnapping, repeatedly raping and attempting to murder a woman he hooded and carried in the boot of his car between assaults. The judge said the details of the case were 'truly horrific' but added, 'I find little point in saying that this was one of the worst cases to come before the court because my experience is that when I do that a probably worse case comes before me the following week.'[17] The women working at the Rape Crisis Centre knew better than anyone that this was true – and that the horrific stories unfolding in the courts represented just a tiny proportion of those which were unfolding in families and communities all over the country.

In May 2001, the DRCC repeated its demand for separate legal representation after a woman fled the witness box in distress during cross-examination by counsel for the man she had accused of rape. A garda went to the woman and tried to calm her by telling her that the cross-examination was what was regarded as normal. The judge commended the garda's honesty, but since he felt the integrity of the court had been interfered with he discharged the jury and the trial collapsed.[18]

In January 2002, the Medical Council found Dr Moira Woods guilty of professional misconduct for her management of several cases of alleged child sex abuse at the SATU during the 1980s. This followed complaints from five sets of parents. The inquiry began in 1992. Out of 55 charges, 13 were upheld. The Council found that she 'failed to gather all the available evidence and/or did not follow the protocols established by the SATU and/or failed to review additional information received after preliminary findings had been reached'.[19] One of the parents was Eddie Hernon, who had lost access to one of his children for three and a half years as a result of Woods' assessment that the child had been sexually abused. 'It has destroyed the last 17 and a half years of my life,' Hernon told a reporter at the *Irish Catholic*. He blamed 'the small clique of radical feminist ideologues who wish to paint all men as potential child abusers and rapists'. He accused them of attacking 'the biological father and the family'.[20]

Woods claimed afterwards that the Medical Council ruling had created a climate of fear among professionals working with sexually abused children. She said it was 'deeply ironic' that the Council's criticisms of conditions at the SATU in the 1980s were the very issues the SATU had tried to address at the time. It had failed, 'because of lack of co-operation from, among others, the medical profession'.[21]

'No actual injury was inflicted on the victim other than rape.' So said Mr Justice Daniel Herbert in March 2002, explaining why he was not sending a Dublin man to jail for raping a young Dublin woman. Instead, he gave him a four-year suspended sentence and wished him well. 'This was not a vicious rape,' the judge said. 'He did not jump out of the bushes and attack the woman. It was just something that happened between them, but he went too far.' The man had threatened to kill the woman and left her with bruises all over her body. When she managed to escape, she had run, terrified, to the nearest house with a light on.[22]

As far as the staff of the Rape Crisis was concerned, it was the judge who had gone too far this time. In a furious letter to the papers the 28 women expressed their outrage. The judge had shown a 'flagrant lack of understanding of rape'. Rape by a stranger who jumped out of the bushes was no better or worse than the sort of rape experienced by 80 per cent of callers to the DRCC, that is, rape by someone known to them. Rape was 'one of the most devastating of human experiences'.

The women described the 'terror, helplessness, humiliation and pain' that impacted on every aspect of a rape victim's life. The immediate effects included 'shock, panic, terror, recurrent and intrusive flashbacks, sleeplessness and nightmares'. Longer term, victims might experience 'dramatic mood swings, self-blame, guilt, loss of trust in relationships, sexual difficulties, impaired concentration and memory and difficulty in coping with normal routines'. The women said rape was 'profoundly under-reported' and that the Herbert judgment reinforced 'dangerous myths' about the crime and could well deter other victims from reporting it. 'What hope can there be for a victim when faced with the possibility of a court case presided over by a judge who demonstrates such archaic attitudes?' The judge had noted that there was 'only one' aggravating factor – that the rapist had threatened to kill his victim while raping her. Rape victims were already marginalised in a system weighted against them. This 'reprehensible' sentence had caused 'public outrage' and the system had to change.[23]

Politicians also condemned the sentence. Monica Barnes said it was depressing. 'I thought we worked long and hard to get rid of that mindset,' she said. The chief executive of Victim Support, Lilian McGovern, said the organisation had been bombarded with calls from angry members of the public. 'It is farcical to suggest that a rape is only a rape,' she said.[24] Olive

Braiden, who had been appointed chairwoman of the government's new Crisis Pregnancy Agency, said it was 'very disturbing'.[25]

The morning after the Herbert judgment, the mother of the raped woman did an emotional interview on RTÉ's *Gerry Ryan Show*. She said her daughter was so distressed she could hardly speak. 'It was like as if my daughter was on trial, not him. We feel so hurt. I don't know where to begin to sort this out, to make an end to it so that my daughter can heal,' she said. 'How could any judge say this man isn't a danger to women?' The DPP went on to appeal the leniency of the sentence, and in 2003 the Court of Criminal Appeal ruled that the judge had given disproportionate weight to the circumstances of the rapist and far too little to those of the victim. The man was jailed for four years.

In the same week as the Herbert case, the outrage expressed by the Rape Crisis Centre over the reduction in the sentence of the rapist in the X case, and its concern over his release after three years without supervision, was shockingly vindicated. The 52-year-old rapist was convicted of kidnapping and sexually assaulting a 15-year-old girl. On his release from prison in 1998, he had been given a licence to drive a taxi. He had picked the girl up on the northside of Dublin and driven her to a lonely backstreet where, he told her, there were no CCTV cameras, before assaulting her.

This was the man of whom Supreme Court judge Mr Justice Hugh O'Flaherty, on behalf of the learned judges in the Court of Criminal Appeal, had said in 1995, 'The court is convinced it is not dealing with a man who is likely to re-offend.' He was deemed a 'hardworking good family man'. Jailing the man for three and a half years in 2002, Judge Pat McCartan said that he was 'a serious menace' who had to get his 'proper deserts'. The judge said he should never have been allowed to drive a taxi and banned him from doing so for ten years. The young woman the man had sexually assaulted said she was angry. The sentence was too light and was 'disgraceful' given that it was his second offence, she said. Allowing him a taxi licence had been 'like putting a paedophile in a playground'.[26] The man lost an appeal against his conviction in 2003.

The Rape Crisis Centre had to struggle constantly to find the funds needed to provide its increasingly wide range of services to a constantly growing number of clients, women and men. Women still accounted for 81 per cent of callers to the Centre in 2000, but the number of men was growing, at 19 per cent. A quarter of the rapes reported to the Centre were of women by husbands or male partners. Most of the male callers had been raped or sexually abused by men, and 41 per cent of them were raped as adults.

At a conference about male victims of domestic violence in Navan in 2000, *Irish Times* columnist John Waters declared, 'This is war.' He told the audience that 'for 30 years feminists have attacked men' and that the 'domestic violence industry' was about 'trying to take children away from their fathers'. Waters has written repeatedly about the subject, referring to 'the highly lucrative domestic violence industry' run by 'feminist ayatollahs' talented in using propaganda.[27] Dr Warren Farrell told the conference, organised by the AMEN group, that he had analysed 50 studies on domestic violence and found that 'men and women batter each other about equally' but women were more likely to start it and to inflict greater violence. Women drove men to suicide, 'a female type of domestic abuse'.

There was another industry, too, he said, which involved the 'systematic use of false accusation'. Women were training children 'into victimhood and an anti-male attitude' and this was 'child abuse'. The writer Erin Pizzey claimed that lawyers told women 'the fastest route to divorce is to claim violence and sexual molestation of children'.

Commenting on the conference, Women's Aid director Denise Charlton said most studies showed that 95 per cent of domestic violence was male. Don Hennessy, co-ordinator of the Cork Domestic Violence project, said that out of 1,500 families the project had worked with in which there was violence, there were just ten in which women were named as the primary abuser, and in just two cases did that turn out to be true. 'Abusers always minimise and often deny,' he said.[28]

The following year various groups objected to a new school initiative for transition year and senior cycle secondary school students, the 'Exploring Masculinities Programme'. They claimed it was a waste of time and intruded on family matters. The Rape Crisis Network cited well-known cases of sexual crime within the family and declared its support for the 'excellent' programme. It welcomed its challenge to the myths of sexual violence, its exploration of the links between porno-graphy, sexual exploitation and poverty and its exploration of relationships between men and women and 'how power can be abused, and cause harm' in such relationships. Fiona Neary of the Network said that the programme emphasised communication and recognising emotions. Referring to concerns about the high rate of suicide among young men, she said it would 'enable more young men to reach out for support during times of crisis'.[29] One man, replying to Neary's letter to the papers, claimed the Exploring Mascul-inities Programme started from the basis that 'all men are bad and evil' and that it was a feminist conspiracy.[30]

In 2001 visiting sociologist Michael Kimmell, a spokesman for the US-based National Organisation for Men Against Sexism said 'the single most obdurate and intractable gender difference around the world is violence'. Speaking about the controversies raised in Ireland he said: 'What we need is solid, reliable, survey data, based on a nationally representative sample of Irish people, who would be asked about their experiences of violence.'[31] The Rape Crisis Centre, along with the Royal College of Surgeons in Ireland, was about to present the startling results of just such a survey.

18

THE HIDDEN PART OF THE ICEBERG

Forty two per cent of women and 28 per cent of men in Ireland have experienced some degree of sexual abuse or sexual assault in their lifetime. Ten per cent of women have been raped, as have 3 per cent of men. Twenty-one per cent of women and 18 per cent of men have suffered attempted penetrative or other serious sexual abuse. Six per cent of women were raped as children, as were 3 per cent of boys. These were some of the findings of the Sexual Abuse and Violence in Ireland (SAVI) report that was carried out by the Royal College of Surgeons for the Rape Crisis Centre and published in 2002. 'That's a lot of people in Irish society,' said Professor Hannah McGee, who led the groundbreaking survey of 3,000 people. The report followed another, smaller survey by the Health Research Board, which found that almost 40 per cent of Irish women had experienced domestic violence. 'This is the hidden part of the iceberg,' said McGee.[1]

SAVI found that women and girls were more at risk than men and boys, and the risk of abuse remained equally high for women from childhood to adulthood, whereas the risk for men decreased threefold from childhood to adulthood. Those who experienced child sexual abuse were significantly more likely to be subjected to sexual violence as adults. The 'overwhelming majority' of abusers of children and adults, male and female, were men. The proportion of adults experiencing sexual violence was found to be rising. Disclosure to professionals was 'strikingly low'. Just 12 per cent of victims had told a counsellor or therapist and just 10 per cent of women and 6 per cent of men had reported what happened to the gardaí. Almost half (47 per cent) of those who revealed that they had been raped or in some way sexually abused said that they had never told a single other person about it.

McGee is head of the health services research centre at the college and the convenor of its research ethics committee. 'We were approached by the DRCC in 1999 in the context that sexual violence was very important and very hidden. There were a lot of myths and strongly held views without evidence,' she said. 'It was a complex task and the DRCC worked very hard to get funds from Atlantic Philanthropies [an American charitable foundation] to research how best to do it.

'After consulting widely in the US and UK, we decided an anonymous telephone survey was the best and only realistic option.'[2]

Geraldine Connolly and Olive Braiden had set up a well-balanced steering group including representatives of the college, the Departments of Health and Justice and expert independents. 'We were worried about how a vulnerable person who had been abused would react to our questions,' said McGee. 'We structured them in such a way as to lead gradually to the most sensitive ones. We got some former clients of the Rape Crisis Centre to act as expert advisors. People's definitions of rape and abuse are so diverse that we made the questions very specific, requiring a yes or no answer. We knew we'd be faced with people who were unwilling to believe our findings – we were extremely careful. The information we got is very explicit.'

The team trained 15 people to do the interviews and the DRCC provided support and debriefing for the researchers. The Economic and Social Research Institute generated the phone numbers to ensure anonymity. The ESRI also devised a quota system based on the census to ensure that the survey reached as wide a range of people as possible. Researchers offered participants the DRCC's freephone number and phoned back a few days later to check on their well-being.

The SAVI report is a huge resource. As well as providing a wealth of statistical information on the incidence of sexual violence, it covers a wide range of related issues. Participants were asked how the abuse affected them and about their beliefs about sexual violence. Men were found to be more likely to believe in the myths of rape than women. Ten per cent of men and 4 per cent of women believed, for example, that a person could stop a rapist 'if they really wanted to'. Forty per cent of men and 26 per cent of women believed that men who raped men must be homosexual.[3]

Smaller studies were carried out to assess the risks of sexual violence among 'marginalised sub-groups' not reached by the main survey. These found that, for example, 49 out of 100 homeless women surveyed had suffered serious sexual violence. Traveller women said that if their community found out someone was attending the Rape Crisis Centre, 'they'd destroy her with talk'.[4] There are chapters on those with learning disabilities, on those in psychiatric services, on prisoners and on prostitutes. One worker at the Ruhama project (a support service for women in prostitution) when asked what measures might help combat violence against prostitutes replied: 'Start looking for men who commit such crimes and be really serious about it.'[5]

The report recommended a public awareness campaign about the startling prevalence of sexual violence, that information on existing services should be made widely available and that barriers to disclosure be removed. It commended programmes that taught children about lowering their risk of abuse, but said strategies should also be devised to get adults, and not just professionals, to take responsibility for protecting children. It emphasised the 'gendered nature of sexual violence' and the fact that a significant number of perpetrators of violence against women were partners. This needed to be addressed 'at the level of public attitudes and in psychosocial and law enforcement settings'. New services should be set up, and there should be a 'systematic programme of Irish research'. Finally, a 'consultative committee on sexual violence' should be set up by the government to ensure that the recommendations of the SAVI report were implemented.

'The SAVI report shows an extraordinary level of hurt that is around among adults,' said McGee. 'This isn't just a problem for individuals – it is a problem for society. If this was a disease, there'd be clinics all over the place. President McAleese launched the report at a conference in Dublin Castle and what was most touching and useful about her speech was that she said she was there to thank those who had taken part in the survey, for helping the rest of us to understand.' McGee praised the DRCC for 'investigating the iceberg'.[6]

'The Rape Crisis Centre has always been a leader – it has always been outspoken and the SAVI survey furthered that,' she said. 'They were a vanguard when they started out in the 1970s. They de-stigmatised sexual violence and used public figures well to take away the shame. They recognised that it is important to rescue the people drowning in the river, but that it is also essential to go upstream and find out who is pushing them in.'

Speaking at the conference at which the SAVI report was launched, Professor David Finkelhor, the director of the US Crimes Against Children Research Centre, said it revealed that Ireland had a 'more serious problem' with child sex abuse than the rest of Europe and North America. Breda Allen highlighted the low level of reporting. 'The big reason is the legal system,' she said. 'It switches the onus from the alleged perpetrator to the victim.'[7] Launching the DRCC's annual statistics in May 2002, Geraldine Connolly said that there had been a 20 per cent increase to a total of 10,000 genuine calls to the Centre's counselling line in 2001. SAVI had indicated that only 12 per cent of victims had spoken to a professional. 'That is a fairly scary picture,' she said.[8] Connolly had been the driving force behind the survey, and she was largely responsible for devising its innovative methodology.

The report was well received. It gave a picture of Ireland which was 'truly horrific', according to one editorial. Its main message was that 'silence aids abuse'.[9] Journalist Patsy

McGarry described it as 'a merciless unearthing of the secret world of the Irish Catholic male'.[10] Ailbhe Smyth said it was 'a profoundly sad, shameful and sobering expose of the cruelty suffered by so many for so long'.[11]

Muireann O'Briain was appointed as chief executive officer of the Rape Crisis Centre in April 2002, shortly after the publication of the SAVI report. 'It was a brilliant piece of work, a landmark,' she said, looking back. 'It validated all we had to say. The methodology the DRCC developed has had a big impact on research since then. Geraldine Connolly was excellent.' O'Briain cited the report when she took issue with columnist Kevin Myers, who, referring to British rape statistics, accused 'feminologists' of using rape as a 'weapon of choice'. Praising the 'remarkable women' associated with the Rape Crisis Centre, she said they had campaigned long and hard for the male and female victims of sexual violence. 'Victims of sexual assault feel bad enough already,' she wrote, 'without important research into their situation being turned into a feminist conspiracy. Such research enables service providers to plan for the future and to put prevention programmes in place.'[12]

After Olive Braiden's resignation, the DRCC had been without a director for 18 months. Braiden was among those surprised that the board did not appoint internally. O'Briain is a barrister and former registrar at the Labour Court. She had also worked for an agency which combated child pornography and had just returned to Ireland after managing it for three years in Thailand. 'I didn't apply for the DRCC job because I assumed they'd want someone with a therapeutic background,' she said. 'They headhunted me.'

She devised a strategic plan for the Centre, which the board approved. 'It enabled them to see a way forward and to deal with problems related to the building, finance and education issues,' she said. 'When they got the Leeson Street building, they got a good deal, but it has become cumbersome and it costs a fortune to repair. In my time, we literally had to stop the roof falling in.' The Centre had acquired the basement (the former Fanny Hill's) in 1999 and received funds from the then Minister for Health, Micheal Martin, to transform it into training rooms and offices. This gave the education and training departments space, as well as providing an office for the volunteer co-ordinators. However, problems persist, such as lack of adequate disability access.

The Dublin RCC had drifted away from the Network of Rape Crisis Centres during the late 1990s, though it had worked during this time with the Network to obtain EU funding for a counselling programme for rape crisis volunteers. This was run at University College Cork. After Olive Braiden's departure, acting director Geraldine Connolly 'did a lot of bridgebuilding', according to Fiona Neary, executive director of the Network. 'Dublin had been involved in the early years but there had been tensions,' said Neary. 'It was so much better funded, and had so much higher a profile than the other Centres. Inevitably it had more power.'[13]

After the Network secured EU funding to set up a European Network of Rape Crisis Centres in 1999, Connolly participated in its first conference in Dublin, attended by 48 Centres from 28 countries. The DRCC is also now involved in the NGO Coalition of Violence Against Women, set up in 2000, and including Rape Crisis Centres, Women's Aid, the Network of Refuges, the support group for women in prostitution, Ruhama and the travellers' support group, Pavee Point. O'Briain consolidated the return to the Network. 'Solidarity makes your voice stronger,' she said.[14]

O'Briain highlighted once again the 'insensitive' legal system which meant that counsellors had to warn victims about the trauma they would face if they went to court. Improvements had been made, but huge changes were still needed, she said.[15] Following a radio interview in which she referred to defendants having the services of 'expensive lawyers', she was rebuked by Mr Justice Paul Carney at a conference on the trial of sexual offences in 2003. 'This expression is not a million miles away from the expression "dirty raincoat lawyers" and represents a remarkable position to be taken by someone who herself holds a patent of silk from the government,' he said. He said good quality advice was essential to the working of the Central Criminal Court, where, he pointed out, 40 per cent of those charged pleaded guilty following legal advice.

'The next time I heard the director on the radio she was saying that there was no such thing as a false sexual charge,' Carney said. 'This is not the experience of the courts. In relation to the balance of rape cases which are contested, there is a majority of acquittals.' O'Briain was out of the country at the time. Breda Allen, chairperson of the DRCC's board, said the DRCC left determination of whether a report was false or not to the state. 'It is not for us to decide,' she said. Carney said he had a third concern relating to the DRCC, in relation to victim impact reports. He said he had recently received one such report from a senior counsellor at the Centre, which stated, 'the severity of the sentence imposed will determine the degree to which the victim becomes reconciled with the justice system'. Carney said this represented 'a serious abuse of process'. He praised the Centre, however, for its 'excellent' work in caring for victims of rape.[16]

Undeterred, O'Briain went on to launch a strong attack on the legal profession, declaring that the DRCC was 'sickened by the aggression' shown towards rape victims by defence lawyers. Their behaviour, she said, went 'way beyond the boundaries of reasonable protection for the accused, to the detriment of the health and well being of the witnesses themselves'. She described how a recent client at the Centre had been subjected to three days of 'absolutely gruelling cross-examination' in the witness box, which had left her 'severely re-traumatised'.[17]

One young victim told her story to journalist Kitty Holland. She said a young man had attacked her as she walked home from a party. He pushed her into a field, raped her, told her she was 'a good ride' and left. At the SATU at the Rotunda she met a Rape Crisis Centre volunteer and went on to see a therapist at the Centre. 'Only for her, I don't think I'd have got this far,' she told Holland. It took two years for the case to come to court. The gardaí had told her it was a 'cut and dried' case, but she was unprepared for what happened when she went into the witness box. 'I didn't think I was going to have chunks torn out of me for three whole days. I didn't think I was going to be made out to be someone I'm not, to have that taken from me,' she said.

During the cross-examination, she said, defence counsel suggested that it was inevitable that her clothes had been in disarray after the incident: 'Isn't that what happens when you make vigorous love on the grass?' At one point, she had an epileptic seizure. Counsel for the state said 'very little', which angered the woman. 'I would have liked him to do more – I was on my own – there was no one speaking for me,' she said. The jury returned a verdict of 'not guilty'. The woman said she had been 'torn apart' and had not got justice.[18]

The DRCC's anger about the Irish legal system was vindicated when, later that year, Professor Liz Kelly published research which showed that more rape victims were denied justice in Ireland than anywhere else in Europe. Research she conducted at the London Metropolitan University found that in the period 1993–7 there was a conviction rate of just 2 per cent. Between 1998 and 2001 it fell to 1 per cent. In England and Wales the figure was 8 per cent. In France it was 32 per cent and in Hungary it was 54 per cent. 'It is inconceivable that 99 per cent of men and women who report rape are not telling the truth,' Professor Kelly said. 'There is still a culture of scepticism about reports of rape, viewing them differently to other crime, and this is supported by judicial statements.' This meant rapists operated in a 'culture of impunity'.[19] Ireland needed to radically rethink the way its investigative and legal systems treated rape victims, she concluded. The Network of Rape Crisis Centres went on to secure funding for a major research project into Ireland's appalling attrition rate, to be conducted under the supervision of Professor Tom O'Malley at the National University of Ireland, Galway, from 2005 to 2008.

'The toxicology service has remarked to SATU that levels of alcohol in the samples they test for us are only seen in one other source – the coroner's office.' This was what Dr Mary Holohan, head of the SATU, told the Joint Oireachtas Committee on Health and Children in 2003. She said staff were often asked to determine whether women had been sexually assaulted or not, since they could not, themselves, remember. The doctor was speaking at a time when there was considerable alarm about the potential availability and use of the so-called 'rape drug' rohypnol. She said there had been no positive tests for rohypnol in Ireland ever. Women who claimed their drinks had been spiked 'needed to believe that is what happened', she said. She drew attention to the alarming levels of drink being consumed by very young girls.[20] Dr Holohan suggested that the government should sponsor hard-hitting TV ads showing the degradation resulting from excessive drinking. Senator Mary Henry called for 'tough enforcement' of the law to ensure that underage children couldn't buy alcohol.[21]

However, when a senior garda claimed that women were wasting garda time and scarce hospital resources by making false allegations of rape after excessive drinking, the DRCC described his comments as 'extremely unhelpful'. Muireann O'Briain said that the DRCC's experience was that 'hardly any false allegations are made'. She said women should be aware that drinking too much made them vulnerable, but this didn't change the fact that 'people don't ask to be raped'. She said gardaí should advise women that 'because of the vulnerable position they may have been in, they will find it difficult to prove that they did not consent'. Women had a right to report rape no matter what the circumstances, 'and to be taken seriously when they do'.[22]

In 2004, Mr Justice Paul Carney said there was a 'significant and surprising' number of cases coming before the courts with the scenario of a woman becoming tired at a party, finding a bed to lie down on and waking up to find a man having sexual intercourse with her. He said that while these events constituted the crime of rape, he was at a loss to know how to deal with them following a decision by the Court of Criminal Appeal. In a case involving anal and vaginal rape, the appeal court had set aside a sentence he had given, even though it was in his view a lenient one. It had also found Carney to be 'in error' for approaching sentence without leaving open the possibility of a non-custodial sentence and for attaching great weight to being consistent. Carney called for more guidance from the appeal court.[23]

The issue of false allegations arose again when the legal advisor to the British False Memory Society (BFMS), Margaret Jarvis, claimed at a press conference in Dublin that the Commission to Inquire into Child Abuse encouraged people to accuse innocent people of abusing them. She also said that the therapy system was 'a machine for manufacturing false allegations'. Counsellors, Rape Crisis Centres and therapists who encouraged people to say their problems were due to past abuse were part of an 'industry' which was indulging in a 'very, very damaging process' and the 'corruption of young lives'. Jarvis had just held a meeting in Dublin, she said, with people falsely accused, and she was providing them with analysis and information. Ms Florence Horsman-Logan of the Let Our Voices Emerge (LOVE) group said that 'more than 30 per cent' of abuse allegations in Ireland were false.

However, survivors groups reacted angrily, and Angela McCarthy of the DRCC said victims of abuse could be driven back into silence following 'extreme language and disparaging remarks' at the press conference. She said these could 'encourage a new myth or form of denial, namely that a large percentage of abuse allegations are false, malicious or driven by a desire for compensation'.[24]

Muireann O'Briain's period as chief executive officer of the DRCC was not an entirely happy one. Although she was held in high regard by some staff, she came into conflict with others. After 18 months as CEO, she left. Rosemary Daly was appointed CEO in February 2004. Daly had become well known as a passionate spokeswoman for the Irish Haemophilia Society. She said that while she was new, she wanted to be true to the vision of the women who set the DRCC up. They were 'very strong, courageous women who set out ... to change how women are treated', she told Mary de Courcy in an interview for a psychotherapy journal.

'I think they were labeled as mad feminists in an effort to put them down by those who didn't like what they are saying. I'm very happy to be a feminist ... I'm a woman and proud to be.' She said she felt people still didn't want sexual violence to be talked about. 'I see all of us in the DRCC as working towards healing. You can feel it in the building when you come in,' she said. 'I said one day that my style of management would be to be on the bottom holding them up rather than at the front leading the charge, that my metaphorical arms are strong enough to hold and support those who are doing the work.' She said she felt her role was to be like a parent, supporting the work of the counsellors 'and in the meantime to be changing attitudes around sexual violence and abuse in a lobbying capacity'. She said the image of the DRCC had to be 'an all encompassing service that embraces everybody; for all genders, creeds, nationalities and for those with disabilities'.[25]

Daly referred to the fact that non-nationals were coming in growing numbers to the DRCC, many of them referred by social workers, doctors and solicitors. Some were asylum seekers or refugees; others were migrant workers. In July 2004 the Mayo Rape Crisis Centre, along with the Irish Refugee Council, claimed the Irish authorities had behaved with 'brutal insensitivity' to a Burundi woman who was refused asylum. Olivia Ndayishimye had been repeatedly raped and had seen her son and her mother killed. She had been attending the Mayo centre for counselling.[26]

The Ruhama project revealed in 2004 that it was aware of 70 women that had been trafficked into Ireland in the previous year to work in the sex industry, including lap-dancing clubs. They were under the control of violent men, and Ruhama had helped 15 of them escape. They included Eastern Europeans and Africans. An 18-year-old Romanian woman reported to the gardaí that she had been brought to Ireland when she was 15 by a Romanian man who promised her a 'great future' but in reality held her captive, subjected her to horrific violence and made her have sex with up to 200 men. Her plight was exposed after she was admitted to hospital having been beaten up. She told her story to journalist Kitty Holland.[27]

Angela McCarthy, head of clinical services at the DRCC, said this was an increasingly important part of the Centre's work. 'Some of these women carry the aura of war with them when they walk in to the Centre,' she said. 'Some of them are severely traumatised. They may have experienced torture, rape, beatings and bereavement, sometimes of many members of their families. They find themselves isolated and in a foreign culture, struggling to adapt and sometimes facing racism and hostility. They have a lot of anxiety. Often it is impossible to address the trauma in their past until their everyday difficulties are sorted out to some degree. We end up trying to help them to get English classes, sorting out accommodation, maternity clothing, and that sort of thing. They can't afford childcare and we don't have facilities here for babies and children. We also see unaccompanied minors aged 16 to 18, and they are in a very lonely position.

'This has been a challenge for our therapists to adjust to different cultural attitudes and work with such severely traumatised clients. We are mindful of the risk of secondary traumatisation for the therapists and the need to provide support for them. My own working experience in war-torn countries has been very useful, and so has the fact that I used to be a French teacher.'

Under Rosemary Daly's direction, the Centre applied for funding for an advocacy worker to help women in these situations with their practical needs, so that counsellors can concentrate on their therapeutic needs. McCarthy has written about the issues arising from such work. Language may present a problem. Facial and body expressions are also often different to those with which the DRCC workers are familiar. Some women might be veiled. The client is likely to have internalised the cultural attitudes of their country of origin. A woman may feel she has dishonoured her family. A man may expect to be treated with contempt for revealing that he has been raped. 'Their traumatic experiences are framed within a context of high levels of cultural blaming, shaming and punishing.' The therapist needed to explain that, 'we are there to support them and not to judge them'. Therapists also needed to 'work on our own unconscious prejudices and biases'.

Clients often expressed intense anxiety about the official interview they face in seeking asylum status: 'A female client may be doubly anxious because she knows she will be expected to give a detailed account of her experience of rape,' McCarthy wrote, in an article co-authored by Mary de Courcy.[28] The Centre sometimes provides victim impact reports as part of the appeal process for asylum seekers who have been refused refugee status. The DRCC's statistics for 2004 showed that 5 per cent of its clients were non-nationals. McCarthy pointed out that the Centre had no funds to pay interpreters.

Nor had it adequate funds to provide enough counsellors to dispose of its waiting list. This, Rosemary Daly said, had to be closed for periods of around a fortnight, so that people didn't end up waiting more than six months. The statistics for 2004 also showed that 20 per cent of the almost 12,000 callers to the DRCC were aged between 15 and 17. Rosemary Daly said the figure was 'shocking', particularly since those aged under 18 could not get on-going counselling without parental consent. 'The difficulty is that if the abuse takes place in the home, they can't get this consent,' she said. Angela McCarthy said teenagers were a 'powerless section of society'. Most victims were under 30. As usual, the overwhelming majority of callers were women, with 11 per cent of them men. For the first time, the annual report included figures for 'drug rape' cases, which represented 3 per cent of cases. Daly suggested the figure might be even higher, since some women might be reluctant to seek help 'as memories are often unclear'.[29] Mary Holohan at the SATU continued to insist that alcohol was the drug responsible for the fact that a third of cases seen there had memory loss.[30] Daly said women should be careful. However, it was not women's drinking habits that caused rape. 'The big question is, why do men rape women?' she said. 'What kind of society do we have when we have to say this is what men do and therefore we should do x, y and z? We should be looking at the attitudes of young men. We should be educating instead of just trying to clean up the mess when the hurt has already been caused.'[31]

As a writer in the *Star* rather crudely put it, 'There is no way you can ever blame a woman for being raped, no matter how drunk she was at the time ... the blame must lie with the man.' The writer added, 'these young girls are not slappers – they're just drunks.' Women drank because they felt bad about themselves and hated their bodies. 'We rely on blokes to reassure us we are not the Loch Ness monster. And a few bottles of the hard stuff helps women flirt with men and secure his flattering attentions. Unfortunately, the unlucky ones get more off the man than they bargained for or wanted ... We should drink less and love ourselves more.'[32]

RTÉ presenter Gerry Ryan took up the same theme during an interview with Rosemary Daly and Hannah McGee on the findings of the SAVI report. 'Nobody deserves to be raped even if they're walking down O'Connell Street naked on ecstasy,' he declared. Ryan was interviewing the women about the 'roadshow' the DRCC had embarked on to, as Daly put it, 'have a national conversation' about the prevalence of sexual violence and the silence of its victims. Muireann O'Briain had done the preparatory work for the series of seminars before her departure. They were held in Tralee, Dundalk, Wexford and Athlone for an audience consisting of health care workers, community and youth workers and the public. They included presentations by local Rape Crisis Centres. Daly said on the *Gerry Ryan Show* that when one SAVI researcher had asked a person why they'd never told anyone about the sexual violence they'd suffered, they replied that no one ever asked.

'Over 25 years ago when the Rape Crisis Centre was starting out, the word rape was never mentioned. It just was not talked about,' Daly said. There was still, in 2004, a sense of 'blame and shame' attached to it. 'That is the barrier we have to remove.' McGee said on the programme that while the Stay Safe programme had been effective in primary schools, there was still a pressing need for more education in life skills in secondary schools. Daly said there would be people listening who 'may have lived in silence' with abuse and she urged them to call the DRCC. Ryan read out a text message which had just been sent to the programme: 'I'm 17. I've been abused by my father for 10 years. I told a chaplain and got an ultimatum to tell my mother who already knows.' Daly read out the DRCC helpline number. 'How long does it usually take for someone to be fixed?' asked Ryan. 'Will any of us ever be fixed?' Daly replied. 'The joy would be to be able to move forward and lead a productive life without sexual violence being the main item on your agenda every day when you open your eyes. It is not your life. It is not you.'[33]

When Amnesty International launched its 2004 campaign against violence against women, Daly said it was 'fantastic' to have the issue put into its international context. She shared the view, expressed by Colm Ó Cuanachain, secretary general of the Irish section of Amnesty, that 'taboo, cultural consent, ignorance, acquiescence and heartbreak all conspire to silence the majority'. Violence against women, Ó Cuanachain said, was 'systematic, endemic and universal'. Amnesty drew attention to the 15,000 dowry killings of women each year in India, to the 'honour' killings of women in Asia and the Middle East and to the 120 million girls who suffered genital mutilation. Inequality made women vulnerable, he said.

The Council of Europe reported that violence against women was the greatest cause of death and injury in women aged 16 to 44. In more than nine out of ten incidents of domestic violence reported to gardaí, the perpetrator was a man and the victim a woman. People needed to pledge, said Ó Cuanachain, 'not to do it, or permit others to do it, or tolerate it, or rest until it is eradicated'.[34]

Daly said she'd gone into the DRCC 'in awe of the past history of the place'. At her desk in Leeson Street, she began to read up on material about rape and was horrified. She said it 'reduced me to tears and made my stomach turn'.[35] She decided she needed to know what it was like 'at the coalface' – so she took part in the DRCC's training course for volunteer telephone counsellors. 'I was blown away by the levels of care given by the therapists and volunteers, and by the quality of work being done by the training department – they travel the country and they are hugely in demand,' she said. She found staff somewhat demoralised, emerging from a second period without a director. 'I worked on building a sense of cohesion among them, and on improving links between staff and the board, which were weak.' Daly also worked on developing outreach programmes which were planned for the Dochas Centre – the women's prison at Mountjoy – and for Tallaght. A pilot programme for Dochas started in April 2005.

Launching an exhibition hosted by the DRCC at the Axis Centre in Ballymun, Daly spoke again of the need to constantly raise the subject of sexual and domestic violence. The exhibition of 365 international posters about violence against women was put together by Galway garda Colm Dempsey. The programme note was written by Tanya Brown, whose sister, Nicole Brown Simpson, was murdered. O.J. Simpson was controversially acquitted of the murder. 'Without education and awareness campaigns, women and children of all ages will feel helpless, hopeless and completely alone,' wrote Brown. Daly described the exhibition as spectacular. 'When you see it first you are bombarded by colour. It's only when you have a closer look that you will see the bleakness and pain underneath.'[36]

Daly experienced some frustration in her role. She wanted to do 'frontline' work with clients. She felt the board of the Centre was too set in its ways, a criticism shared with others connected to the Centre. 'The organisation has been there a long time and has certain ways of operating,' she said. 'I wanted to change things.' In December 2004 she resigned. One senior staff member expressed regret that Daly had left after such a short time. 'She was working in a very careful and diplomatic way to bring about change,' she said.[37] The DRCC immediately appointed Irene Bergin to replace her. Bergin had formerly worked as development manager at CARI and as director general of the ISPCA.

'We as a society have still not faced up to the prevalence, nature and underlying causes of violence against women,' said

Kate Mulkerrins of the Network of Rape Crisis Centres at the opening of an EU conference on violence against women in Dublin Castle in 2004. She said that after 25 years of campaigning by Rape Crisis Centres, 'we still manage to end up bottom of the league in Europe' in terms of bringing rapists to justice. At the conference, the president of the Irish Human Rights Commission, Dr Maurice Manning, said the case for an EU directive on violence against women was 'unanswerable'. He said it was a 'matter of regret' that the EU constitution was 'silent on the subject'.[38] Criminologist Dr Clare Leon told a conference that 90 per cent of sexual crime in Ireland did not result in a conviction.

The McColgan children had been 'trapped in a system that failed to protect them'. The story of another family similarly trapped was exposed when, in 2004, a former soldier from Donegal was sent to prison for life for the serial rape of two of his daughters and four of his nieces. His wife had first complained of his offences in 1987 and gardaí had sent a file to the DPP, but he was not charged. A health board intervention meant that he was barred from the family home for a period, but he was allowed back. He admitted abusing the children and left the army with an honourable discharge. The rapes continued for 13 more years. One of the girls told the court the man had ruined all their lives.

Sentencing anomalies have continued. A teenage boy from Dublin who raped a 50-year-old man was given a suspended sentence. Mr Justice Carney said there were 'exceptional circumstances' meriting a non-custodial sentence. These included the remorse of the rapist, his early guilty plea and the fact that the victim was 35 years older and 'of a stocky build', whereas the defendant was 'a reedy young man' who had been experiencing difficulties over his sexual orientation which had since been resolved. The chairwoman of the DRCC, Breda Allen, appealed to other victims not to be discouraged from reporting rape to the gardaí.

It emerged in 2004 that in the previous year just eight sex offenders in prison had completed a programme designed to stop them re-offending. Just over 100 prisoners had completed it in the 10 years since it was set up.[39] The DRCC had called again for more emphasis on such programmes following the 2003 conviction of a man who was sentenced to 14 years in jail for rape. Twelve years earlier he had raped another woman and had served nine years in jail. He had also assaulted a third woman and attacked gardaí with a slashhook when they tried to capture him. Gardaí said his appetite for violence could not be underestimated and that they had no doubt he would rape again if freed. The mother of his most recent victim said he should have been jailed for longer. 'If he gets his freedom he will attack again,' she said. Breda Allen commented: 'The likelihood is that if he was kept in for 25 years he could re-offend.'[40] Attitudes to victims continue to be problematic. In 2002 a judge expressed disgust at the 'pig ignorance' of a community that ostracised a teenage girl after she alleged sex abuse against her father, who was later convicted.[40]

During the trial of Marc Dutroux for the murder of four young girls in Belgium it emerged that he had honed his methods during a spree of abductions, rapes and torture during the 1980s. He had served 6 years of a 13-year sentence before being released in 1992 to look after his grandmother. He was soon constructing the tunnels and dungeons he would use to hide his next set of victims. He had got the idea from another convicted rapist while in prison.[41]

19

A Good Place to Be

In 1979, 79 people sought help from the DRCC. In 2003, 15,717 people did so. In 1979, the Centre had raised £600 on the Reclaim the Night march. In 2003, it had around €800,000 in government grants and raised a further €300,000 through fundraising. In 1979, it consisted of a group of less than 20 volunteers. In 2004, it had 30 staff and more than 70 volunteers. In 1979, it had an answering machine in a room in someone else's office. By 2004, its large Georgian house in Dublin 2 is too small for the still-expanding organisation.

Annie Gallagher intended 20 years ago to become a volunteer at the Centre but realised early on in the training course that it was not for her – instead she offered to help with fundraising. She and her colleague Collette Schutz work in a tiny office behind the reception area of the Centre. 'One of our first big events was the Peter O'Brien fashion show in 1986,' she recalled. 'He was the wonderboy from Finglas who had become the lead designer with Chlöe. It was huge to get him. He was on *The Late Late Show* talking about it and we had the Concert Hall. It was mould-breaking, really – a far cry from the parish hall. It was the start of us believing in ourselves. Our fundraising was sexy – we were very popular.'

She praised the contribution made by fundraiser Kevin Flanagan over many years. 'Kevin organised a lot of events. He was a ballet dancer and he was well connected with all the aerobics groups. For years he ran the DRCC stepathons which raised thousands of pounds,' she said.

'After the board was set up and the Friends of the Rape Crisis Centre, I was invited to be fundraising co-ordinator. Mary Henry was chair of the Friends – she was very motivating and focused. She wrapped herself around her committee. Ireland was really beginning to come to terms with the fact that rape was happening and the impact that had on the public was that people wanted to appease their consciences. The more horrific the case which came into the public eye, the more support we got. People couldn't bear the idea that the Rape Crisis Centre would cease to exist.' In 1993, U2 divided the proceeds of one of its concerts among several charities, including the Rape Crisis Centre. Back in the 1980s, Hazel O'Connor made a single and donated the proceeds to the Centre. The Alternative Miss Ireland contest was held in its aid.

Singer Máire Ní Bhraonain has also done much to support the Centre. 'In 1993 Aengus Roche thought up our first golf classic, and at that golfer John Baker approached us and helped us organise it as an annual thing,' said Schutz. 'Clannad became our patrons and from then on it was the Clannad Golf Classic in aid of the DRCC. It is still one of our staples and John Baker is still our MC. David Harvey was the force behind the corporate quiz and Pat Kenny has always been the questionmaster. When it was seen that *men* were supporting us, corporate Dublin weighed in and we were able to start pitching things at a very high level. We were rubbing shoulders with the guys people read about in the business pages. It became prestigious to be associated with the Rape Crisis Centre. The cloud of suspicion and discomfort about rape lifted somewhat.' Gallagher agreed. 'We got the reputation of people who put on a good gig,' she said. 'Our summer lunch is organised by Jo Supple, aka Miss Candy, and then there's the Ball in October. We appeal to aspiring BMW types, but also to the wider public. The Women's Marathon is always a big event for us. We always get great support from two radio stations, FM104 and 98FM.'

'Ireland is a better place because of the work of the Rape Crisis Centre. We've established ourselves as a viable repair service for people who've been damaged,' said Graham Crisp, chairman of the board's fundraising section. 'But fundraising for the Centre was never all that easy. Rape is such a difficult subject. The big multinationals avoid it, and so do a lot of the big local companies. It is sensitive. We're a relatively small charity. Still, we are more secure now than ever before. Our flag-day is still our biggest event – it raises about €50,000. We're hoping that with closer links now with the Network of Rape Crisis Centres that will lead to a common approach across all areas of policy and funding.'

Accounts officer Naomi Patton joined the Centre in 1987. Her first day at work was her 21st birthday. Funding was in crisis. 'There was a huge deficit. I was shocked when I realised how bad it was. Everything was written into big ledgers. We trundled along – and then there was the audit by the Revenue and the audit by the EHB. I was completely and utterly scared stiff. The EHB accountant, Martin Gallagher, would come in and study every item. In fact he went on to become a very good friend of the Centre over the years. Our accountant, Dermot Keogh, has been a real rock for the Centre, too.' Patton said she joined the Centre knowing nothing about sexual violence. 'I've huge respect for the work that goes on here,' she said. 'The Centre has changed a lot but it has been constant in the support it gives to the people who most need it. I love working here. I love the Rape Crisis Centre.'

Volunteering is still the frontline of the DRCC's services. Volunteers keep the helpline open 24 hours a day seven days a week, covering overnights and weekends, while paid staff run it during office hours. These volunteers don't meet with clients face to face. Another group of volunteers operates a rota to provide accompaniment to support rape victims attending the SATU at the Rotunda Hospital. Volunteers may also accompany clients to court.

'I was a rape victim and a victim of child sex abuse myself, so I knew the value of the service offered by the Centre even though I hadn't availed of it,' said Mel Connors, a volunteer on the helpline. After interview, she did the DRCC's training, an intensive programme over four weekends, in 2002. It involved discussions, role plays and listening to tapes of people talking about their experience of sexual violence. There were talks about the myths of rape, suicide and child abuse. She then joined the telephone counselling rota and now covers four shifts a month.

'There was enormous validation for me in the training,' she said. 'And my own experience means I understand when someone says to me that they weren't believed or nothing was done. As a volunteer, I'm very comfortable realising you're not there to find solutions. I don't feel under pressure – you are there to bear witness. You don't judge. It is really interesting work. You can be talking to someone about something that happened two hours ago or thirty years. People live strange and difficult lives with great courage. It can be quite inspiring.'

Ruth Walsh was a SATU volunteer for the maximum two years before becoming an outreach speaker for the Centre. 'With the SATU you've to be available to head up to the Rotunda at short notice. Ideally, you want to have some time with the victim before they go for the medical examination. Some don't want to talk, others do. Sometimes they ask about what lies ahead. We tell them they'll be treated sensitively. We let them know the Rape Crisis Centre is here, too, if they need it,' she said. 'Last night I was asked to do a talk to a church group. I brought notes and an overhead projector but when I got there it was this fabulous African service of praise with singing and dancing and children everywhere. I just shouted a few things down the mike and gave the pastor some leaflets. There was a child hanging onto my leg showing me a truck. It was a bit different from the usual attentive rows of sixth formers in their uniforms. But I think it was important – the pastor wanted to show the people that there are services here that they can avail of.'

Walsh has accompanied several women to court. 'Sometimes the person has been alienated from their family, and sometimes even the family is with the defendant,' she said. 'In one case, I was able to protect someone from the press. In another, I sat beside a woman and kept her from having to sit beside her relatives.'

The volunteers are organised by and supported by Mairead Mallon, the full-time head of volunteer services, Maria O'Loughlin and Elaine Claffey, both part-time volunteer co-ordinators working in the basement office. 'This department is where all the energy vibrates from,' said Claffey. 'This is where you bring in the community, those who care. The energy rises through the Centre.' Training courses are held once or twice a year. 'There's huge interest,' said Mallon. 'We are open 365 days a year and we never have a gap. We have professional women in high-powered jobs, and we have housewives. They want to 'give something back', and for some, to 'get something back' in a human way. We don't look for qualifications – it is more about qualities. Our volunteers go the extra mile.'

Given the DRCC's ambition to eradicate sexual violence, education and training have always been a central part of its work. Leonie O'Dowd is head of training, and Eve Daly is education officer. 'Most rape victims will never come for therapy, so we try to enhance the ability of other workers to meet needs as they encounter them. We run courses for therapists, school counsellors, gardaí, youth workers, addiction workers, legal aid workers, workers with the homeless and others. The judges have held out, though they could really do with it. We'd love to do more work with the gardaí – at present we train the trainees for three hours in groups of 40 or 50, but we hope through an initiative of the Network to do in-service training as well. We consult with the group first and then design the course to suit their needs. We also do courses about preventing and dealing with sexual harassment in the workplace and bullying. We do a lot of work for the statutory sector.

'We discuss the myths of rape, because if, for example, a garda firmly believes that most rape allegations are false, then that will do damage. The myths are still very much the same as they were when the Centre opened, but there are a few new ones. For example, that all priests are dangerous to children.

Or that the child abuser is a man in a white van. The man who killed the little English girl Sara Payne did have a white van, but it was coincidental. It is about getting people to face the reality: that most victims know their attacker and that it is in the family that children are most at risk. We get people to explore their attitudes to, for example, situations about which they might be quite judgemental. We discuss things like the too early sexualisation of children.

'In the training, it is important to allow people to have a chance to talk about how they are facing these things. Operating the Department of Health guidelines, Children First, is a nightmare. People used to think that if you reported abuse that was more or less the end of it, but now they know that it may lead into a long-drawn-out process which may not lead to effective intervention. We spend time talking with people about what it is like to work with children who they know are being abused but nothing is being done about it.

'Increasingly, we put a lot of emphasis on resourcing the workers vis-à-vis vicarious traumatisation. We are conscious of the sensitivities of the people we're training. This stuff resonates with people – we invite them to participate but we don't push them. We do a little focusing exercise every day just to check if people are feeling fragile. One thing people find really helpful is understanding that how their clients relate to them isn't personal. In the past year, we've developed a template about the dynamics of abuse which play out between client and counsellor and between staff and people in authority in organisations. Workers can move from being a support to trying to rescue people, to backing off and feeling helpless. We discuss the need to "abuse-proof" systems, to look at checks and balances around power and consultation. If you are working with trauma and abuse, staff tend to adopt roles, the abusive parent, the parent who doesn't listen, the child who's pathologically good, the child who's acting out ... organisations have to actively combat this.'[1]

Maria Byrne joined the Centre in 1995 to provide secretarial support to the board and as Olive Braiden's personal assistant. 'I moved from the corporate sector where I was used to having my own office,' she recalled. 'Here, I had a small laptop and a desk in the corner of the phone counselling room. It was really strange. I had to be very quiet because people were counselling. But I loved it – there was a lovely serene working atmosphere. I learned a lot listening to the counsellors. I'd have had no inkling before that about the worst sort of things. Working as relief on the switchboard and on the reception desk, I began to meet clients face to face.' As other senior workers left, Byrne began to acquire more duties. She has been the administrator of the DRCC since 2000.

The work of the Rape Crisis Centre is constantly evolving. 'In training now, we're involved in equality issues,' said Angela McCarthy. 'The period the Centre was set up was one of struggle. We're in a different era now. Women haven't won all their rights but it has changed. We are up and running. We're in a more confident position.'

Fiona Neary of the Network of Rape Crisis Centres said the Dublin Centre had made a huge contribution. 'It gave credibility to Rape Crisis Centres nationally, it gave excellent training and it demonstrated that the law can be changed,' she said. 'It is excellent that it is now firmly part of the Network. We need to work together and have coherent leadership. There is so much work to be done over the next generation. There are critical gaps in services, and there's a huge amount of educational work to be done. We know very little about ending sexual violence, which is really our aim.'[2] The Network was campaigning to change the law so that defendants could no longer conduct their own defence in rape trials. The existing situation had seen several men opt to conduct their own cross-examination of the woman alleging rape against them.

Director Irene Bergin said she had 'huge respect' for her staff and volunteers. 'We have no problem getting volunteers at a time when many organisations do,' she said. 'That says a lot about the esteem people have for the Rape Crisis Centre. It's a difficult place to work. We won't stop rape because it's a crime as old as Christ. It has always been there. But we can help the women and men who come here to get better.'

Bergin said the feminist ethos was still important in the

Centre. 'Women have suffered huge discrimination because of their gender. Most perpetrators of rape were men – a growing number of the Centre's clients are also men. 'We are seeing more men and also more women from new communities, some of them from very strong male cultures. We need translation services,' she said. Bergin said the Centre needed to find ways of reaching younger clients. 'We need to lobby for political change, too.'

Shirley Cummins is a former insurance worker who gave it up to study psychology and religion. While at college, she became a SATU volunteer at the DRCC, then, after two years, went into its outreach department, before getting a full-time job at the Centre as a telephone counsellor. There are two full-time and four part-time phone counsellors. 'It is a privilege to do this work. People are traumatised but they have such courage,' she said. 'There is a huge variety to the calls we get – you can be giving information, listening, pointing people in the right direction for something they need. It is a brilliant service that we offer. We never stop. Everyone at the Rape Crisis Centre is here not because they have to be, but because they want to be here.'

The first person clients and visitors meet when they come into the DRCC is receptionist Dorothy Cogan. She sits at the front desk, which always has a bunch of fresh flowers on it, in the bright hall. She joined the Centre in 1986. 'It is wonderful,' she said. 'The clients are amazing. They are so courageous. Working here really makes you believe in the human spirit. The Centre has changed a lot – it is much more professional now and so much busier. There are a lot more men now and a lot of women of different nationalities. In the olden days, I was the housekeeper and I used to have tea with clients. That doesn't happen now – things are more formal. But so many clients over the years have told me how safe they feel here. They sense an atmosphere of calm when they come in that door. This is definitely a good place to be.'

Reclaim the Night march, Anne Connolly with megaphone, October 1978.

Anti-Amendment Campaign platform: Anne O'Donnell, Jean Tansey, Noreen Byrne and Moira Woods.

The front door of the Ra
Crisis Centre on Leeson St

Annual Report 1984: Anne O'Donnell, Bernie Purcell and Barbara Egan.

Emma Hussey (former Chairwoman of the DRCC Board), Olive Braiden and Mary Henry (founder of Friends of the Rape Crisis Centre) in 1991.

Martyn Turner cartoon of the X case.

Meeting Padraig Flynn in 1992: Olive Braiden, Frances Fitzgerald, Anne Taylor and Rosin McDermott.

President Mary Robinson with Bosnian women at Áras an Uachtaráin in 1993.

Workout Against Rape: Politicians at a fundraising event in 2002.

Clockwise above: Olive Braiden and Mr Justice Paul Carney in July 1999. The late Joe Robbins (former Chair of the DRCC board). President Mary McAleese and Geraldine Connolly (former Head of Training and Education, DRCC). Muireann O'Briain (former Director).

Angela McCarthy (Head of Counselling, DRCC), Miriam MacGillicuddy (Labour Councillor, Tralee), Vera O'Leary (Director, Tralee RCC), Inspector Barry O'Rourke (Tralee Garda Station) and Rosemary Daly (Former Director, DRCC) at the SAVI Roadshow in 2004.

25th anniversary, May 2005: Naomi Patton (Accounts Officer), ie Gallagher (Funding Co-ordinator), Bertie Ahern (Taoiseach), Irene Bergin (Director) and eda Allen (Chair, Board of Directors).

NOTES

1 RECLAIM THE NIGHT

[1] Interview with the author, July 2005.
[2] Interview with the author, June 2004.
[3] Interview with the author, June 2004.
[4] *Sunday Journal*, 22 October 1978.
[5] *The Irish Times*, 14 October 1978.
[6] Interview with the author, June 2004.
[7] Interview with the author, June 2004.
[8] Interview with the author, June 2004.
[9] Interview with the author, June 2004.
[10] Interview with the author, June 2004.
[11] Lyn Madden and June Levine, *Lyn: A Story of Prostitution*, Cork: Attic Press, 1987, p. 29.
[12] *Sunday Journal*, 15 October 1978.
[13] *The Irish Times*, 23 October 1978.
[14] *The Irish Times*, 19 October 1978.
[15] Ibid.
[16] Ibid.
[17] *The Irish Times*, 23 October 1978.
[18] Ibid.
[19] *The Irish Times*, 24 October 1978.
[20] *Galway Advertiser*, November 1978.
[21] *Spare Rib*, December 1978.
[22] Interview with the author, June 2004.

2 THE CAMPAIGN AGAINST RAPE (CAR)

[1] June Levine, *Sisters*, Dublin: Ward River Press, 1982, p. 284.
[2] IWU discussion paper, quoted in Linda Connolly, *The Irish Womens Movement*, Dublin: Lilliput, 2003, p. 133.
[3] Interview with the author, July 2004.

[4] Interview with the author, July 2004.
[5] Judgment delivered 7 April 1978, HM Court of Criminal Appeal, Belfast.
[6] *The Irish Times*, 10 April 1978.
[7] Sarah Nelson, *Incest: Facts and Myths*, Edinburgh: Stramullion, 1982.
[8] Stephen Rae, *Guilty*, Dublin: Blackwater Press, 2002, p. 26.
[9] There is a full account of these crimes in Stephen Rae, *Guilty*, Dublin: Blackwater Press, 2002, pp. 1–26.
[10] London RCC, *Sexual Violence: the reality for women*, London: Women's Press, 1984.
[11] Ibid.
[12] Unpublished letter from WAR, 15 November 1977.
[13] Unpublished paper presented to WLC, 1977.
[14] Unpublished manifesto against rape, Des Feministes Revolutionnaires, circa 1977.
[15] Unpublished minutes of CAR, 13 September 1977.
[16] Interview with the author, July 2004.
[17] Interview with the author, July 2004.
[18] Résumé of policy and membership requirements, RCCG, November 1977.

3 TAKING ON 'THE ANCIENT ATMOSPHERE OF RAPE'

[1] Interview with the author, July 2004.
[2] From *Living and Loving*, 1969, quoted in *The Field Day Anthology of Irish Writing*, Vol. 5, Cork: Cork University Press, 2002, p. 1416.
[3] DRCC, First Report, 1979.
[4] *Evening Press*, 20 February 1979.
[5] 'Peer Counselling', DRCC archive.
[6] RCC archive.
[7] Interview with the author, July 2004.
[8] June Levine, *Sisters*, Dublin: Ward River Press, 1982, p. 57.
[9] Interview with the author, July 2004.
[10] Interview with the author, July 2004.
[11] History of the Pleas of the Crown 629, 1736, quoted in the CSW's 'Submission on Rape in Ireland', 1978, p. 10.
[12] Ibid., p. 10.
[13] Senate report, 4 April 1979.
[14] *The Irish Times*, 5 April 1979.
[15] Quoted in *The Field Day Anthology of Irish Writing*, Vol. 5, Cork: Cork University Press, 2002, pp. 223–4.
[16] DRCC Annual Report, 1981.
[17] *Irish Press*, 29 October 1980.
[18] *The Irish Times*, 28 November 1980.

[19] *The Irish Times*, 2 April 1981.
[20] *The Irish Times*, May 1981.

4 ANGER

[1] *Evening Herald*, 15 May 1980.
[2] DRCC, Second Report, 1981.
[3] Leeds Revolutionary Feminist Group, conference paper 1979, published in *Love Your Enemy?*, London: Onlywomen Press, 1981.
[4] Minutes of DRCC meeting, 20 June 1983.
[5] Interview with the author, October 2004.
[6] Interview with the author, July 2005.
[7] Interview with the author, January 2005.
[8] DRCC, Second Report, 1981.

5 MEDDLING WITH THE MORAL LAW

[1] Quoted in Emily O'Reilly, *Masterminds of the Right*, Cork: Attic Press, 1988, p. 55.
[2] *In Dublin*, 8 July 1982.
[3] Letter to *Irish Press*, 9 January 1981.
[4] RTÉ interview, 23 July 1980.
[5] *The Irish Times*, 3 June 1981.
[6] *Irish Press*, 3 June 1981.
[7] Ibid.
[8] *Status*, October 1981, p. 27.
[9] *In Dublin*, 8 July 1982.
[10] Ibid.
[11] Quoted in O'Reilly, op. cit., p. 63.
[12] *In Dublin*, 6 August 1982.
[13] Quoted in O'Reilly, op. cit., p. 70.
[14] *Irish Independent*, 16 April 1982.
[15] *Irish Press*, 30 March 1982.
[16] *The Irish Times*, 6 May 1982.
[17] *The Irish Times*, 21 May 1982.
[18] Interview with the author, July 2004.
[19] Minutes of DRCC meeting, 13 February 1978.
[20] Minutes of DRCC meeting, 13 April 1982.
[21] *The Irish Feminist Review*, Cork: Women's Community Press, 1984, p. 10.
[22] Minutes of DRCC meeting, 26 April 1982.
[23] Interview with the author, August 2004.
[24] Quoted in 'The Abortion Referendum – the case against', issued by the Anti-Amendment Campaign, 1982.
[25] *Irish Press*, 12 July 1982.

26 *Irish Independent,* 24 June 1983.
27 *Sunday Independent,* 21 August 1983.
28 RTÉ *Today Tonight* programme, August 1983.
29 Interview with the author, August 2004.
30 Interview with the author, October 2004.
31 Letter to *The Irish Times,* 5 September 1983.
32 *The Irish Times,* 2 September 1983.
33 *The Irish Times,* 6 September 1983.
34 *Irish Independent,* 9 September 1983.

6 'WHAT SORT OF LADIES ARE WE DEALING WITH HERE?'

1 Letter of resignation by Nuala Fennell, June 1981, quoted in *The Field Day Anthology of Irish Writing,* Vol. 5, Cork: Cork University Press, 2002, p. 201.
2 *Evening Press,* 23 February 1983.
3 Quoted in *The Irish Times,* 11 May 2003.
4 DRCC Annual Report, 1983.
5 Quoted in Gene Kerrigan and Pat Brennan, *This Great Little Nation,* Dublin: Gill & Macmillan, 1999, p. 111.
6 Nell McCafferty, *A Woman to Blame: the Kerry Babies Case,* Cork: Attic Press, 1985.
7 Ailbhe Smyth, 'The Women's Movement in the Republic of Ireland', in *Irish Women's Studies Reader,* ed. Ailbhe Smyth, Cork: Attic Press, 1993, p. 250.
8 Interview with the author, July 2004.
9 Interview with the author, July 2004.
10 DRCC meeting minutes, 26 April 1982.
11 Interview with the author, July 2004.
12 DRCC meeting minutes, 4 October 1982.
13 Interview with the author, February 2004.
14 Interview with the author, February 2005.
15 Interview with the author, June 2004.
16 Interview with the author, July 2004.
17 *Sunday Press,* 1983.
18 'Rape', Health Education Bureau, 1983, p. 9.
19 DRCC Annual Report, 1983.
20 *Irish Medical Times,* 17 February 1978.
21 DRCC meeting minutes, 26 April 1982.
22 DRCC meeting minutes, 2 July 1984.
23 Quoted in Susan McKay, *Sophia's Story,* Dublin: Gill & Macmillan, 1998, p. 84.
24 Ibid., p. 167.
25 Ibid., p. 160.

7 LIFTING THE VEIL OF SILENCE

[1] *The Irish Times*, 14 October 1982.
[2] RTÉ interview, 12 January 1984.
[3] RTÉ radio interview, 26 June 1984.
[4] Letter in DRCC archive, 22 October 1984.
[5] *The Irish Times*, 17 January 1985.
[6] Incest Survivors Anon, 1982.
[7] NARA league, 1980.
[8] 'Information on Child Sexual Abuse and Incest', advice sheet 17a, ICCL, 1985.
[9] ICCL, Report of the CSA Working Party, 1988.
[10] *Medical Monthly*, February 1984.
[11] *Sunday Independent*, 25 February 1979.
[12] *The Irish Times*, 28 May 1982.
[13] *The Irish Times*, 5 March 1982.
[14] *The Irish Times*, 21 January 1984.
[15] Interview with the author, July 2004.
[16] *Irish Independent*, 23 August 1983.
[17] *Sunday Independent*, 20 January 1985.
[18] *Irish Catholic*, March 1985.
[19] DRCC meeting minutes, 11 March 1985.
[20] DRCC meeting minutes, 19 August 1985.
[21] *The Irish Times*, 21 January 1985.
[22] *The Irish Times*, 8 February 1985.
[23] *The Irish Times*, 20 February 1985.
[24] *Sunday Tribune*, 27 January 1985.
[25] *Irish Press*, 3 March 1985.
[26] Interview with the author, September 2004.
[27] *Irish Press*, 3 October 1985.
[28] *Evening Press*, 3 October 1985.
[29] DRCC meeting minutes, 4 November 1985.
[30] *Irish Press*, 5 December 1985.
[31] *Evening Herald*, 16 October 1985.
[32] DRCC meeting minutes, 25 February 1985.
[33] *The Irish Times*, 24 July 1985.
[34] *Evening Press*, 6 November 1985.
[35] 'Counselling Adolescents and Adults Who Have Suffered Sexual Abuse', DRCC booklet, 1986.
[36] Interview with the author, August 2004.

8 MOVING ON

[1] *Evening Herald*, 15 May 1986.
[2] *Evening Herald*, 7 April 1986.

[3] *The Irish Times*, 24 November 1986.
[4] *Evening Herald*, 14 November 1986.
[5] *Irish Press*, 13 November 1986.
[6] *Evening Herald*, 14 November 1986.
[7] *The Irish Times*, 24 November 1986.
[8] DRCC archive.
[9] *The Irish Times*, 14 April 1986.
[10] *Sunday Tribune*, 12 October 1986.
[11] *Irish Press*, 13 November 1986.
[12] *Irish Press*, 24 July 1986.
[13] *Irish Press*, 7 October 1986.
[14] *Irish Press*, 14 August 1986.
[15] *Sunday Tribune*, 5 October 1986.
[16] *Evening Press*, 20 October 1986.
[17] *Irish Independent*, 8 October 1986.
[18] *This Great Little Nation*, op. cit., p. 46.
[19] *The Irish Times*, 3 June 1987.
[20] *The Irish Times*, 22 June 1987.
[21] *Irish Press*, 24 February 1987.
[22] *Evening Press*, 2 March 1987.
[23] *Irish Press*, 28 February 1987.
[24] RTÉ interview, 1 December 1987.
[25] *Irish Press*, 7 December 1987.

9 AGGRAVATING CIRCUMSTANCES

[1] *Evening Herald*, 18 April 1988.
[2] *The Irish Times*, 2 June 1988.
[3] *People (DPP)* v. *Tiernan* 1988, IR250.
[4] RTÉ radio interview, 2 June 1988.
[5] *Futureline,* Vol. 4, December 1986.
[6] *Sunday Tribune*, 15 May 1988.
[7] Adjournment debate, Dáil Eireann, Vol. 384, 16 November 1988.
[8] *The Irish Times*, 11 November 1988.
[9] *The Irish Times*, 18 November 1988.
[10] Interview with the author, July 2004.
[11] Interview with the author, October 2004.
[12] *Sunday Tribune*, 12 October 1986.
[13] *Sunday Tribune*, 19 October 1986.
[14] Interview with the author, July 2004.
[15] Interview with the author, November 2004.

10 'NOT ONE IOTA OF POWER'

[1] *Irish Press*, 16 January 1989.

[2] *Irish Independent,* 22 November 1989.
[3] *The Irish Times,* 16 November 1989.
[4] *Irish Independent,* 19 October 1989.
[5] *Evening Press,* 1 October 1989.
[6] *Evening Press,* 29 September 1989.
[7] *Evening Press,* 22 August 1989.
[8] *Evening Herald,* 2 November 1989.
[9] *Evening Herald,* 2 June 1989.
[10] *The Irish Times,* 17 February 1989.
[11] DRCC Annual Report, 1988.
[12] Evaluation Report, p. 36.
[13] Ibid., p. 49.
[14] Ibid., p. 50.
[15] *The Irish Times,* 13 February 1990.

11 A Rebirth of Optimism

[1] DRCC meeting minutes, 12 June 1989.
[2] DRCC Annual Report, 1989.
[3] *The Irish Times,* 14 February 1990.
[4] *The Irish Times,* 17 February 1990.
[5] *Irish Independent,* 28 February 1990.
[6] *The Irish Times,* 26 February 1990.
[7] Interview with the author, August 2004.
[8] Letter in DRCC archive, 18 May 1990.
[9] RCC press release, 31 July 1990.
[10] Interview with the author, September 2004.
[11] Deirdre Walsh and Rosemary Liddy, *Surviving Sexual Abuse,* Cork: Attic Press, 1989.
[12] *The Irish Times,* 11 January 1990.
[13] *Irish Independent,* 18 January 1990.
[14] *The Irish Times,* 25 September 1990.
[15] *Sunday Press,* 11 February 1990.
[16] *Irish Press,* 12 December 1991.
[17] *Irish Press,* 7 November 1990.
[18] *Irish Press,* 1 November 1990.
[19] *The Irish Times,* 27 March 1990.
[20] *The Irish Times,* 20 September 1990.
[21] *Irish Press,* 23 March 1990.
[22] Interview with the author, August 2004.
[23] *Evening Herald,* 18 February 1991.
[24] *The Irish Times,* 17 July 1991.
[25] *Evening Herald,* 17 July 1991.
[26] *The Irish Times,* 17 July 1991.

27 *Evening Herald,* 20 July 1991.
28 *Irish Press,* 8 February 1991.
29 *The Irish Times,* 23 February 1991.
30 *Sunday Tribune,* 17 February 1991.
31 *Evening Press,* 13 February 1991.
32 *The Irish Times,* 23 February 1991.

12 UNTHINKABLE PROSPECT

1 Quoted in Myrtle Hill, *Women in Ireland,* Belfast: Blackstaff, 2003.
2 Letter, 6 December 1990.
3 From 'Women and the Law in Ireland', 1988, quoted in *The Field Day Anthology of Irish Writing,* Vol. 5, Cork: Cork University Press, 2002, p. 329.
4 *Irish Press,* 7 May 1990.
5 *The Irish Times,* 10 November 1990.
6 *Irish Independent,* 22 April 1991.
7 RTÉ, 4 December 1990.
8 Ibid.
9 *The Irish Times,* 10 December 1990.
10 *Evening Herald,* 21 May 1991.
11 *Sunday Independent,* 4 August 1991.
12 *Irish Press,* 30 August 1991.
13 *Evening Herald,* 7 August 1991.
14 *Sunday Independent,* 4 August 1991.
15 *Irish Press,* 30 August 1991.
16 Dáil Eireann adjournment debate, Vol. 410, 10 July 1991.
17 *The Irish Times,* 10 July 1991.
18 *The Irish Times,* 27 July 1991.
19 *The Irish Times,* 27 July 1991.
20 Gemma Hussey, unpublished diaries.
21 *The Irish Times,* 5 August 1991.
22 *Irish Press,* 1 August 1991.
23 *Irish Independent,* 19 August 1991.
24 *The Irish Times,* 19 August 1991.
25 *The Irish Times,* 14 August 1991.
26 *Sunday Independent,* 4 August 1991.
27 *The Irish Times,* 8 August 1991.
28 *The Irish Times,* 7 August 1991.
29 *The Irish Times,* 13 August 1991.
30 *Irish Independent,* 16 October 1991.
31 *The Irish Times,* 14 August 1991.
32 *The Irish Times,* 7 August 1991.
33 *Irish Independent,* 3 August 1991.

[34] Letter in DRCC archive, 14 August 1991.

[35] *Evening Press*, 18 November 1991.

[36] *The Irish Times*, 13 September 1991.

[37] DRCC archive.

[38] *The Irish Times*, 3 September 1991.

[39] Letter in DRCC archive, 22 August 1991.

[40] DRCC archive.

[41] Statement from DRCC board, 26 August 1991.

[42] *The Irish Times*, 14 August 1991.

[43] Gemma Hussey, op. cit.

[44] Letter from Rory O'Hanlon to Bertie Ahern, 15 October 1991, DRCC archive.

[45] Interview with the author, September 2004.

[46] *Irish Independent*, 30 December 1991.

[47] *The Irish Times*, 18 December 1991.

13 A Country 'Dizzy with Shock and Anger'

[1] *Sunday Tribune*, 18 August 1991.

[2] *Sunday Tribune*, 25 August 1991.

[3] *Irish Independent*, 16 November 1992.

[4] *The Irish Times*, 15 February 1992.

[5] *Late Late Show*, RTÉ, 21 February 1992.

[6] *Irish Press*, 20 February 1992.

[7] *Irish Independent*, 20 February 1992.

[8] *The Irish Times*, 15 February 1992.

[9] *Irish Independent*, 26 February 1992.

[10] Fine Gael press release, 18 February 1992.

[11] *Newsweek*, 2 March 1992.

[12] *European*, 12 March 1992.

[13] *Evening Press*, 27 February 1992.

[14] *Evening Herald*, 26 February 1992.

[15] *Evening Herald*, 9 July 1992.

[16] Letter to *The Irish Times*, 18 March 1992.

[17] *Sunday Tribune*, 2 August 1992.

[18] Kate Shanahan, *Crimes Worse than Death*, Cork: Attic Press, 1992, p. 16.

[19] *Irish Press*, 16 July 1992.

[20] Shanahan, op. cit., p. 15.

[21] Report on the *Gerry Ryan Show*, *Irish Press*, 17 July 1992.

[22] *News*, RTÉ, 16 July 1992.

[23] *The Irish Times*, 17 July 1992.

[24] *Irish Independent*, 25 July 1992.

[25] *Star*, 17 July 1992.

[26] *Irish Independent*, 21 July 1992.

[27] *Morning Ireland,* RTÉ, 17 July 1992.
[28] *Sunday Independent,* 19 July 1992.
[29] *Irish Press,* 18 July 1992.
[30] *Irish Press,* 21 July 1992.
[31] *Star,* 22 July 1992.
[32] *Evening Herald,* 29 July 1992.
[33] *Irish Press,* 7 August 1992.
[34] *Evening Herald,* 5 August 1992.
[35] *Star,* 5 October 1992.
[36] *Sunday Press,* 25 October 1992.

14 RAPE AS A WAR CRIME

[1] *The Irish Times,* 28 January 1993.
[2] *Evening Press,* 2 March 1993.
[3] *Evening Herald,* 3 March 1993.
[4] Kieron Woods, *The Kilkenny Incest Case,* Dublin: Poolbeg, 1993.
[5] *Sunday Tribune,* May 1993.
[6] Kilkenny Incest Investigation Report, 1993.
[7] Letter to *The Irish Times,* 24 May 1993.
[8] Interview with the author, October 2004.
[9] *Sunday Independent,* 18 July 1993.
[10] *Irish Independent,* 16 July 1993.
[11] *Evening Herald,* 17 July 1993.
[12] *Sunday Tribune,* 9 May 1993.
[13] DRCC statement, 19 July 1993.
[14] *Sun,* 18 July 1993.
[15] *Sunday Tribune,* 28 March 1993.
[16] DRCC report, 1993.
[17] *Irish Press,* 31 May 1993.
[18] *Sunday Independent,* 10 October 1993.
[19] DRCC press release, 10 September 1996.
[20] *Cork Examiner,* 27 October 1993.
[21] *Cork Examiner,* 8 September 1993.
[22] *Irish Independent,* 9 December 1993.
[23] *Sunday World,* 19 December 1993.
[24] *Sunday Independent,* 12 December 1993.
[25] *Sunday Independent,* 19 December 1993.
[26] *The Irish Times,* 27 December 1993.
[27] Interview with the author, August 2004.

15 FROM STAY SAFE TO FR BRENDAN SMYTH

[1] Quoted in *The Irish Times,* 30 June 1993.
[2] *Sunday Tribune,* 20 March 1994.

[3] *Sunday Press,* 1 March 1992.
[4] *Irish Independent,* 18 October 1993.
[5] *Irish Independent,* 27 October 1993.
[6] *Irish Independent,* 21 October 1993.
[7] *The Irish Times,* 30 June 1993.
[8] *The Irish Times,* 12 January 1994.
[9] *The Irish Times,* January 1994.
[10] *Irish Independent,* 22 February 1994.
[11] *The Irish Times,* 24 February 1994.
[12] *The Irish Times,* 3 March 1994.
[13] *The Irish Times,* 23 February 1994.
[14] *Irish Press,* 7 February 1995.
[15] *The Irish Times,* 25 June 1996.
[16] Interview with the author, September 2004.
[17] *Irish Independent,* 30 December 1994.
[18] Statement from DRCC, DRCC archive.
[19] *The Irish Times,* 14 November 1994.
[20] *The Irish Times,* 9 December 1994.
[21] *Cork Examiner,* 23 November 1994.
[22] DRCC board meeting minutes, 21 November 1994.
[23] DRCC board meeting minutes, 25 January 1995.
[24] *Tuesday File,* RTÉ, November 1994.
[25] *Sunday Tribune,* 24 August 1997.
[26] *Evening Press,* 15 March 1995.
[27] *Irish Independent,* 15 March 1995.
[28] *Evening Herald,* 14 March 1995.
[29] *Irish Independent,* 15 March 1995.
[30] *The Irish Times,* 18 March 1995.
[31] *The Irish Times,* 20 March 1995.
[32] *Cork Examiner,* 24 April 1995.
[33] *The Irish Times,* 3 April 1995.
[34] *Sunday Independent,* 19 March 1995.
[35] *Sunday Tribune,* 12 March 1995.
[36] *The Irish Times,* 22 March 1995.
[37] *Star,* 19 January 1996.
[38] *Sunday World,* 15 March 1998.
[39] *Sunday Independent,* 28 January 1996.
[40] *Guilty,* op. cit.
[41] *Irish Independent,* 13 January 1996.
[42] Statement from DRCC, DRCC archive.
[43] *Irish Independent,* 21 February 1996.
[44] DRCC board meeting minutes, 26 February 1996.
[45] *The Irish Times,* 29 February 1996.

[46] Interview with the author, August 2004.

[47] Interview with the author, July 2004.

16 RAISING PROFOUNDLY SILENCED VOICES

[1] 'Report of the Working Party on the Legal and Judicial Process for Victims of Sexual and Other Crimes of Violence Against Women and Children', Dublin: NWC, 1996.

[2] Interview with the author, October 2004.

[3] *The Irish Times*, 10 October 1995.

[4] ICCL report of the CSA working group, 1988, p. 114.

[5] *Irish Independent*, 18 April 1996.

[6] *Irish Independent*, 24 December 1996.

[7] *The Irish Times*, 23 October 1997.

[8] *News of the World*, 19 April 1998.

[9] DRCC consent form.

[10] *Sunday Tribune*, 30 November 1997.

[11] *The Irish Times*, 18 December 1998.

[12] *Women's Way*, 28 November 1997.

[13] *The Irish Times*, 8 December 1997.

[14] *The Irish Times*, 25 April 1994.

[15] DRCC board meeting minutes, 7 March 1995.

[16] *Irish Independent*, 26 October 1999.

[17] Andrea Dworkin, *Life and Death*, London: Virago, 1997, p. 74.

[18] *The Irish Times*, 28 July 1998.

[19] *Sunday World*, 9 April 2000.

[20] *Evening Herald*, 8 October 1996.

[21] *Irish Independent*, 12 September 1997.

[22] 'Report of the Working Party on the Legal and Judicial Process', op. cit. pp. 43–5.

[23] *Evening Herald*, 8 October 1996.

[24] *Women's Way*, 16 October 1992.

[25] *The Irish Times*, 26 February 1997.

[26] Interview with the author, July 2004.

[27] *Irish Independent*, 8 September 1997.

[28] *Evening Herald*, 8 October 1997.

[29] *The Irish Times*, 26 November 1999.

[30] 'The Legal Process and the Victims of Rape', DRCC, 1998.

[31] *Irish Independent*, 30 March 2000.

[32] 'Women and War', DRCC archive, 10 April 1998.

[33] Letter to *The Irish Times*, 31 July 1998.

[34] Faoiseamh is the counselling service set up by the Conference of Religous in Ireland in 1997 to counsel victims of abuse by members of religious orders.

[35] June Goulding, *A Light in the Window*, Dublin: Poolbeg, 1999.

17 A Shocking Tolerance of Rape

[1] *The Irish Times*, 28 September 2000.
[2] *Irish Independent*, 16 August 2000.
[3] *Star*, 29 January 2000.
[4] *The Irish Times*, 18 May 1999.
[5] *The Irish Times*, 6 March 2002.
[6] *Sunday Independent*, 26 September 1999.
[7] *Irish Independent*, 22 September 1999.
[8] Address by Mr Justice Paul Carney to the Burren Law School, 3 May 2003.
[9] *Irish Independent*, 13 March 2000.
[10] *Sunday Business Post*, 10 March 2000.
[11] *Irish Independent*, 5 June 2002.
[12] *Irish Independent*, 11 July 2000.
[13] *Irish Independent*, 31 July 2000.
[14] *Sunday Tribune*, 16 July 2000.
[15] *Irish Independent*, 29 July 2000.
[16] *The Irish Times*, 10 April 2002.
[17] *Irish Examiner*, 12 May 2002.
[18] RCC press release, 30 May 2001.
[19] *The Irish Times*, 7 January 2003.
[20] *Irish Catholic*, 19 February 2004.
[21] *The Irish Times*, 7 January 2003.
[22] *Sunday Tribune*, 10 March 2002.
[23] *The Irish Times*, 1 April 2002.
[24] *Irish Independent*, 4 April 2002.
[25] *The Irish Times*, 4 March 2002.
[26] *The Irish Times*, 6 March 2002.
[27] *The Irish Times*, 3 December 2001.
[28] *Sunday Tribune*, 2 April 2000.
[29] *Irish Independent*, 7 November 2001.
[30] *Irish Independent*, 9 November 2001.
[31] *The Irish Times*, 17 January 2002.

18 The Hidden Part of the Iceberg

[1] *Irish Independent*, 22 March 2002.
[2] Interview with the author, August 2004.
[3] SAVI, p. 157.
[4] Ibid., p. 211.
[5] Ibid., p. 236.
[6] Interview with the author, August 2004.
[7] *The Irish Times*, 20 April 2002.
[8] *Irish Independent*, 21 May 2002.
[9] *Evening Herald*, 19 April 2002.

[10] *The Irish Times*, 4 May 2002.
[11] *Gay Community News*, June 2002.
[12] Letter to *The Irish Times*, 1 August 2002.
[13] Interview with the author, September 2004.
[14] Interview with the author, September 2004.
[15] *Irish Independent*, 22 July 2002.
[16] *The Irish Times*, 7 April 2003.
[17] *Irish Independent*, 30 August 2003.
[18] *The Irish Times*, 30 August 2003.
[19] *Irish Independent*, 30 October 2003.
[20] *The Irish Times*, 20 March 2003.
[21] *Sunday Independent*, 26 January 2003.
[22] *Irish Independent*, 20 February 2003.
[23] *The Irish Times*, 18 February 2004.
[24] *The Irish Times*, 19 February 2004.
[25] *Inside Out*, Journal for the Irish Association of Humanistic and
    Integrative Psychotherapy, No. 44, Summer 2004, pp. 23–8.
[26] *Irish Independent*, 15 July 2004.
[27] *The Irish Times*, 13 May 2004.
[28] 'Psychotherapy and cross-cultural clients', *Inside Out*, Journal for the
    Irish Association of Humanistic and Integrative Psychotherapy,
    No. 43, Spring 2003, pp. 14–19.
[29] *The Mirror*, 20 July 2004.
[30] *Irish Examiner*, 29 November 2004.
[31] *Irish Independent*, 20 September 2004.
[32] *Star*, 10 August 2004.
[33] *Gerry Ryan Show*, RTÉ, 28 April 2004.
[34] Letter to *The Irish Times*, 29 April 2004.
[35] *Irish Examiner*, 10 February 2004.
[36] *Irish Examiner*, 6 October 2004.
[37] Interview with the author, February 2005.
[38] *The Irish Times*, 25 May 2004.
[39] *The Irish Times*, 29 December 2004.
[40] *Irish Independent*, 11 October 2003.
[41] *Irish Independent*, 22 November 2002.
[42] *Irish Independent*, 9 March 2004.

19 A GOOD PLACE TO BE

[1] Interview with the author, January 2005.
[2] Interview with the author, January 2005.

INDEX